A THEORY OF WEALTH DISTRIBUTION
AND ACCUMULATION

A Theory of Wealth Distribution and Accumulation

MAURO BARANZINI

CLARENDON PRESS · OXFORD
1991

Oxford University Press, Walton Street, Oxford OX2 6DP
Oxford New York Toronto
Delhi Bombay Calcutta Madras Karachi
Petaling Jaya Singapore Hong Kong Tokyo
Nairobi Dar es Salaam Cape Town
Melbourne Auckland
and associated companies in
Berlin Ibadan

Oxford is a trade mark of Oxford University Press

Published in the United States
by Oxford University Press, New York

British Library Cataloguing in Publication Data
Baranzini, Mauro
A theory of wealth distribution and accumulation.
1. Wealth
I. Title
339.2
ISBN 0-19-823313-2

Library of Congress Cataloging in Publication Data
Baranzini, Mauro.
A theory of wealth distribution and accumulation/Mauro Baranzini.
p. cm.
Includes bibliographical references and index.
1. Income distribution. 2. Wealth. 3. Saving and investment. 4. Income
distribution–Mathematical models. 5. Wealth–Mathematical models. 6. Saving and
investment–Mathematical models. I. Title.
HC79.I5B338 1991 339.2'01'5118–dc20 90-42927
ISBN 0-19-823313-2

Typeset by KEYTEC, Bridport, Dorset

Printed and bound in
Great Britain by Bookcraft (Bath) Ltd.
Midsomer Norton, Avon

To
Evelina, Moira, Timothy,
and Linda

ACKNOWLEDGEMENTS

I WANT to express my gratitude to all those institutions and persons who contributed to the realization of this research programme. Thanks are first due to The Queen's College, University of Oxford, for providing research facilities during my stay as a research student and as a lecturer and tutor in economics (1971–84), to the Centre for Research in Economic Analysis (CRANEC) of the Catholic University of Milan (1982 onwards), and finally to the Institute for Economic Sciences of the University of Verona (since 1987). Shorter stays at the Universities of Cambridge (1976), MIT and Harvard (1976), Berkeley (1979), and Zürich (1983) have also been helpful. Finally financial support from the Swiss National Science Foundation and the Italian Consiglio Nazionale delle Ricerche is gratefully acknowledged.

The debts accumulated since the early 1970s in the preparation of this volume are numerous. First of all Pietro Balestra, now at the Universities of Geneva and Dijon, encouraged me to take up this field of research while I was a graduate student at the University of Fribourg in Switzerland. At Oxford, where I stayed initially with a Florey European Studentship of The Queen's College and with a Swiss Science Foundation Fellowship, my thesis supervisors David W. Soskice (University College), John S. Flemming (Nuffield College, now at the Bank of England), and James A. Mirrlees (Nuffield College) gave generously of their time and ideas and continuously forced me to rethink and defend my position on numerous issues. My D.Phil. thesis examiners Walter A. Eltis (Exeter College) and Hywel G. Jones (Linacre College) also provided precious insights and suggestions on various parts.

As often happens with a thesis after its acceptance (in my case back in 1976) it comes to be completely rewritten and extended to include new perspectives and issues. In my case the analysis has been extended to include an integrated macro-economic framework and to take into account the numerous contributions of the fast-growing literature in the field of inter-generational transmission of wealth and income distribution. I owe, for this second and crucial phase, a great debt to Luigi L. Pasinetti (then at King's College, Cambridge, and now at the Catholic University of Milan) who prompted my interest for the classical and post-Keynesian theories of production, distribution, and accumulation, and who encouraged in so many ways my work on that topic. The weekly discussions that I have had the privilege to have with him over these last ten years have helped me enormously to widen my horizon and to improve my understanding of our science; his penetrating criticism has been a continuous stimulus for my research.

Over many years I have also had the benefit of conversations with and advice from numerous teachers and colleagues, of whom I would particularly like to thank David L. Bevan (St John's College, Oxford), Heinrich Bortis (University of Fribourg), Carlo Casarosa (University of Pisa), Alvaro Cencini (University of Dijon), Roberto Cippà (Swiss National Bank), John Enos (Magdalen College, Oxford), Nicholas H. Dimsdale (The Queen's College, Oxford), Ferdinando Meacci (University of Padua), Alberto Quadrio Curzio (Catholic University of Milan), Roberto Scazzieri (Universities of Padua and Bologna), and Bernard Schmitt (Universities of Fribourg and Dijon). Other colleagues, students, and anonymous reviewers have provided detailed advice and criticism with regard to content, style, and presentation. I am also indebted for editorial assistance to Adrian Pollock. Responsibility for all remaining errors remains entirely and unreservedly with the author.

University of Verona   M. B.
and The Queen's College, Oxford
October 1989

CONTENTS

Despite the difficulties in modelling bequests empirically, it is clear that the subject merits further work at both the theoretical and the empirical level. For some households, although probably a minority, bequests are likely to represent one of the main motives for accumulation of wealth.

> M. King, 'The Economics of Saving:
> A Survey of Recent Contributions', in
> K. J. Arrow and S. Honkapohja (eds.),
> *Frontiers of Economics,* 1985.

This paper suggests the importance of and need for substantially greater research and data collection on intergenerational transfers. Life-cycle models of savings that emphasize savings for retirement as the dominant form of capital accumulation should give way to models that illuminate the determinants of intergenerational transfers.

> L. J. Kotlikoff and J. H. Summers,
> 'The Role of Inter-Generational Transfers
> in Aggregate Capital Accumulation', 1981.

Although much research has been done on the intra-generational distribution of income and wealth, much less work has been done on inter-generational effects; research in both areas is needed for a complete understanding of the subject.

> P. L. Menchik, 'Inter-Generational
> Transmission of Inequality:
> An Empirical Study of Wealth Mobility',
> *Economica,* 1979.

The major theories of distribution have been concerned with the distribution of income between social classes, or the owners of the factors of production, categories which are often assumed to be coterminous. In the final analysis, however, one must surely be interested mainly in the distribution of income between households, or between groups of individuals who share their incomes and expenditures. ... The distribution of income between persons is undoubtedly related to the factor income distribution, but it is necessary to build a bridge between the two.

> H. Lydall, *A Theory of Income Distribution,* 1979.

The capitalists' class may possibly accumulate without regard to the return, but if working-class saving is interpreted in life-cycle terms, then it is very likely to be influenced by the rate of interest.

> A. B. Atkinson, *The Economics of Inequality,* 1975.

Introduction

THE purpose of this volume is to provide a general framework for the macro-economic theory of income distribution and wealth accumulation, especially by focusing on the laws which regulate the behaviour of individuals and social groups within a given institutional set-up. In this way it is possible to reconsider the theoretical issue of savings accumulation, i.e. the 'supply side' of the process of capital accumulation, income distribution, and profit determination, by concentrating on the historical reasons that are at the basis of 'class distinction', as well as 'generation distinction', in modern economic analysis. Additionally, in order to provide a more comprehensive picture of the macro-economic models of growth and income distribution, the implications of market imperfections and of a different dynastic approach to the issue of bequest saving, as well as of interest-uncertainty, in the patterns of wealth accumulation are explicitly considered. In this way it is hoped that additional light will be thrown on the mechanisms that lead to different paths of wealth (savings) accumulation and hence on its distribution among socio-economic groups; in other words a number of normally exogenous assumptions come to be explained within the model, thus providing more comprehensive answers to the problems of growth and income distribution.

In order to expand our knowledge in this field of analysis the following qualifications have been introduced, representing a break with the standard model of enquiry which has characterized the macro-economic literature of the last thirty years or so. First, socio-economic classes (which are at the centre of most classical, post-Keynesian, and neo-Ricardian models) are no longer considered as exogenously given according to a specific 'property right' (associated with a given 'withdrawing capacity'), income composition, or propensity to save, but are considered, in a more endogenous manner, as the outcome of long-term institutional, behavioural, and economic forces modelling the socio-economic structure of society and successive generations. Secondly, the complex process of income distribution and wealth accumulation and distribution among groups and classes is no longer postulated exclusively in terms of class-struggle (as is the case with most of the above-mentioned models), but is seen also, and especially in certain cases, as the outcome of different intertemporal and inter-generational allocations of consumption, and of life-cycle and bequest savings. As a matter of fact the micro-economic analysis of consumption- and saving-behaviour of the life-cycle theory allows us to study the intertemporal allocation of consumption, which cannot be confined to the life-cycle horizon of a single individual, but may concern different individuals and generations with a longer horizon (the latter by introducing the concept of inter-generational transmission of wealth or accumulated savings).[1] A third element concerns the inclusion in the analysis of some of the mechanisms that in the long run may accelerate the process of concentration or dispersion of income, life-cycle savings, and inter-generational wealth among individuals, groups, or socio-economic classes sharing a common behaviour. Among such mechanisms the following may be anticipated: (*a*) the presence of diversified investment opportunities allowing for holdings of different portfolios; (*b*) a different weight attached to the importance of inter-generational bequests; and (*c*) a different composition of the human capital/physical capital ratio. More specific hypotheses have been left out; but they may be easily incorporated, as for instance a different initial wealth endowment, a different life expectancy, and explicit investment in human capital stock. The explicit consideration of these long-term mechanisms is expected to throw additional light on the sort of reasons that may lead to a historical distinction among classes in a growing economy, both in a deterministic and stochastic context; furthermore it may be possible to identify the counteracting tendencies of this process, that is the movements towards a lower concentration or dispersion of economic property in general, which may ultimately change the general set-up of the economic system.

As already pointed out, the introduction of both inter-generational wealth (as distinct from life-cycle savings) and of a bequest discount rate (besides a life-cycle consumption discount rate) is bound to widen the concept of 'class-struggle'. In classical, post-Keynesian, and neo-Ricardian models the distribution of income, and consequently of wealth, depends on the factors of production (and their relative 'rights of property') or the socio-economic classes which are identified with a specific factor of production even if they may earn income from other sources. The introduction of inter-generational wealth and of its relative discount rate shifts the distribution struggle between generations, since a

---

[1] This element is particularly important in a model of distribution and accumulation which is based on long-term built-in mechanisms like steady-state growth; such mechanisms may be more easily connected with specific tendencies of concentration or dispersion of income and wealth (see, on this point, Phelps Brown, 1988, pp. 436–64) based on long-term time-periods such as those among generations, rather than on short- or medium-term reallocation of disposable income among factors of production or classes as usually considered by traditional models.

given generation may decide to consume more during its life-cycle and to leave less to the next generation or vice versa. We shall enquire into the conditions which determine the various decisions of socio-economic classes and of the resulting relative strength of such classes at the present time.

From a more general point of view there are various ways in which generations may be interlinked in economic terms. The first, obvious one is the long-term rate of growth that a given society chooses: a high rate of growth will ensure a higher consumption per capita later on and vice versa. The second way is connected with the public debt, a mechanism through which a part of present (and past) public expenditure is debited to the next generation(s). A third way is inter-generational transfer of wealth which will be one of the central points of this analysis. This approach should help towards understanding some aspects of the complex issue of the relations between generations and of the way in which 'allocation' of consumption takes place in a truly long-term sense.

In order to tackle this research programme the integrated structure of these issues is considered in the first two chapters, which are mainly dedicated to theoretical and methodological perspectives and in which consideration is given to the general framework of analysis of the neoclassical and post-Keynesian models characterized by a fundamentally different vision of production, capital accumulation, and income determination and distribution. Hence the 'scope and method' of alternative frameworks of analysis are fundamental in providing an answer to the questions which are addressed here. This will be achieved in part by encapsulating some fundamental elements of both frameworks in order to obtain an integrated and much more comprehensive structure. Such encapsulation will not consist of a simple mixture of the two modern approaches—which of course seem to be incompatible since they are very different in scope and method—but in grafting a number of aspects of the micro-economic foundations of the neoclassical theory into the macro-economic structure of the post-Keynesian model, the latter being characterized by a fixed capital/output ratio and by the absence of the traditional neoclassical production function. The consideration of socio-economic groups (or classes), as opposed to single individuals, will also reinforce the post-Keynesian structure of the model of distribution and accumulation; but the greater flexibility of the savings ratio of the socio-economic groups, their patterns of allocation of consumption over the life-cycle, and their patterns of inter-generational transmission of wealth should give a clear 'allocationist' emphasis to the study of distribution and accumulation, so ensuring a much wider approach.

The relationship between (and superimposition of) the macro- and micro-economic foundations in an integrated model of growth, distribution, and accumulation has so far been one of the weakest points of the theory, and a number of scholars have pointed this out without, however, carrying out further enquiry. Recently one of the major representatives of the Cambridge school pointed out that:

There is no incompatibility between [the] way of conceiving and of investigating the behaviour of single individuals and the conception of a general framework of satisfactory economic growth for the economic system as a whole ... [T]he two fields of investigation are completely separate from each other. We may well consider an economic system that fulfils the more basic requirements of structural efficiency but at the same time has 'local' situations of micro-economic inefficiency. The opposite is also possible: micro-economic efficiency at the level of consumers and/or producers and structural inefficiency—for example less than full employment and idle capacity (Pasinetti, 1987, p. 997).

The two different levels of analysis, which in the case of Pasinetti quoted here tackles the problems of efficiency in the process of growth, are described in the following way:

(i) A first fundamental stage consists in sketching out a set of general conditions that the process of growth must fulfil in order to be considered 'satisfactory'. At this first stage, only basic problems are faced, such as those of compatibility among production sectors, final demand composition and over-all avoidance of waste. These are problems that concern what we may call *structural efficiency*.

(ii) Once the conditions of satisfactory growth (structural efficiency) have been fulfilled, a second stage follows in which the way becomes open to the investigation and solution of a series of, so to speak, 'local' problems of efficiency, at the level of the single individuals. For these 'local' problems, the procedures and methods of maximization under constraints may well be appropriate in many circumstances; even though never in an exclusive way. We may talk in this respect of 'local' or *micro-economic efficiency* (Pasinetti, 1987, p. 997).

The 'method' expounded by Pasinetti may indeed be applied to the analysis here, which has however a somewhat different 'scope'. We are in fact not only concerned with the issue of structural efficiency in the process of growth, but also with:

1. At the *macro-level* the problems of steady-state equilibrium growth, defined in a framework where the rate of neutral technical progress, the rate of population growth, and the constant capital/output ratio are all exogenously given, where investment is determined by full-employment conditions, and where the investment-equals-savings condition is ensured by redistribution of income between wages and profits and/or among classes with different propensities to consume; and

2. At the *micro-level* the issue of income distribution and wealth distribution and accumulation which will ensure that the amount of savings generated by the system will equal full-employment investment. The savings behaviour, which differs according to the characteristics of the various socio-economic classes, may be explained in terms of intertemporal utility-maximization, both with respect to life-cycle consumption and the inter-generational bequest. In this way the issue of distribution and accumulation comes to include the very long run by linking one generation to the next.

This approach allows us to retain the most important qualifications of the macro-economic model focusing on the laws of profit determination and on the functional distribution of income (and avoiding many of the difficulties associated with the neoclassical framework, such as the determination of the marginal productivity of the productive factors, or the absence of imperfect markets and residual incomes), and at the same time take advantage of a number of instruments of the neoclassical micro-theory, which considers the rational behaviour of individuals faced with the choice between consumption and saving within a given framework of constraints.

Clearly, in order to achieve the necessary 'scope' two different methods at different stages (macro- and micro-economic respectively) will be used; but as Pasinetti (1987) has pointed out, due to the fact that the levels of analysis are quite different, there is no particular reason to talk of 'incompatibility' between the two approaches.[2]

Another important issue dealt with in this volume concerns the impact that the inter-generational transfer of wealth (resulting from previous

[2] The emphasis placed on the distinction between 'marginalist' and 'non-marginalist' theories (the latter being mainly represented by the classical, Keynesian, and neo-Ricardian models) differs widely among scholars. Neo-Ricardians tend to emphasize the difference among theories which allow for factors' substitutability and those which do not. Sen (1970) suggests a typology of growth models where neoclassical or marginalist models are 'closed' by marginal product factor pricing, and where Keynesian models are 'closed' by an independent investment function, corresponding to the level of economic activity ensuring full employment to the system. In other terms, as Brems (1979) has suggested, the neoclassical model is characterized by an aggregate production function that permits substitution between factors of production, while the post-Keynesian model is characterized by an aggregate production function of the fixed-coefficient variety. More recently Darity has written: 'What will separate neoclassical and Keynesian approaches is the environment with which these optimizing entrepreneurs are confronted on the key dimension of uncertainty. The neoclassical world is one of perfect foresight. The Keynesian world is one of *subjective* uncertainty. ... The neoclassical approach to "uncertainty" reveals the substance of the difference. "Rational expectations", for example, is *still* perfect foresight about the *systematic* determinants of a variable output about which expectations are being formed. Thus neoclassical economics really ends up doing "risk" analysis, rather than uncertainty. ... It is Knightian risk that pervades a neoclassical world, while it is Knightian uncertainty that pervades the Keynesian world' (Darity, 1981, pp. 978–9).

savings) has on the framework of wealth accumulation and income distribution among classes and types of income. Only truly dynamic models, with a long-term horizon, are in a position to yield exhaustive answers to this problem, which is particularly relevant if we think that at least one-half of the total wealth of most industrialized nations is transmitted from one generation to another and has relatively little to do with life-cycle consumption- and savings-allocation.[3]

As King (1985, p. 285) and many others have pointed out recently, the mechanisms which determine the inter-generational transfers of wealth deserve more attention, both at the theoretical and empirical level. But the process of wealth accumulation is not confined to the progressive increase of capital, but has wide implications for the formation and perpetuation of different classes. Not surprisingly Atkinson (1986) has pointed out that the forces that must be taken into account to explain the mechanisms of income distribution must be considered with particular detail in the framework of long-term analysis. Hence the historical reasons which account for the formation and perpetuation of different classes in general and for different patterns of consumption and saving will be brought to the fore.

The type of analysis considered in this volume has been conventionally labelled as 'functional distribution theory'. It is not directly concerned with the distribution of income among single individuals, but it seeks primarily to explain (*a*) the reward that the factors of production receive and (*b*) the way in which it is assigned to them. Secondly, it seeks to explain the role that different socio-economic classes (as distinct from individuals) have in the process of accumulation of wealth, both life-cycle and inter-generational, and hence on the distribution of income among factors of production and classes. However, the link between 'functional' (i.e. macro) and 'personal' (i.e. micro) distribution is not as clear-cut as it might seem. For instance once factor prices (or payments or rewards) are determined, according to endogenous or exogenous elements (or a combination of both), then knowledge of the distribution of ownership of these factors may be relevant for the

---

[3] The introduction of bequests raises a number of relevant questions which we shall deal with only partially, including the way in which the bequest motive enters the donor's utility function, the division of the legacy among children and recipients in general, the timing of gifts, and the important issue of allocation of expenditure on children's education (cf. King, 1985, p. 282). In the specialized literature there exist two schools of thought concerning the relevance of the share of inter-generational bequests in the total national wealth of industrialized countries; the first maintains that it amounts to about two-thirds, while the other holds that it is much less significant (see Chapter 1). Professor Phelps Brown (1988, pp. 440–1) stresses that 'the proportion of one-half for lifetime savings can be accepted as the order of magnitude arising from a careful and well-founded estimate' for both US and UK.

determination of the personal distribution of income and wealth. For example if given types of factors of production are exclusively or predominantly owned by socio-economic groups, knowledge of factor shares might help to identify, at least in part, the shares of such groups, and it is hence necessary to understand the personal distribution of economic power. It should be emphasized that this knowledge is essential, since there might be other factors at work which account for the distribution of income and wealth.

It is worth pointing out that these kinds of relationships are, at least in general terms, more direct in neoclassical distribution theories, where the macro level is the straight aggregation of the micro-level, and where there exists no element of market imperfection or of residual income. More refined is the picture for a number of other theories, like the classical and post-Keynesian, where the link between macro- and micro-economics is not straightforward, and where the same framework of analysis may be completely different. The point is that it is worth while to pursue the enquiry into the possible complexity of links between 'functional' and 'personal' distribution theories, even by trying to maintain unaltered the general framework of analysis which in this study is that of a post-Keynesian model.

In order to understand and explain economic phenomena it is necessary to integrate them into a preconstructed theoretical framework. This has been the case with all theories of income determination and distribution, as well as of capital distribution and accumulation. In other words the explanation of certain facts is directly connected with their integration into a given conceptual framework.

Another important feature of this study concerns the possible morphogenesis of socio-economic groups or classes, i.e. the analysis of the forces which account for the tendencies of progressive concentration or dispersion of accumulated savings and wealth which, among other things, modify the economic relationships among groups as well as among successive generations. Morphogenesis is a relevant aspect within this framework since it may explain one of the important mechanisms at the basis of economic development. A thoughtful outline of the forces accounting for concentration or dispersion of wealth in modern economic societies has been recently provided by Phelps Brown (1988, ch. 15). In particular he stresses that the dispersion of wealth may occur as a result of: (*a*) a fall in the value of holdings (since the proportion of assets held in the form of stocks and shares rises with the size of the holding, the wealth of the top 1 per cent of holders is particularly vulnerable to a fall in the stock-market); (*b*) the drawing down of savings to maintain a sustained level of consumption after retirement; (*c*) transfers in the donor's lifetime for various reasons; and finally (*d*) dispersion at death, due to a large number of children and/or other ways of transmitting inter-generational wealth. Besides these forces of dispersion we find a number of fairly powerful ones accounting for the progressive concentration of wealth, namely: (*a*) an unequal distribution of personal income; (*b*) different propensities to save; (*c*) a different portfolio composition and hence a differentiated mean rate of return; (*d*) an unequal distribution and/or concentration of bequests at death due to a small number of children; and finally (*e*) the life-cycle accumulation of savings.

A number of these forces will be included in the analysis that follows, isolating in a progressive manner those elements which seem to be particularly relevant for the study of the overall steady-state path of accumulation. However, this approach will also have to consider, more or less explicitly, the role of institutions in the process of distribution and accumulation. A number of contributions (for example Bortis, 1988; and Baranzini and Scazzieri, 1990, ch. 1) have recently pointed out that most economic models focusing on the long-term structure of growth, distribution, and accumulation can, in general, more efficiently incorporate institutional aspects of our socio-economic systems. The historical development of our industrialized systems cannot be explained simply on the basis of quasi-mechanical and symmetrical day-to-day decisions based on optimal allocation of resources. Such a view may be useful to explain the short-term behaviour of our economies, but the long-term process of development ought to be explained by a sort of 'common track', representing a special framework within which the behaviour of classes must be pushed through.[4]

Bortis (1988, p. 9) states that the analysis of the institutional framework is particularly useful for the comprehension of the dynamics of the process of economic growth. More precisely, with a specific microeconomic framework (as defined at the beginning of this Introduction), different institutional settings yield different solutions, characterized by different strategies of capital accumulation, different roles of technology, and, of course, different structures of the composition of demand. This latter aspect is particularly-important, since recent works (for example, Pasinetti, 1981) have emphasized the impact of changes in the composition of demand on the structure of the economy, and hence indirectly on the process of capital accumulation. More specifically changes in the

---

[4] This requisite of stability and independence at the same time is efficiently performed by the 'institutional framework' with particular reference to: (*a*) the influence of different socio-economic settings, with respect to consumption, saving, and bequest behaviour; (*b*) the non-economic constraints at the basis of the macro- and personal distribution of income and wealth; and (*c*) the role of the public sector and its influence through monetary and fiscal policies.

composition of demand, and not simply in the level of demand, have a profound influence on the way in which the labour force, technology, and resources in general are employed and allocated in a dynamic productive process.

Institutions have an impact on the composition of demand in various ways among which the following may be mentioned:

1. They affect the structure of prices, and in most economies the public sector directly or indirectly influences the determination of a number of prices of goods and services.

2. They influence the distribution of disposable income and wealth, through the structure of direct and indirect taxes (estate duties included) and hence the structure of demand, which varies according to the level of the disposable incomes of individuals.

3. They affect the dynamic of the system of prices, and therefore the dynamic of distribution of technology. More generally institutions may represent an obstacle or a stimulus to the process of technological change. In this way the system of prices, which may be heavily conditioned by the institutional setting, will influence the cost of production, the distribution of income, and hence the composition of both supply and demand at the same time.

Pasinetti (1981) has exhaustively considered, from a general point of view, some of these issues by rejecting the idea of a specific institutional setting, but by taking into consideration a limited number of extra-economic elements, such as the rate of population growth and the natural level of profit, while leaving aside other aspects of the institutional setting as the market structure (which of course has a greater impact on the macro-economic system), the tax structure, and explicit interventions in the price system or directly in the productive sector with incentives and disincentives. Of course the introduction of all (or a number of) these elements would allow for a partial refinement of the model, and would most probably provide additional insights into a framework of analysis so far wholly unexplored.

It is clear that a model which, at least at the micro-level, focuses on the mechanisms determining the distribution of available income between consumption and saving, ought to specify what saving really means and implies. If we recall the framework of models of development, savings are often regarded as a cause or means of growth, and not a direct outcome of it. This role is less clear in neoclassical standard models, where savings equal investment simultaneously. Within the post-Keynesian model the causal relationship is clear: savings adjust to the amount of investment which is determined *ex ante* by the entrepreneurs' 'animal spirits' and ensures a given rate of growth of the system.

In the models considered in this volume the role of savings becomes even more important, not only because it must ensure an equilibrium growth to the system and, at the same time, an optimal allocation of the resources of families, but also because it becomes the main element through which the dynamic of capital accumulation and the reasons behind the formation of different classes in economic terms can be studied. The allocation between consumption and savings will also enable us to study the mechanisms which are at the basis of the distribution of the inter-generational capital stock among the various socio-economic classes.

Before bringing this Introduction to an end we want to reconsider some of the implications for an analysis like the present one, of groups, classes, or dynasties of given socio-economic individuals, instead of single individuals. The first and most important implication of this approach is that in this way some of the difficulties associated with aggregation are avoided, and at the same time one of the characterizing requirements of post-Keynesian models is fulfilled. Speaking more generally, the analysis of the behaviour of specific socio-economic classes places itself half-way between the individualistic approach of the neoclassical model and the social-welfare function originally proposed by Bergson (1938). This may turn out to be a wise choice since it avoids any precise drawbacks as pointed out by Balogh, himself a strenuous supporter of the free-market economy:

A consumer's behaviour must not be impulsive; he must be assumed to have considered all the possible choices open to him and to have fully understood their implications. The consumer must not only be rational, but his tastes must be constant; any change in tastes would make the kind of comparisons discussed here impossible in principle. ... In particular, he must not be influenced in his own choice by the consumption, conspicuous or otherwise, of others. In other words, in sociological parlance, the consumer must be entirely 'inner-directed'—an 'island of utility' (Balogh, 1982, p. 79).

To such a restricted conception of human behaviour may be opposed the following opinion expressed by Arrow on the social-utility function:

The operational and epistemological basis of the social welfare function is never analysed. Individual preferences refer, however shakily, to conceivably observable behaviour. Whose behaviour or whose judgement is referred to in the social welfare function is never clarified. Presumably, the function is an expression of the ethical attitudes of any particular observer, but this attitude leaves open all the problems which centre about the concept of political or social obligations; why should any individual accept policies inconsistent with his own social welfare function? (Arrow, 1967, p. 736).

The approach followed in this volume, as pointed out above, may well be placed between these two extremes, since groups of individuals, families, or dynasties, which have specific qualifications and common interests, will be considered. The specific qualifications refer, in particular, to the kind of income perceived by all social groups, or to the proportion of the various incomes earned, and to the particular view of the process of savings and capital accumulation. The classes that I have envisaged, following one of the dominant traditions in economic thought, are large enough to absorb significant deviations from the average, but not sufficiently large and heterogeneous as to run into the dangers pointed out by Arrow. In this sense the analysis here differentiates itself neatly from the life-cycle models which consider the existence of individuals only, without grouping them into subclasses and classes.

The definition of classes may, additionally, be related to the decisions to save and to invest, as they are seen by Keynes:

Saving is the act of the individual consumer and consists in the negative act of refraining from spending the whole of his current income on consumption. Investment, on the other hand, is the act of the entrepreneur whose function is to make the decisions which determine the amount of non-available output, and consists in the positive act of starting or maintaining some process of production or of withholding liquid goods. It is measured by the net addition to wealth whether in the form of fixed capital, working capital or liquid capital (Keynes, 1930, p. 172; quoted by Darity, 1981, pp. 987–8).

Hence the classes of consumers or workers and entrepreneurs or capitalists may also be distinguished on this ground. This adds to the argument that the members of a given class have a fairly strong common profile; in this case the social-welfare function of the group acquires a special configuration and avoids, at least in general terms, the drawbacks pointed out by Arrow.

As is well known, post-Keynesian economics may be divided into two broad research programmes: the first one, especially developed in the UK and continental Europe, focusing on the real and mainly macroeconomic aspects of income distribution, capital accumulation, growth, taxation, price, and disequilibrium theory in general. The second, which has been particularly developed in North America, has mainly focused on the monetary side of these issues, as well as on certain microeconomic phenomena.

The best-known works in a broadly defined field of post-Keynesian micro-economics are those of Wood (1975), Eichner (1976), and Marglin (1984). Wood, who comes closer than the other two authors to the research programme of this volume, provides a 'new theory of what determines the profit margin of the individual company and the share of profits in national income'. According to Wood the aim of each firm is to grow as fast as possible, subject to two constraints, the opportunity frontier and the finance frontier. In this context the profit margin and the rate of growth of the firm's output are determined by the intersection of the opportunity frontier and the finance frontier. Furthermore macro-economic equilibrium requires that the additional demand created by additional investment be equal to the increase in output made possible by investment. Thus, once the ratios of saving and of autonomous expenditures to income and the capital/output ratio are given, the macro-economic equilibrium rate of growth is determined. As Wood (1975, pp. 108–11) points out, if this rate of growth is introduced into the macro-version of the finance frontier, then the equilibrium share of profits in national income is also determined, since competition ensures that the finance constraint is binding.

Although important, these contributions are, however, mainly theories of the firm which leave rather untouched the relationship between firms and families, or producers and consumers, from which can be built a more general framework of the macro-economic distribution of income and accumulation.

In a general way one of the purposes of this volume is to bridge the gap between the two research programmes of post-Keynesian economics, first by integrating the micro- and macro-economic issues relative to income distribution and wealth accumulation, and secondly by considering the role of market imperfections in the generation of different socio-economic classes. It is hoped that an analysis of this type might help to strengthen the scientific ties between different groups of researchers sharing a common interest in economic science. As Morishima has pointed out: 'International friendship among economists of different schools of thought is more important than that of the same school, especially in such a difficult period of history when political and economic interests are giving rise to so many conflicts' (Morishima, 1977, p. 61).

PART I

The Modern Macro-Economic Model of
Income Distribution and Wealth
Accumulation: Theoretical Perspectives

1

Theoretical Perspectives

1.1 SCOPE AND METHOD OF THE VOLUME

1.1.1 Scope

The main aim of this volume is to enquire theoretically into the process of accumulation, distribution, and transmission of savings in a capitalist society. In particular the aim is to focus on the forces which account for the formation of two types of accumulated savings (inter-generational assets or bequests and life-cycle savings) and on their respective role in the determination of the distributive equilibrium variables of the model.

The relevance of inherited wealth for the distribution of income and wealth itself has been stressed in a large number of recent studies:[1] for example Atkinson (1970, 1972, 1975), Atkinson and Harris (1978), Bevan (1974, 1979), Bevan and Stiglitz (1978), Flemming (1979), Harbury and Hitchens (1979), Kotlikoff and Summers (1980, 1981), Kurz (1984), Laitner (1979), Lydall (1979), Meade (1966b, 1973), Menchik (1979), Menchik and David (1983), Phelps Brown (1988), Shorrocks (1979), Tomes (1981, 1982), and many others.

Harbury and Hitchens (1979), for instance, challenge the commonly held view that inheritance is no longer a main factor in the distribution and perpetuation of wealth, and show, on the basis of more than fifteen

---

[1] Although there is general agreement about the relevance of inherited wealth, there is less agreement concerning its share in the total wealth of modern nations. A number of scholars (as King and Modigliani) maintain that the highest estimate suggests that the share is about one-quarter or one-third (the remaining part being made up by life-cycle savings); while another group of scholars (as Kotlikoff and Summers, as well as Atkinson, and Bevan) puts the proportion between one-half and two-thirds, at least for the majority of cases. As we have mentioned in the Introduction Phelps Brown (1988, pp. 440–1) has recently calculated that for the UK and USA an estimate of one-half seems to be correct for recent decades. (This issue has recently been discussed exhaustively in Kessler and Masson (1988), pp. 1–11 and pp. 23–8. Unfortunately this volume came to our attention too late for consideration here of some of their findings.) It must be said that for a theoretical and macro-economic analysis like the present one the size of inter-generational assets (relative to the whole national wealth) is of little importance, since its mere existence is bound to play a fundamental role in the determination of the equilibrium values of the system. In addition, the presence of a specific class for which inter-generational wealth plays a decisive role in the determination of its total disposable income reinforces the proposition of treating the process of formation and transmission of inter-generational wealth in its own way. For these, and other reasons, it is clear that the inclusion of the bequest motive in our model remains valid even if it were to make up a relatively small proportion of the total wealth of a community.

years of detective work on successive generations, that inheritances or inter-generational capital, remain a factor of the utmost importance.[2]

If inheritance plays such an important role in the process of accumulation and distribution (i.e. concentration) of wealth, then it must also be relevant in the formation and distribution of income, both functional and personal, and also in the determination of the profits-rate. Such a view is shared, among many others, by King (1985) and Kotlikoff and Summers (1981). King (1985, p. 285), for example, stresses that in spite of the great obstacles in modelling inheritances empirically, 'it is clear that the subject merits further work at both the theoretical and the empirical level'. And he adds that for a specific set of households 'bequests are likely to represent one of the main motives for accumulation of wealth'. This latter statement may, at first sight, justify the division of households into socio-economic classes which, on one side, give emphasis to life-cycle savings, and, on the other, give more emphasis to the distinction between consumption and savings in a life-cycle framework. The same argument is taken up by Kotlikoff and Summers who state that: 'life-cycle models of savings that emphasize savings for retirement as the dominant form of capital accumulation should give way to models that illuminate the determinants of inter-generational transfers' (Kotlikoff and Summers, 1981, p. 706).

For these reasons it seems that the issue of inheritance and inter-generational transfers must be incorporated in theoretical models of income distribution and profit determination which have been put forward in the last three decades and which have been at the centre of the so-called 'Two-Cambridges' controversies on capital theory and income distribution. Such an issue has already been considered, at least from a partial point of view, in the neoclassical literature, although the main focus has not been on defining the influence of inheritance on the *functional* distribution of income and wealth (with the notable exception of Bevan, 1974; Atkinson, 1974b; and Britto, 1972, 1979). Much more interest, in this context, has been shown in the study of the impact of inheritance on the personal distribution of income and wealth. Among studies of this kind we find those of Atkinson (1971, 1975, ch. 6), Atkinson and Harrison (1978), Bevan (1974, 1979), Blinder (1973,

---

[2] Though Harbury and Hitchens recognize that it is difficult to unravel the complexities of the process of the transfer of inter-generational wealth, they state that: 'If judgement must be reserved about *trends* over time, one firm conclusion seems almost unequivocally to stand out. It is that inheritance is the major determinant of wealth inequality. The regression analysis attributed some two-thirds of the inequality of the distribution of wealth in 1973 to inheritance. . . . It is difficult to avoid the conclusion that inheritance has been the most important single source of wealth inequality in the fairly recent past in twentieth-century Britain' (Harbury and Hitchens, 1979, p. 136).

1976), Brittain (1973, 1977), Flemming (1979), Harbury (1962), King (1985), Meade (1966*b*, 1973), Menchik (1979), Oulton (1976) and Phelps Brown (1988). The review *Economica* dedicated a whole issue to this question in November 1979, with contributions by A. S. Goldberger, P. L. Menchik, J. S. Flemming, D. L. Bevan, J. P. Laitner, and A. S. Shorrocks.

1.1.2 Method of analysis

We now come to the method of analysis, and more precisely to the general framework that we have chosen to adopt.[3] In our opinion the influence of inheritance and bequests on the functional distribution of income and wealth may be more exhaustively and convincingly considered in a (modified) post-Keynesian framework, and this for various reasons. Among the most important are the following: the possibility of considering different socio-economic classes; the non-acceptance of the marginalistic postulate following which the payment of the factors of production is based on their marginal productivity, so allowing for elements of market imperfection or elements of monopoly which also may take part in the process of distribution; and the long-term horizon of the model, which adjusts itself well to the issue of inheritance or inter-generational transfers that, by their very nature, may be analysed only in a long-term framework. The other differences between the various theoretical frameworks in which these issues may be considered (and their main implications) are dealt with in the sections below.

Of course, in order to set the problem in an appropriate perspective, it will be necessary to introduce into the chosen model substantial additions, which will not alter the basic postulates of post-Keynesian theory. This will be achieved first by giving to it some micro-foundations, since inheritance motives may be considered only within the context of a household or dynasty (classes being made up by a given number of households or dynasties with given common distinguishing economic features); and secondly by introducing a sort of 'rational and optimal behaviour' of individuals who first consider the possibility of leaving a given bequest to their children (compatible with the requirements for growth of the system), and then proceed to allocate their consumption and savings in order to maximize their total utility. (Alternatively we shall also attach a given utility to the inter-generational bequest and to the allocation of consumption and consider the conditions under which

---

[3] In Baranzini (1976) a number of issues associated with the same problem were considered within a neoclassical context, and a number of analytical results were reached that will be compared to those obtained in the present volume. The interpretation of the differences between the two frameworks will bring out new perspectives for this area of enquiry.

the accumulation of the inter-generational capital stock satisfies the requirements for steady-state growth.)

These procedures are clearly more compatible within a neoclassical or marginalist framework, which is basically micro-economic in its foundations, though there is no major objection to providing the post-Keynesian model with such micro-foundations, provided that the most important qualifications are retained. Such qualifications refer to a given capital/output ratio; to the circularity of the system according to which it is investment, exogenously determined by employment conditions, which governs overall savings; and to the equality between investment and savings ensured by changes in the distribution of income among classes rather than by changes in the level of economic activity as in the case of the traditional neoclassical model.

The other important qualification of the post-Keynesian model concerns the saving propensity of the classes, which normally is supposed to be fixed and exogenously given; in the model adopted here this will not be the case, and the saving propensity of the classes will be a function of most parameters of the model including the equilibrium interest rate which influences the income of individuals via their accumulated savings (on which an interest rate is earned). In this way one moves away from comparative static analysis towards a much more long-term one, encompassing two or more generations with their inter-generational bequests and their life-cycle plans of savings, consumption, and dynastic accumulation.

From this point of view post-Keynesian economics may be considered a 'research programme' in continuous evolution and refinement. In the 1950s and 1960s, mainly through the works of the Cambridge economists Nicholas Kaldor, Joan Robinson, Richard Kahn, and Luigi Pasinetti, the main development of post-Keynesian theory was generalizing Keynes's theory to the long run, to encompass questions of income distribution and profit determination in a full-employment situation. On this point it is interesting to note what Pasinetti thinks:

[T]he main concern of post-Keynesian economists has been that of generalizing Keynes's theory to the long-run, although I do not think it would be correct to take this as implying a criticism of Keynes's short-run approach. Keynes was indeed primarily concerned with the short run, because he wanted to explain how a capitalist system may fall into a depression, at any point of time, owing to the lack of effective demand. This leaves the long run completely open for investigation. Economics is after all concerned both with short- and with long-run processes, and it appears to me quite natural that Keynes's analytical breakthrough in short-run economics should be pursued into the long run (Pasinetti, 1984–5, p. 246).[4]

[4] Bortis (1988) links post-Keynesianism to classical economics, stating that 'Post-

Since the late 1960s several additional developments and extensions have taken place in post-Keynesian economics. We shall mention here those with a direct or indirect reference to the problems of long-run distribution and accumulation.[5]

A first step was taken by the introduction of uncertainty into the monetary post-Keynesian model, mainly developed in the USA. We find here the works of Davidson (1978), which give uncertainty a central role in the explanation of accumulation and effective demand, and Minsky, who underlines the importance of volatile long-run expectations for the determination of capital accumulation, and gives particular emphasis to financial stability in the determination of the dynamics of a capitalist system. Kregel's (1976) contribution on 'Economic Methodology in the Face of Uncertainty' should also be mentioned: in this paper Kregel stresses that long-run growth and capital accumulation can be handled by making simplifying assumptions about liquidity preference and consumption and allowing for the effects of changes in capital stock. In Chapter 7 consideration is also given to uncertainty in the consumption- and saving-plans of households (via the rate of return on accumulated savings) and it is shown that in certain cases it may explain the existence of different classes of financial capital owners.

Another major line of research of post-Keynesian economists has been pursued to provide some kind of micro-foundations for the model, with particular regard to the theory of the firm. Two of the most important steps in this direction have been those of Wood (1975) and Eichner (1976, 1986).[6] Eichner enquires into the micro-foundations of the corporate economy, in the conviction that orthodox micro-economic theory has little relevance to the contemporary situation of large industrial systems. He situates his contribution in an 'alternative body of

Keynesianism is nothing but a projection of Keynesian short-run theory into the medium and long-term on classical (Ricardian) lines' (Bortis, 1988, p. 71); or 'to simplify somewhat, post-Keynesianism could thus be called *a synthesis of Ricardo and Keynes*' (Bortis, 1988, p. 1).

[5] Harcourt (1981) distinguishes between three different strands of Keynesianism: (*a*) Keynesian fundamentalists (represented by Paul Davidson, Hyman Minsky, and Sidney Weintraub); (*b*) the Robinsonians (represented by Joan Robinson, Richard Kahn, Michael Kalecki, and Jan Kregel); and (*c*) the neo-Ricardians (represented by Krishna Bharadwaj, John Eatwell, Piero Garegnani, Murray Milgate, and Luigi Pasinetti). To the Robinsonians we should add Geoffrey Harcourt himself.

[6] In the preface to his second volume he states that: '[There is a] need to abandon the supply-and-demand framework of the orthodox theory if a realistic model of the US and other advanced market economies is ever to be constructed. Indeed, it can be argued on the basis of the essays contained in this collection that supply and demand curves, with price as the common explanatory variable, play the same role in economic analysis that a belief in Divine intervention plays in scientific work in general: it is an extraneous element which obscures the factors actually at work. The proof that the US economy can be modelled more realistically by abandoning the conventional supply-and-demand framework will be found in the following essays' (Eichner, 1986, p. viii).

theory' founded on the 'managerial, behaviouralist, institutionalist and post-Keynesian literature', which he labels as the 'new micro-economics'.[7] He defines it as follows:

The new microeconomics is intended, first and foremost, to provide a more useful model of firm and industry behaviour. Instead of viewing the firm as merely the cat's paw of an impersonal market, it regards the business enterprise, especially when it takes the form of a modern corporation, or megacorp, as an important source of independent decision-making within the economy.... The decision of how much to invest is far more important to the firm's continued success than the decision of how much to produce, with the decision of what price to charge being more closely tied to the former than to the latter (Eichner, 1986, p. 28).

In the intention of Eichner the new micro-economics is meant to provide a more convenient and exhaustive foundation for macro-economics analysis. In his words:

The output, price, investment, and finance decisions made at the firm level are critical in determining the macrodynamic behaviour of the system as a whole, and if that macrodynamic behaviour, as represented by the growth of output and employment as well as by the rise in the average price level, is to be adequately explained, it is necessary that the macro model rests on a solid micro foundation (Eichner, 1986, p. 28).

Eichner presents in detail the 'distinguishing centerpiece' of the new micro-economics of the firm, a model of mutually determined investment, prices, external finance, and output, first considered in a deterministic world and secondly by introducing three types of uncertainty: major product innovation, inter-firm competition, and changes in government policies. The model has also been used to throw additional light on the 'stylized' historical facts of recent decades, i.e. the secular rise in prices and the uneven expansion of the industrialized economies.

We must also mention Wood's (1975) model, which attaches a particular importance to the effects of uncertainty and ignorance about the future on capital markets by rejecting the traditional marginalist choice of maximand and specification of constraints. Wood focuses on the strategic role of retained earnings in the financing of private investment and maintains that, in general, profits are determined by investment. His macro-economic relationships depend on his detailed micro-economic modelling of the individual firm. (In this field see also Kaldor, 1966; and Mastromatteo, 1989a, 1989b.)

A third important line of research of post-Keynesian economics is that

---

[7] Among the post-Keynesian contributions in this field Eichner quotes those of Kalecki, Steindl, Joan Robinson, Sylos-Labini, Vickers (1968), Harris, and Coutts, Godley, and Nordhaus (1978).

pursued mainly by Pasinetti (1965, 1973, 1981). His analysis contains elements which may be placed between the fields of macro- and micro-economics, since it considers the productive (and consumption) system as a set of vertically integrated sectors, hence with an important disaggregation of the macro-economic model. Pasinetti develops an original theoretical treatment of the problems of reaching and maintaining full employment in a multisector economic system with: (*a*) a growing population, (*b*) different rates of technical progress in different productive sectors (an element which has acquired an increasing importance in recent decades), and (*c*) changes in consumers' preferences according to Engel's law. Pasinetti explicitly considers the requirements for full capacity utilization and full employment of the labour force, in the framework of both stable and changing prices.

This approach represents a break with the traditional analysis usually presented in terms of input–output analysis, and presents a scheme in terms of vertically integrated sectors. The great advantage of such an original approach is that it allows for an exhaustive examination of the process of economic growth on the formation of prices and hence on the distribution of income and wealth, and on employment and the dynamics of production in general. In his work Pasinetti leaves aside the analytical tools of marginalist economics by reviving the approach of classical economists in a framework which is basically of a (post-) Keynesian nature. (On this point see, for instance, Baranzini and Scazzieri, 1990, sect. 1.6.)

A fourth research programme of post-Keynesian economics, although less co-ordinated than the previous one but more directly connected with the theme of the present volume, is represented by the large literature stemming from the original Kaldor (1956)–Pasinetti (1962) model of economic growth, income distribution, and profit determination. This literature will be classified in detail in sect. 2.3. Generally speaking this research programme has been motivated by the desire of 'relaxing assumptions, trying new hypotheses, introducing complications of all sorts' into the original two-class model. According to Pasinetti:

The considerable amount of literature that was generated by this theorem has gone through two phases. A first phase was characterized by explorations on what happens *outside* the range within which the theorem holds; and here the contribution that has become most renowned is that of Meade (1963, 1966) and Samuelson–Modigliani (1966), who—in an effort to bring back some relevance for the neoclassical theory of marginal productivity—have analysed the range within which workers' savings are so high as to make their coexistence with the capitalists impossible on a long-run equilibrium-growth path. . . . In a second phase that has followed many authors have proceeded to relaxing assumptions, trying new hypotheses, introducing complications of all sorts. This second phase has only led to a strengthening of the original Cambridge Theorem (i.e. Kaldor's approach) which has been emerging as surprisingly much more robust to changes of assumptions than the Meade–Samuelson–Modigliani Dual, while the symmetrical aspects, on which Meade, Samuelson and Modigliani relied so much, have been receding in the background and falling out of the picture one after another (Pasinetti, 1989a, p. 25).

Table 1.1 presents a schematic representation of the broad field of analysis covered by post-Keynesian economics in general, with special reference to the topics of price determination, income distribution, and capital accumulation. The list is naturally not exhaustive of the whole 'research programme' and does not even include some of the works which are quoted in the first part of this volume. The distinction between macro- and micro-economics is of course maintained, even if it is sometimes difficult to label a specific theory as belonging to one or other of the fields. It may be noted that a notable effort has been made to provide the post-Keynesian scheme with some micro-elements; and the purpose of this volume is that of providing some foundations for the completion of the box at the bottom on the right-hand side, concerning the micro-economics side of the large field of consumers' allocation of consumption, savings, and wealth. To this is added a specific field of analysis, corresponding to the 'sectorial' or 'inter-industry' analysis formulated by Pasinetti, who considers production, distribution, and consumption dynamics within the disaggregated sectors of the economy, but without descending to the single-firm's level.

1.2   THE CONCEPT OF WEALTH

This volume deals primarily with the mechanisms connected with the supply-side accumulation of life-cycle savings and inter-generational dynastic wealth (or financial capital). It does not deal with the complicated process of productive capital formation and accumulation, which is mainly determined by entrepreneurial activity responding to various demands. Clearly the two processes are strictly interlinked since, in general and in the long-run, the process of formation and accumulation of physical capital must be matched by corresponding abstention from present consumption for future consumption. However, this distinction between the two acts is made easier by the overall macro-economic feature of the post-Keynesian model: the amount of physical investment that entrepreneurs will choose is determined by the technologically given K/Y (capital/output) ratio, normally subject to full-employment conditions.[8] In order to ensure equilibrium the total supply of savings will

---

[8] As Bortis (1976, 1984) has suggested it may be determined by other specific requirements, not necessarily implying full employment.

Table 1.1 Post-Keynesian theory: seminal research programmes for price theory, economic growth, and distribution

	Primarily field of price theory, production and functional distribution of income	Primarily field of consumer demand, allocation and accumulation of wealth
Macro-economic level	Kalecki (1939, 1954, 1971a), Robinson (1956, 1962), Kaldor (1956, 1960a, 1962), Pasinetti (1962, 1974a), Wood (1975, 1978), Pasinetti (1966c)	Kalecki (1939, 1954, 1971a), Robinson (1956, 1962), Kaldor (1956, 1960a, 1961, 1966, 1976), Pasinetti (1962, 1974a, 1981, 1989a)
'Sectoral' or industrial level	Pasinetti (1965, 1977a, 1981, 1988a), Leon (1967), Goodwin (1967)	Pasinetti (1965, 1977a, 1981, 1988a)
Micro-economic level	('New Micro-Economics') Eichner (1973, 1976), Kregel (1976), Sylos-Labini (1962, 1974, 1979), Vickers (1968), Harris (1974), Moss (1978), Wood (1975, 1978), Coutts, Godley, Nordhaus (1978), Harcourt and Kenyon (1976)	Issues of wealth and wealth accumulation (both life-cycle and inter-generational); allocation of consumption and savings over the life-cycle

have to equal total physical investment; and the mechanisms which make this equality possible will be studied in this volume. More specifically, the term 'wealth accumulation' is used to indicate the decisions of individuals or families to save for a specific objective, while the term 'capital accumulation' will, more generally, refer to the wider process through which a society increases its potential to produce a flow of goods and services.

It may be argued that there is no generally accepted definition of wealth; rather there are a number of alternative wealth concepts. This does not represent a major problem for our analysis, at least once a precise strategy has been defined. It will however play an important role in the context of uncertainty within the model of long-term accumulation (see Chapter 7), since the existence of non-specified forms of alternative assets may explain a particular behaviour of a given class.[9] Parents, for instance, can pass on to their children advantages of education, genetic talents, social contacts, or, as will be assumed throughout this work, money wealth. All these elements may lead a privileged child to accumulate above-average wealth through, for example, 'the possession of "superior" education or genes or through social

[9] On the difference between income and wealth one can be more straightforward. While income can be defined as a 'flow of goods or services', wealth is usually thought of as being a 'stock' of goods and services. The definition of wealth may however cause some misunderstanding, as pointed out by Pasinetti: 'The principal distinction to be made is that "abundance of goods" might mean an endowment, or fund, of existing goods, i.e. wealth as a stock of commodities or claims, or it might mean a sizable periodic flow of goods and services, i.e. wealth as a flow of commodities or income. These two meanings are often confused, even today. Yet they embody very different concepts. Although the two kinds of wealth are not, of course, unconnected, the relation between the two is not at all simple or clear; nor is it unchanging with the evolution of the economic systems themselves. The fact is that, when speaking of the wealth of single individuals, one usually finds it most convenient to refer to the concept of wealth as a stock (to the size of their total ownership). But, when speaking of rich and poor countries, one usually refers to the average income per head of their inhabitants, i.e. to their average annual ability to produce goods and services' (Pasinetti, 1977a, p. 2). Although the two concepts are interrelated (since in general, there ought to be a positive relationship between stock of wealth and annual production of goods and services), it is clear from a historical point of view that the stock of wealth is a much more important variable than the annual flow of income resulting from it: the accumulation (as well as the distribution among classes or among dynasties) of wealth is a dynamic concept which ought to be considered over a long period of time. The behavioural parameters used in this context should also be connected with long-term variables, such as life-cycle savings- and consumption-plans or the inter-generational transmission of wealth. In the traditional post-Keynesian model of growth and income distribution (à la Kaldor–Pasinetti) the link between the distribution of income and the distribution of wealth is represented by a fixed (exogenously given) propensity to save of the socio-economic classes of the system. If one differentiates between life-cycle and inter-generational capital stock (the former being a function, among other parameters and variables, of the rate of return on capital) then the interaction between distribution of income and wealth accumulation becomes more complicated, and the link necessitates further enquiry. This methodological point is taken up again in Chapters 2 and 3.

contacts made at school, which lead to business opportunities in later life, or even to a wealthy spouse' (Harbury and Hitchens, 1979, p. 3). So the question of wealth distribution, both at the personal and functional level, remains crucial for theoretical economists as well as policy-makers. Consider for example the macro-economic policies' objective of efficient allocation of resources, growth, price stability, and full employment. The pursuit of these objectives is liable to be influenced by the distribution of wealth:

The effectiveness of investment may be illustrated by capital/output ratios, for the estimation of which real rather than financial assets are then mainly relevant. There is likely to be more interest too in assets as plant and equipment than in the stock of dwellings. Nevertheless, financial assets are also relevant to such matters as savings propensities when the effectiveness of counter-inflationary policies are under discussion (Harbury and Hitchens, 1979, p. 4).

Clearly in both marginalist and post-Keynesian contexts the way in which wealth (or financial capital) is accumulated represents an important question, because it exercises a direct influence on the level of consumption (think of the relevance of the composition of consumption in any sectoral analysis) and on the impact that it has on investment activity (directly on the availability of finance in a marginalist model). Hence, functional distribution of income has an important impact on the personal distribution of income, on the process of savings and wealth accumulation, and on the distinction between life-cycle and intergenerational bequests. This will, later, exercise its influence on the distribution of income.

1.3 THE ACCUMULATION OF PHYSICAL CAPITAL: SOME CONCEPTUAL ELEMENTS

Since the pattern of accumulation of physical capital is strictly connected with the supply side of savings it may be worth considering some aspects of the former; a number of the following points will be reconsidered in due course, especially in connection with the institutional and distributional framework. As pointed out by Nell (1987, pp. 14–15) the process of accumulation of capital has mainly been considered in one or other of two general frameworks. The first and more common is that which sees it 'as an extension of the productive potential of an economy with a given technology, which may be improved in the process'; this view is based on the idea of steady growth and on the 'conception of capital as productive goods or, in more sophisticated versions, as a fund providing command over productive goods' (Nell, 1987, p. 14). The second approach analyses 'accumulation or decumulation of capital simply as the adjustment of a particular factor of production to its equilibrium level, as determined by supply and demand'. Obviously within this latter framework the focus of analysis is the allocation of scarce resources, maybe governed by the distribution of consumption and savings or other elements, so leaving the real forces of the process of capital accumulation in the background.

However, according to Nell the analysis of the accumulation of capital always needs refining:

Capital must also be understood as a way of organizing production and economic activity, so that the accumulation of capital is the extension of this form of organization into areas in which production, exchange and distribution were governed by other rules. This conception of capital emphasizes the importance of organization; so understood, technology and engineering are not abstract science, they are ways of organizing production, and so have an institutional dimension. Accumulation then implies the transformation of institutions as well as production (Nell, 1987, p. 14).

An alternative way of considering the process of capital accumulation may be that of retaining the general framework of macro-economic steady-state growth with a given technology and where the other macro-economic relationships are determined independently of the micro-economic relationships. However, the relevance of the organization of production and distribution, and of the institutional framework, may be considered at the intermediate level with the introduction of socio-economic classes into the model. Let us consider these elements in detail.

1. *The organization of production*, which concerns above all the definition of the role of the productive factors, which in non-marginalist models are linked to the role of socio-economic classes. Fundamentally the typology concerns the capitalists or entrepreneurs who organize production (and own directly the physical capital stock), the workers who provide labour and life-cycle savings, and in certain cases a class of rentiers.[10] The proportion of the various factors employed in the production process may be determined both endogenously or exogenously (with a fixed capital/output ratio in the post-Keynesian model).

2. *The strictly defined institutional framework*, which concerns first of all the role of the state, via the fiscal structure (on consumption, income, and wealth), via the various types of subsidy, the control on prices, and anti-monopolies legislation. Under this heading one could also consider the way in which education is provided and distributed in the economic system.

---

[10] Note that in a number of models a class may provide more than one factor of production.

3. *The distributional framework*, which concerns all laws and rules which lead to a given distribution both at the functional and personal level of income and wealth. The marginalist framework is based on the concept of marginal productivity of the factors of production; the classical and post-Keynesian frameworks do rely on other concepts and put in the foreground the historical aspects of accumulation and distribution.

Most of these points will be reconsidered in detail below. Here it should be pointed out that the process of accumulation of physical capital is closely associated with the technical, demographic, institutional, and distributional structure of an economic system. This association has a double nature, since the same accumulation process has a strong influence on these factors. This fact has often been underestimated; for instance accumulation may influence the long-term development of technology via variations in the composition of demand (due to improvements in the standard of living) or the utilization of different proportions of productive factors. Accumulation may also influence the demographic structure: the inter-generational transmission of wealth of a number of dynasties may be better achieved with a smaller than average number of children; moreover the process of accumulation allows for a higher standard of living and hence may influence the composition of the average family.

The accumulation process leads of course to changes in the distribution of income and wealth, both at the functional and personal level.[11] This is especially true in classical and post-Keynesian models, although in a different way, and is even more important if accumulation causes the appearance of market imperfections. This leads us to the fourth argument, i.e. the influence that accumulation has on the institutional framework. Accumulation, as has often been pointed out, during early stages requires concentration of economic power which is often, but not necessarily, institutionalized; at a later stage it often requires the intervention of the public sector which takes steps to check restrictive practices (for instance through anti-monopolies legislation), to enforce a given degree of price control, and/or to regulate the economy in general.

1.4 THE PROCESS OF WEALTH ACCUMULATION AND SOCIO-ECONOMIC CLASSES

The identification of social, institutional, and economic classes in the process of income formation and distribution has permeated most of the

---

[11] On this point see e.g. Adelman and Taft Morris (1971).

macro-economic models since the physiocrats of the seventeenth century. This may well be due, among other things, to the fact that until a few decades ago most societies were characterized by the existence of closed classes, with little or no mobility, each with a high degree of homogeneity.[12] The relevance of the existence of classes in bringing about a given distribution has been recently summarized by Phelps Brown as follows: 'Not only are people grouped by origin, moreover, but the levels that they can ever attain are limited from the outset— limited both by the qualifications they are able to acquire and by the posts that are open to them. The inequality of income and wealth, in other words, is simply one expression of class structure' (Phelps Brown, 1988, p. 471).

From an economic point of view this means that certain groups of people do share a common behaviour, like a high propensity to consume and a low propensity to save; or a high propensity to endow their children with financial assets; or a high propensity to reinvest in the productive process; or in the case of pensioners, a very low income with a fairly high propensity to consume. There are however various parameters by which classes may be identified, aiming in particular at socio-economic phenomena. Among these we may consider:

1. Different endowments (human and physical capital in particular).[13]

---

[12] According to Joan Robinson: 'A nation is made up of groups and classes with conflicting interests. The only example of a human society without internal conflicts was Robinson Crusoe, and even he may have suffered from ambivalence. An economy is an entity consisting of groups with conflicting interests held together by rules of the game' (Robinson, 1956, p. 16). The relevance of socio-economic classes in the process of wealth accumulation is discussed in the sections that follow.

[13] The question of heritability of intelligence has been widely debated in the literature, starting from the observation that looking at a national population one is confronted with large differences in intelligence as measured by IQ tests. To what extent are these differences the result of variations in genetic make-up, and to what extent are they the outcome of differences in life-experience? In other words, what weight of the variance in IQ-test scores may be attributed to genetic variance, and what weight may be attributed to socio-economic and environmental variance? This question is relevant in the context of studies similar to the present one, since if the IQ variance is due to socio-economic reasons, then it ought to be considered as an endogenous variable. Moreover one could argue, as Goldberger (1979, p. 326) does, that if the IQ variance is largely of a genetic nature, then it is bound to be immutable, while if the IQ variance is largely due to socio-economic or environmental conditions, this may be eradicated (at least in principle). On this point, which has intrigued generations of scientists, opinions differ widely. Goldberger (1979, p. 326) quotes the geneticist C. O. Carter as maintaining that it is 'evident to any experienced and unprejudiced observer that the major part of the variation of intellectual ability in school children in Britain is genetic' (*The Times*, 3 Nov. 1976). By providing new, more adequate, statistics Goldberger observes that the IQ correlation within families 'weakens as the biological and/or social distance increases'. The opinion that genetic variance accounts for a high share of the IQ variance has been rejected by other authors as well: Jencks puts this figure at about 45 per cent, while Kamin showed that a number of these empirical correlations had been wrongly calculated and distorted.

2. Different sources of income, or predominance of a given type of income (from labour, capital, land, etc.).
3. Different propensities to consume and to save (average and/or marginal).
4. The predominance of 'life-cycle' or 'inter-generational' capital stock owned.
5. Different propensities to leave a bequest to the next generation (under the form of human capital or education, physical or financial capital, and/or social contacts).
6. Different bargaining positions which may lead to different economic rewards, for instance in terms of income. This element refers also to the existence of residuals in certain functional theories of income distribution, where factors are not paid according, say, to their marginal productivity, but according to their particular role in the productive process.

Clearly this list is not exhaustive, although it incorporates most of the criteria on which physiocratic, classical, post-Keynesian, and neo-Ricardian models of distribution have been constructed and developed. (Not to mention also certain neoclassical models as those of Samuelson and Modigliani (1966a, b), Meade (1963, 1964, 1966a), Stiglitz (1967), Sato (1966), Britto (1969, 1972), and Balestra and Baranzini (1971) which have taken into account the hypothesis of different socio-economic classes.)

It is also clear that some of the criteria may apply simultaneously in certain cases. As a matter of fact institutional principles in most societies tend to link points 1 and 2; on the other hand most models of distribution (in particular post-Keynesian and neo-Ricardian) have postulated a strict relationship between points 2 and 3 due to the different role in the accumulation process assigned to each class. Points 4 and 5 are also strictly connected, since under normal conditions a higher propensity to leave a bequest will tend to increase the relevance of the inter-generational capital stock (or inheritances) through time for a given dynasty or class. The same argument may be applied to point 1,

---

Goldberger (1979, where all references are provided) concludes by stating that for a right assessment of the relevance of heritability it may be convenient to focus on earnings. On this point he rejects three propositions: (a) that inter-generational mobility is low (i.e. that a son's earnings closely resemble those of his father); (b) that environmental improvements cannot produce much change in an individual's earnings; and (c) that the genetic factor, an important determinant of an individual's earning capacity, cannot be changed. On the question whether 'equalizing common environments would eliminate only a small proportion of earnings variance', Goldberger (1979, pp. 346–7) is less definite because it would seem much more functional to 'provide appropriate rather than mechanically equal environments, that is to optimize rather than equalize the development of earnings ability'. (On this point see also, for an exhaustive treatment, Phelps Brown, 1988, pp. 473–8.)

concerning the endowment of a given class, which in the case of the physical capital is strictly linked with points 4 and 5.

One should however be careful in assuming certain relationships as given, since institutional aspects may in certain cases not apply in a traditional sense, but may register relevant changes. One clear example, often quoted in the post-Keynesian literature, relates to Kaldor's (1955–6) seminal model of profit determination and income distribution: in this model one class (the workers) draws its income entirely from work and saves a small but positive share of its income. However, this class does not own (directly) the resulting accumulated savings nor does it earn the relative interest income on them. It is, as pointed out in Balestra and Baranzini (1971, p. 244), as 'if the workers hand over their savings to the capitalists without getting any sort of compensation in return'. This led Pasinetti to refine the model by stating that:

In any type of society, when any individual saves a part of his income, he must also be allowed to own it, otherwise he would not save at all. This means that the stock of capital which exists in the system is owned by those people (capitalists and workers) who in the past made the corresponding savings. And since ownership of capital entitles the owner to a rate of interest, if workers have saved—and thus own a part of the stock of capital (directly or through loans to the capitalists)—then they will also receive a share of the total profits (Pasinetti, 1962, p. 270).[14]

This passage is particularly important since it shows that the relationship between ownership and its reward is not always a direct one. Suffice it to mention differentiated interest rates on accumulated savings (considered by a number of scholars—see Sect. 2.3 below—including Pasinetti, 1974, ch. 6) according to whether the investment is done in a direct way or not; and also death duties, which in certain cases may mean that a large proportion of inter-generational capital stock is transferred to the public sector in the form of taxes. Other cases may be found in the literature.[15]

---

[14] In this way the distinction among factors of production no longer corresponds to that of socio-economic classes, since in this specific case, through their accumulated savings, workers earn a wage income and a share of profits of the system. This is just one example of 'earnings overlapping' for a given class, which is bound to give a higher rate of flexibility to the model considered.

[15] A somewhat similar problem arises when the division of an estate among the children (which may play an important part in the process of wealth concentration or dispersion) does not take place on equal terms, so preventing the overall steady-state growth of the system. A study made by the British Royal Commission on the Distribution of Income and Wealth in 1977 (and quoted by Phelps Brown, 1988, pp. 452–4) shows, for a fairly large sample, that in half the estates with two or more children, the bequests to the children were equal. For the other half 'it can be calculated that on average the most-favoured child received 74 per cent of the property bequeathed to two children, and about 51 per cent where there were three or four children' (Phelps Brown, 1988, p. 453).

To conclude, it should be added that the socio-economic and historical parameters by which classes may be identified are numerous and are combined according to the main criteria of the various schemes of analysis. Emphasis on the parameters varies from model to model, as institutional backgrounds tend to change continuously, and also according to the priorities chosen and to the particular political system envisaged.

1.5 INCOME, OWNERSHIP OF WEALTH, AND EXISTENCE OF CLASSES

The task of studying the relationships between the distribution of income and the accumulation of personal or dynastic wealth is made more complicated by the following factors:

1. The classes to be found in a given society do not always correspond with the broad categories of income.
2. The motives behind the accumulation of wealth or capital differ widely, and may include a desire for life-cycle savings, a wish to make inter-generational transfers, or even 'consumption repugnance'.
3. The demographic constraints (i.e. the number of children per family, life-expectancy, length of retirement, or length of education) vary widely among classes and even within the same class.
4. There exists a certain degree of class mobility, which tends to reduce or to magnify class distinctions.
5. The relationship between wealth and relative income tends to differ according to the type of investment and to its size; this may be an additional element in the concentration or dispersal of the financial aggregate stock.

Of these five factors which profoundly affect relationships among social classes and between successive generations the first one is considered here, the others being analysed in later sections and chapters. During this exposition the existence of other factors of class distinction not listed here will also be considered.

As pointed out in Baranzini and Scazzieri (1986, pp. 36–40), a relevant difference between 'production oriented' and 'exchange oriented' theories, closely connected with the definition of income and wealth distribution, is to be found in the 'social class' vision and 'individualistic' vision associated with the two lines of research respectively. Sir John Hicks uses the term 'political economy' for production-oriented theories (classical and post-Keynesian for instance) and 'catallactics' for exchange-oriented ones (as neoclassical) and states that: 'political economy is always in some sense socialist, catallactics individualist; though one cannot make that fit the history unless one distinguishes between means and ends. The Old Political Economists were socialists (or at least "social") in the ends they set up; but they were individualist in practice, because they held that individualism was the way to the achievement of their social ends' (Hicks, 1976, p. 213).

This point is also taken up by Harris who emphasizes that within the marginalist framework the distribution of the product is 'conceived in terms of a society of atomistic individuals' and tackled within the sphere of exchange (both of factor services and of products). Moreover he maintains that:

Underlying this neoclassical analysis is the conception of a society *without* classes, defined either in terms of appropriation of the product according to divisions in property ownership, as in Classical economic analysis, or in terms of a social-production relation (the capital–labour relation) based on control of labor in production, as in Marxian theory. In this respect, there is a fundamental division between the substance of neoclassical theory on the one hand and that of Classical and Marxian theory on the other. Without classes in the above sense there can be no meaningful distinction between income from property and income from work (Harris, 1978, pp. 19–20).

According to the marginalist scheme distribution is determined by marginal productivity and the quantity of each factor employed. Consequently the basis on which a given share of the product accrues to a given group of people, dynasty, or class has no particular importance, except for the marginal productivity of the factor owned.

As pointed out in the preceding paragraph, the definition and identification of social classes or groups in economic terms is not easy. A social class may be defined broadly as a group of individuals who share one or more common attributes. In a number of post-Keynesian models of distribution two attributes do, in principle, overlap for both classes. Those who directly own physical means of production and whose income is mainly derived from this ownership make up the capitalist or entrepreneuriał class, which in general exhibits a higher than average propensity to save (and reinvest). On the other hand those who do not own physical means of production (i.e. physical capital), or only indirectly, and whose income is mainly derived from work (or from capital) have a lower than average propensity to save: they are labelled as workers.[16]

Of course other criteria are used to divide the population into classes,

---

[16] More or less the same scheme is to be found in physiocratic and classical theories, where the distinction between property rights (capital, labour, and land) and propensities to consume and to save is even more pronounced.

or to subdivide them to provide for more realism so giving more flexibility to the model. The point is, as Craven (1979) argues, that models that give prominence to this kind of behavioural assumption (relative to saving)

contrast with all models of competitive economies where individuals react only to the direct stimulus of the markets in which they operate and have no appreciable effects on those markets. The comment that might be made on a two-class approach to the problem is that it simplifies the model to such an extent that the interests of each group can be clearly seen and the outcome is fairly easy to work out. However, this is a virtue of the macroeconomic approach to distribution theory, which enables us to see the main forces at work. If the model were made much more complicated, it would be difficult to see how collective action by any group that understood the model could change the outcome in its favour (Craven, 1979, p. 79).

It might be added that the assumption relative to class structure might in certain cases allow enquiry into the conditions in which inconsistencies might arise in the course of the development of a given economic system (and this may be relevant for the study of development economics) or in identifying the cause of pathological aspects of a given system. One might not be able to put forward exact propositions to eliminate such inconsistencies, but it might well be possible to identify their causes and underlying mechanisms.

These aspects are recalled by Walsh and Gram (1980, p. 406) who underline the relevance of assigning ownership of the factors of production to groups or classes which are not necessarily confined to an exclusive role or activity, as in the case of certain post-Keynesian models (see Chapter 2) where a given class can, simultaneously, draw income from labour and accumulated savings (i.e. capital indirectly owned) and where there are also classes who draw their income solely from one factor of production. Of course a similar argument may be applied to the propensity to save, which may be differentiated not according to the class, but according to the origin of the income.

On the other hand the lack of a class structure is more in line with the fundamental principles of the neoclassical model, which is basically micro-economically oriented and dominated by perfect competition. Some of these points are taken up by Walsh and Gram (1980), who by analysing the mechanisms of price formation maintain that in the case of neoclassical theories:

social class is subsumed in the given pattern of ownership of factors, a pattern which may be egalitarian or extremely uneven. This treats class division solely in terms of demand; the preferences of certain consumers happen to have more weight in the balance that determines the allocation of resources and the distribution of output. Production, on the other hand, is analyzed independently of the distribution of these endowments, and thus of social class. There is no counterpart in neoclassical theory to the classical idea that private ownership of produced means of production as such has an important bearing on the analysis of production in a capitalist economy. At the same time, the irrelevance of class relations in production is entirely consistent with the neoclassical view of the economic problem as that of exchange of the productive powers of given resources. Differences in factors ownership may alter the terms of this exchange, it is argued, but not the structure of the theory (Walsh and Gram, 1980, p. 406).

The implications of the existence or absence of a class structure, both on the production and consumption side, seem to be far-reaching. First, according to the socio-economic framework chosen, one provides a different setting for the explanation of the mechanisms at work in an industrialized society and a different approach to the problems of price formation, income distribution, wealth accumulation, and so on. Secondly, the choice is bound to have a major impact on the time-horizon of the model: more static and hence more concerned about the interrelationships among the variables existing at the time in the case of a classless or atomistic society; more dynamic and hence more interested in the 'historical' aspects of the model in the case of the presence of socio-economic groups at whatever level of production, distribution, and consumption. Of course the introduction of the life-cycle hypothesis into a classical or post-Keynesian comparative-statics context will give a longer horizon to the model, allowing for a more comprehensive examination of the factors of wealth accumulation and for a distinction between life-cycle and inter-generational capital stock. This is due to the fact that in this context decisions about savings are not taken from a short-term perspective, but, as Bliss points out:

Saving presumably is not desired for the most part as an end in itself, but rather as a means to future consumption or bequest. The basis of the life-cycle approach is just such a treatment of the decision to save. It is almost a necessary consequence of that approach that the rate of saving of any particular household will vary over the course of its life-span. Of course, the saving rate of a group of households of the same type may be constant, just as the reproduction rate of a group may be constant notwithstanding the fact that the reproduction rate of an individual family varies over its lifetime (Bliss, 1975, p. 137).

The relevance of the role of socio-economic classes has been reconsidered in a number of recent works (see, for instance, Kirman, 1989, and Nell, 1989), from the point of view of both consumption and saving patterns. By discussing the micro-foundations of macro-economics Kirman concludes that:

It is not mere chance that one assumption that leads to strong results as to uniqueness and stability is that society should behave as an individual. Yet we know that to obtain such behaviour individuals' behaviour must be very similar. (See for example the references to the standard literature on this in Stoker, 1984, who deals with this question in detail.) If we are to progress further we may well be forced to theorise in terms of groups who have collectively coherent behaviour. Thus demand and expenditure functions if they are to be set against reality must be defined at some reasonably high level of aggregation (Kirman, 1989, p. 138).

Kirman also points out that making assumptions about agents' characteristics corresponds, in some ways, to making assumptions about the organization and the institutions of the society in which they operate. Institutions, considered in their broader definition as in Baranzini and Scazzieri (1990, ch. 1), also include the patterns of transmission of wealth, of factors property and, consequently, decisions of individuals or dynasties with regard to consumption, saving, and accumulation. It is precisely on such bases that the micro-foundations of macro-economics will be constructed here. This kind of analysis, especially developed in the context of a steady-state model, will throw light on a number of 'regularities or general patterns of behaviour', in the direction suggested by Kirman:

Anyone who makes significant progress in this direction either by examining and explaining how the nature of interaction and communication between individuals may yield regularity at the aggregate level or by explaining how interaction may yield regularity at the aggregate level or by explaining how interaction may yield restrictions on the evolution of the distribution of agents' characteristics, will have made a radical step forward (Kirman, 1989, p. 138).

The point is that 'regularities or general patterns of behaviour' in the framework of long-term growth have to be discovered as a special link between generations. In this sense the 'class struggle' tends to become a sort of 'generation struggle' as already pointed out in the Introduction.

1.6 PROPERTY RIGHTS AND INCOME DISTRIBUTION

As pointed out in Baranzini and Scazzieri (1986, pp. 36–40) property rights are fundamental determinants of distribution and accumulation if the production process requires some form of co-operation from individuals or classes having the power of 'withdrawing' certain essential inputs of the production process.

Distribution of the social product may be explained by considering the property rights of 'classes' of individuals on condition that the claim of any individual to a certain share of the product is determined by the input category, within which that individual may exert his own 'withdrawal capacity'. The idea that land, capital and labour are 'separately appropriated' (Mill, 1965, p. 235), and that each input category is associated with a 'withdrawal capacity' of a different kind, characterizes the classical theories of income distribution.

Social classes remain fundamental in post-Keynesian theories (Kaldor, 1956; Pasinetti, 1962; Joan Robinson, 1962), even if, in the case of Pasinetti, the distinctive feature of each class is given by its saving and consumption behaviour. In Pasinetti's theory, the assumption of 'separate appropriation' of each productive factor is no longer in the foreground, and workers' incomes are made up of wages and interests on accumulated savings. In this type of theory, it is postulated that there are different rates of saving associated with different classes. The overall rate of saving, then, depends on the distribution of income among such categories of individuals (Baranzini and Scazzieri, 1986, p. 38).

What is relevant is that the Kaldor–Pasinetti model of distribution does not accept the 'strong version' of the social-class theory of income and wealth distribution, while maintaining a 'weak' concept of social class,[17] in which the distinctive features are found in its consumption and saving behaviour rather than in its 'rights and entitlements'. The same applies to the life-cycle theory, where the behavioural parameters (for instance the desire to transmit inter-generational bequests) are relevant in determining the level of consumption and investment.

The concept of socio-economic class is not present in neoclassical or marginalist theories where one finds the following assumptions concerning property and rights: (a) different factors of production may be the property of the same individual; (b) any 'withdrawal capacity', if it exists, is exactly the same for all individuals and factors of production; (c) 'individual' decisions are likely to be affected in a more significant way by market signals than by the 'traditional' choices made in the past (such choices depend on custom, social status, etc., rather than on preferences and prices) (Baranzini and Scazzieri, 1986, p. 39).

These qualifications of the neoclassical model imply that income distribution and capital accumulation are completely detached from the behavioural characteristics associated with the ownership of the factors of production (or 'inputs'). For this reason:

Income distribution and capital accumulation (the latter associated with saving behaviour) thus become entirely consistent with the theory of an individualistic market economy, in the sense that they can be explained by exchange relationships between individuals (or even *within* individuals, as in the case of time-preference theory of saving). Institutional constraints such as the differential

---

[17] J. S. Mill's 'withdrawal capacity' helps to give a less impressionist view of classes. For Mill 'The distribution of wealth . . . depends on the laws and customs of society'; and property rights are fundamental determinants of distribution if the production process requires some form of 'co-operation' from individuals who have the power of 'withdrawing' certain essential inputs.

'powers' associated with ownership of different inputs are removed from the picture, as they cannot easily be explained by considering exchange relationships only. In particular, saving behaviour becomes part of the range of phenomena on which a theory of choice and allocation throws light: 'household saving and dissaving emerge from a treatment of intertemporal consumption planning that is formally closely analogous to . . . static consumption theory' (Bliss, 1975, p. 133) (Baranzini and Scazzieri, 1986, pp. 39–40).

The framework of the neoclassical or marginalist analysis will of course be retained for that part of our model which considers the life-cycle theory in order to provide a micro-framework of income distribution and wealth accumulation.

1.7 WEALTH ACCUMULATION AND ALTERNATIVE ECONOMIC THEORIES

1.7.1 Introduction

The process of accumulation may be considered from two distinct points of view (although they are often considered as a unique element in most analyses):

1. From the *investment* point of view, i.e. as a direct input in the productive process. The main problems connected with this area of analysis are of a micro- and macro-economic nature. At the micro-level we need a theory of the firm which explains the behaviour of firms in the face of investment. At the macro-level a theory of investment must define the level of economic activity under given requirements. For instance in the case of the post-Keynesian model the level of investment must, under conditions of full employment, ensure a steady-state growth to the whole system; savings will passively adjust to such exogenously determined level of investment via income and wealth redistribution. This is a field privileged by economic theorists since it concerns, among other things, the issues of optimal growth, income distribution, and so on.

2. From the *saving*, or supply-side point of view, by considering the mechanisms which lead to a given formation of life-cycle or inter-generational savings. This line of research may be carried out, at least from a theoretical point of view, by taking into account:

(*a*) the influence of economic, institutional, demographic, and technical parameters on the patterns of life-cycle accumulation of savings;

(*b*) the relevance of the mechanisms relative to inter-generational transfers of wealth and the influence on these of economic, institutional, demographic, and technical factors; and

(*c*) the peculiarities, composition, and historical relevance of the socio-economic classes taking part in the process of wealth accumulation.

It should be said that the post-Keynesian school of profit determination and income distribution has mainly concentrated on point 1 above, leaving aside the analysis of point 2. This is of course because the post-Keynesian model is essentially of a macro-economic nature, and cannot, as it is usually formulated, capture all aspects of the supply side of savings, especially those connected with the inter-generational transmission of wealth which requires a study of all behavioural parameters of consumers. It is the purpose of this volume to take up this particular issue.

It should be emphasized that the introduction of an essentially micro-economic model (as the life-cycle theory) into a macro-economic structure (as the post-Keynesian model of distribution) does not represent a breaking-point with tradition. As a matter of fact most models, including the Keynesian one, accept that the behaviour of entrepreneurs is determined by past, present, and future events. In the same way, one may assume that the behaviour of consumers, taken as a class, dynasty, or individuals, is based on past, present, and future events. The latter may refer to the level of bequest inherited, to the level of income earned, or to the desire to endow the next generation with a given asset respectively.

In this way the link between the distribution of income and wealth at the macro-level, and saving and consumption behaviour at the micro-level, turns out to be reinforced. For instance, the rate of profit (supposed equal to the rate of interest) influences the level of disposable income of the various groups; on the other hand the level of savings is no longer exogenously determined by constant propensities to save, but may be endogenized via the expected rate of return on all types of accumulated savings.

1.7.2 The links between the integrated macro-model and the micro-model: a first approach

If the constancy of the saving propensities of the classes of the post-Keynesian model of distribution is dropped, the steady-state values of most variables come to be determined by behavioural, institutional, demographic, and technical parameters. In this way one of the main criticisms of this theory of distribution will be lifted, and the saving and consumption patterns become much more flexible.

The links between the macro- and micro-model may be represented, for the moment, as in Table 1.2. (Note that it is assumed, except when otherwise specified, that there is equality between the rate of interest, r,

Table 1.2 The macro-model and micro-model of distribution

The Macro-Model	The Micro-Model
The rate of interest or profits and the distribution of income and wealth are determined by: (*a*) the 'flexible' propensities to save of the groups; (*b*) the equilibrium rate of growth of ⟷ the system; (*c*) the fixed capital/output ratio (i.e. technology)	It determines the 'flexible' propensity to save of the groups and their patterns of consumption, saving, and accumulation via (*a*) the rate of interest on savings ⟷ (present and expected); (*b*) behavioural parameters; (*c*) institutional parameters; (*d*) demographic parameters; (*e*) technical parameters

earned on accumulated savings and the average macro-economic rate of profits of the system, P/K; see also Bliss, 1975, p. 121.) As may be observed the role of the rate of interest is crucial in the determination of the equilibrium variables of the model (where the ratios among the variables remain constant). On the one hand the macro-model determines, in a situation of steady-state growth, the distribution of income among factors of production (and hence the value of the rate of profit) which guarantees an overall level of savings equal to the exogenously given level of investment (precisely defined by the rate of growth of the system in a full-employment situation). On the other hand the micro-model defines the propensity to save, to consume, and to accumulate inter-generational wealth of the dynasties and classes of the system, as a function of economic parameters (the wage-rate and the present and expected rate of interest on inter-generational wealth and savings), institutional parameters (the length of the working period, the level of the pension rate; taxes on consumption, savings, bequests, and so on), demographic parameters (the rate of growth of population, life-expectancy, and so on), and possible technical parameters.

In this way there is a strict interrelation between the two models (where the macro-economic one defines the overall scheme of analysis): income distribution and propensities to save both depend on the interest rate, and in order to guarantee a steady-state growth of the system (where all classes maintain the same relative economic strength, and the ratio among economic variables does not change) there must exist a unique value of the rate of interest (or profits) which at the same time ensures the desired distribution of income and wealth and maximizes the welfare of the classes with respect to life-time consumption and bequests.

1.7.3 The conceptual frameworks of alternative economic theories

At this point it may be interesting to consider, from a more general point of view, the main differences between the neoclassical or marginalist approach to economic theory (in which the life-cycle theory was originally conceived and developed) and the post-Keynesian theory (constituting the backbone of the distribution theory on which the integrated model advanced here is built). As pointed out in Baranzini and Scazzieri (1986, pp. 1–87) marginalist and post-Keynesian theories may be included, respectively, in the 'exchange-oriented' and 'production-oriented' research programmes, characterized by a distinct way of considering and formulating economic models. Broadly speaking, the first research programme deals primarily with resource allocation and 'rational decisions', while the other is mainly concerned with the 'objective laws' of production and distribution of income. These distinct lines of research, as already pointed out, differ according to:

1. *The nature of the commodities considered*. Commodities are connected with the principle of scarcity within 'exchange-oriented' theories, and that of producibility within 'production-oriented' theories.

2. *The vision of the production process*. Classical, neo-Ricardian, and post-Keynesian theories exhibit a 'circular' vision of the productive process, whereas neoclassical or marginalist theories have a 'unidirectional' view of it. The circular vision may be related to a 'closed' system, within which a vital role is played by the 'objective' relationship among the various sectors, as determined by the particular technology of production of the system. This particular aspect of classical, neoclassical, and post-Keynesian models has been extensively treated in Baranzini and Scazzieri (1986, pp. 33–5, 44–7). But a hint to the chain of causal relationships may also be useful at this stage. Indeed, the type of 'causal relationships' to be found in the post-Keynesian model of growth and income distribution has been skilfully described by Bliss:

In the Cambridge model the irritations arising from the interdependent network of influences are circumvented by some special assumptions that have the effect of allowing the state of the economy to be solved out and discussed in three distinct stages:

(1) The rate of interest (here equal to the rate of profit) is determined by a relation, pertaining to the whole economy, between the need for investment funds implied by the growth of the economy and the supply of these funds which is related to the level of profits. From this step is derived the rate of interest.

(2) Given the rate of interest it is possible to determine, independently of demand conditions and the growth rate, the costs of production of all goods in terms of labour (i.e. in wage units) and the techniques of production that the economy will use. From this step come relative prices.

(3) Finally, demand conditions may be brought in to determine the rates of

output, given the techniques of production; and hence the capital–output ratio in value terms for the whole economy; and hence, given the rate of interest, the share of profit in total output. . . .
Here is an undeniably attractive scheme and it is not surprising that economists have found it absorbing. As a decomposable structure it has the advantage of simplicity; given a change in specification one ascertains which steps in the solution procedure are affected and it is then not difficult to work out the consequences and, particularly where an early step is involved, to obtain definite conclusions (Bliss, 1975, p. 121).

Furthermore, in order to differentiate between the marginalist and the classical and post-Keynesian schemes, Pasinetti (1964–5) introduces the concept of 'symmetry' and 'asymmetry', by maintaining that the marginalist model can be represented by a system of interdependent equations, where 'interdependence' means 'simultaneous and symmetric relationships among variables'. Classical and modern classical models (i.e. post-Keynesian and neo-Ricardian in particular) are characterized by the absence of such symmetry: here the relationships among variables are unidirectional, and seldom bidirectional or multidirectional. This asymmetry determines a 'causal relationship' (or 'causal chain') or 'recursivity'. This does not, of course, mean that one may not find a certain number of simultaneous relationships, for instance, in the Keynesian model; but in this case we are simply confronted with subsystems of simultaneous equations, which are incorporated in an explicitly predetermined causal chain. (This aspect has been expounded by Pasinetti, 1964–5, pp. 245–6.)

3. *The criteria of distribution.* Generally speaking, in the 'original' marginalist or neoclassical model income distribution is determined by (*a*) the level of demand for the factors of production, (*b*) the willingness of owners of these factors to lend them to firms, (*c*) technology, which determines the level of factors' productivity, and (*d*) the initial endowment of the factors of production. With (*c*) and (*d*) being exogenously determined, income distribution is entirely determined within the resource market, in which individual owners of resources meet buyers. For the theories belonging to the 'research line of production', i.e. classical, post-Keynesian, and neo-Ricardian, economic as well as technical and demographic factors come into play to determine income distribution and capital accumulation. This is the case of the Ricardian model, and of all post-Keynesian models of income distribution, as we shall discuss in detail in Chapter 2.

4. *The role of social classes.* This aspect has already been considered in Section 1.5 above. 'Exchange-oriented' or marginalist theories usually consider an atomistic society (hence they have an individualistic vision of the economic system) where individuals are sovereign, both in the

consumers' and producers' fields, and where there is an almost complete absence of classes and groups. Instead, classes play a relevant role in 'production-oriented' theories, as in the case of classical, neo-Ricardian, and post-Keynesian models of economic growth.

There remain *three aspects* which differ according to the theoretical framework of analysis chosen, and which will be considered in detail in the following paragraphs since they are particularly relevant to this analysis. The first concerns the *time-framework and the role of economic growth*, the second concerns the role of *long-term capital accumulation*, and the third is relative to the *role of supply and demand*, always of course within the context of marginalist and classical/post-Keynesian theories. Within the context of this analysis questions of 'symmetry' and perfect substitutability of the factors of production in the case of neoclassical theories, and 'asymmetry' and non-substitutability of factors of production in the case of classical and Keynesian frameworks will be considered.

The role of capital accumulation is essential in determining not only patterns of distribution of income, but also the general framework within which the analysis of this volume is to be conducted. Different ways of looking at these phenomena, based on essentially different assumptions, may lead to radically different results, both from an analytical and economic point of view. The general framework of the model requires therefore a thorough consideration. Hence we shall first consider the time-framework and role of economic growth (1.7.4) and secondly the role of capital accumulation (1.7.5) within the two general frameworks, that is, the exchange-oriented and production-oriented theories respectively. It will be recalled that one of the main aims of this volume is that of carrying out a research programme which attempts to incorporate given aspects of one 'paradigm' (the neoclassical one) into the general post-Keynesian framework in the hope of answering a number of original questions in the field of capital accumulation and income distribution.

1.7.4 The time-framework and the role of economic growth

While trade-oriented theories, in their original formulation at least, tend to give more emphasis to static analysis (or comparative static analysis in certain cases), production oriented theories tend to provide a more dynamic approach. This latter statement is surely true for the classical economists (cf. Ricardo for instance).[18]

---

[18] The concept of a scarce commodity seems to fit much better in a static framework, since all factors of production required for the production of other commodities (including those produced in the past) are considered as limited in the same way as natural resources; here again the main problem remains that of maximizing a given function, subject to

The post-Keynesian macro-economic theory may, in a certain sense, represent a special case, since its first elaborations (those of Kaldor, Joan Robinson, and Pasinetti) are of a comparative static nature, although the assumption of steady-state growth clearly requires long-term considerations. For instance, the adaptation of the distribution of wealth among classes to the equilibrium distribution of income is a long process; or any change in the propensities to save of the classes will bring the distribution of income and wealth to a new equilibrium only after a long period (cf. Atkinson, 1969; and Mückl, 1975).

In addition, especially through the works of Pasinetti (1965, 1973, 1981) and a few others, post-Keynesian economics has been expanded to embrace long-term structural dynamics. For these reasons one might maintain that the broad post-Keynesian line of research on growth, income distribution, capital accumulation, and production dynamics is really concerned with the long-run; its main aim is to explain long-run (and additionally 'natural' for Pasinetti) levels of output, employment, and prices. Prior to this, income distribution had to be explained in terms of fixed or slowly changing institutional set-ups.[19]

Here an important element concerning the qualification of feasibility and viability of the marginalist and non-marginalist schemes respectively discussed in Baranzini and Scazzieri (1986, pp. 31–3) should be recalled. In marginalist or exchange-oriented theories the existence of a commodity is not explained by any mechanism of the model, nor is it explicitly explained if the exchanges which take place today are repeatable tomorrow; the reconstitution of factor services is also not exhaustively treated, and there is no reason to suppose that the allocations now yielding an output of commodities will be repeated in the periods that follow.[20] As Walsh and Gram (1980, pp. 404–5) point out 'feasibility in neoclassical theory therefore lacks the dynamic character of viability in classical theory'. Classical, neo-Ricardian, and post-Keynesian theories

various constraints. On the other hand the concept of a producible good or commodity (which is associated with the classical model in particular) is related to the possibility of producing certain commodities, as Ricardo points out, almost without limit, provided labour and land are freely available. In this context the dynamic aspect of the production process is emphasized (cf. Baranzini and Scazzieri, 1986, pp. 31–3).

[19] As already pointed out earlier Pasinetti gets into great detail in the theoretical explanation of the differences between trade theories and production theories. As to the time perspective he writes: 'A particularly important difference between the two [kinds of theory], for theoretical analysis, is that they acquire an opposite practical relevance in relation to time, the former being relevant (in the short run) just when the latter is practically irrelevant, and the latter becoming relevant (in the long run) just when the former becomes irrelevant. This opposition carries with it profound consequences for the theoretical analysis, as it normally induces the theorist to diametrically opposite attitudes to the type of hypotheses to choose' (Pasinetti, 1981, p. 4).

[20] On the significance of 'natural' for Pasinetti see himself (1981), and also Bortis (1990*b*) and Baranzini and Scazzieri (1990, pp. 35–8).

on this precise point are characterized by a different perspective, which may be related to the conditions of viability; here the existence and reproduction of the economy through time take place in a clearly dynamic context.

As to the different roles that economic growth plays in the two theories of exchange and production the following may be recalled:

Generally speaking, one might say that the long-run perspective of most economic theories is closely connected with the rate of capital accumulation of any given system. However, the variables on which the two lines of research tend to focus are different. Neoclassical theories stress the role of factors such as inter-temporal discount rates, rate of interest on accumulated savings, and individual utility functions, thus bringing in the life-cycle allocation of income between consumption and saving. Theories of the classical type also focus on the allocation of income between consumption and saving, but have it determined by (1) technology that yields a given surplus and (2) institutional factors determining saving propensities (Baranzini and Scazzieri, 1986, p. 42).

It must be said that post-classical economists, in general, did not make a direct effort, at least from a theoretical point of view, to expound the fundamental dynamic forces behind the process of growth of the industrialized nations. The issue of long-run dynamics again became the focus of attention after the contributions of von Neumann, Hicks, and Harrod.

One might say that the long-run perspective is connected with the process of capital accumulation, linking one period (or even one generation) to another and so giving a truly dynamic content to the model under investigation. The way in which the other factors of production are brought into use is also relevant in this context. It is thus natural that the next step will be to enquire into the way in which capital accumulation is conceived and treated within each research programme.

1.7.5 The role of capital accumulation

In this subsection a number of issues related to the process of accumulation of physical capital (the demand side of the act of savings) will be considered. Reference will be made to the supply side of savings if necessary. From what has just been said above it may be concluded that since the accumulation of physical capital in an industrialized society is very much a dynamic phenomenon, it is clear that production-oriented theories should be in a better position to throw additional light on the mechanisms that determine the process of distribution of personal or dynastic wealth (and indirectly that of income). This aspect, which has often been only marginally considered, is quite relevant since it is well accepted that there is a strict interdependence between the distribution of income and the distribution of wealth. For, as Pasinetti points out,

By applying the rules of capital accumulation backward in time, as well as forward, the capital stock existing at any arbitrary point of time appears as nothing but the cumulation of all net investments (all capital goods, once in existence, being then constantly replaced) that took place in the past—from nothing at the beginning of the process of capitalistic production to the present stock of capital goods (Pasinetti, 1983*b*, p. 410).[21]

To put it in general terms we may say that the marginalist core does not explicitly include a long-run perspective of the process of capital accumulation. As Lichtenstein (1983, p. 16) has pointed out, capital accumulation is not at the centre of the neoclassical model, since the focus of this theory concerns the way in which individuals or families allocate between consumption and saving.

This aspect is also considered by Harris (1978, ch. 1) who maintains that the problem of accumulation within the neoclassical framework is considered essentially as a matter of exchange of commodities through time. This means that the problem of accumulation becomes the problem of exchange with an additional dimension, i.e. that of intertemporal allocation. Time, in this perspective, enters the model just like any other variable in order to allow for the exchange process to take place, but not primarily to enquire about the process of capital accumulation (which is connected with cumulative processes of various types). Wealth accumulation being related to an individual's consumption decisions, it could well be imagined to come to an end at the death of each individual, provided that generations overlap to a certain degree. In this sense the introduction of a bequest motive, as examined in this volume, helps to overcome this shortcoming.

Summing up, it may be said that for the marginalists the process of capital accumulation is mainly the outcome of the consumption- and saving-decisions of individuals, taken on the basis of their particular requirements; for classical and post-Keynesian theories such a process is more closely related to the continuing and self-sustaining process of expansion of capital as an essential feature of industrialized societies: here the role of social classes is that of providing a larger base for the

---

[21] In the same paper Pasinetti explains the reasons for which the accumulation of consumption goods has to be differentiated from that of capital goods: 'For, while the accumulation of durable consumption goods has no overall relevance and is therefore a matter that may be left to the decisions of the single individuals alone, the process of accumulation of capital goods is essential to the working of the whole production process and therefore cannot but be a matter of concern for the economic system as a whole. This is a crucial point. No industrial society can avoid facing the social implications of the process of capital accumulation' (Pasinetti, 1983*b*, p. 411).

behavioural requirements of the model. A mix of life-cycle optimal consumption- and saving-decisions, with inter-generational transfer of wealth, in a post-Keynesian framework characterized by the presence of social classes and precise requirements for growth could well provide a comprehensive framework of accumulation analysis. Capital (and hence wealth, although indirectly in a system where it is the desire to investment that determines total savings) accumulation may hence be connected with the *viability* of the system, i.e. to its ability to maintain itself through time. Those theories which give particular emphasis to the mechanisms of reproduction (i.e. renewal of resources, renewal of the physical and human capital, and so on) may thus be classified as viable, where the past and future of production is as important as the present level of economic activity. It may also be a matter of priority in the choice of the objectives of analysis. At a closer look one might argue that within the marginalist scheme there is no explicit requirement for a reconstitution of the strength of the factors of production so that the allocation which now yields a given output may or may not be repeatable in the future. A provision for its repeatability may well be introduced in certain circumstances, but does not concern the core of marginalist economics.

The role and mechanisms of long-run capital accumulation were taken up by post-Keynesian economics when the first analyses in the field of economic growth and development were widely published.[22] Post-Keynesian theory shows that there is a strict relationship between the rate of growth of the economy, the distribution of income between social classes, and the price level. It is at this point that wealth and capital accumulation come in, since the total saving of each class is the product of the exogenously (or institutionally) determined saving propensity times the financial capital stock, either made up by previous life-cycle savings and/or by inter-generational bequests. In a steady-state situation (where the capital stock of the classes grows at a constant rate and where the ratios among the economic variables remain the same) it is therefore possible to define, in terms of all parameters of the model, rates of saving as well as the capital share of each class or group of

---

[22] Despite these results many economists still believe that post-Keynesian economics is strictly conditioned by the existence of socio-logically definable classes of wage- and profit-recipients, maintaining that it is restricted to defining distribution in two-class terms. But, as Kregel points out, Pasinetti's (1962) approach provides the basis for a nearly personal distribution of income as well. 'Once wage-earners also receive some non-wage income, say interest on savings, rents, or profits, they must be grouped according to some criterion other than their income source—in terms of their asset preferences, for example. The number of different classes could, in the limiting case, coincide with the number of individual income-recipients. Indeed, Pasinetti's original intention was to extend the theory to many income classes' (Kregel, 1978, pp. 42–3). See also Tobin (1960).

consumers and savers. This share will of course be related in a predetermined way, i.e. through propensities to save, to the distribution of income among classes (and not necessarily among factors of production). In this way it is possible to study the influence of the rate of growth, of technology (i.e. the capital/output ratio), and of the various propensities to consume and to save on the capital share owned by each class or group. It may also be possible, in given circumstances, to study the relevance in equilibrium, of the inter-generational capital stock of each class.

A cumulative process like capital accumulation is bound to remain a strategic variable of the economic system, since from it depends the actual and potential level of economic activity. It is not surprising that so much effort has been devoted to the study of this area. Before closing this paragraph we may briefly consider Keynes's position concerning the accumulation of capital and the 'euthanasia of the rentier', later to be taken up by a number of modern scholars. Keynes himself did not explicitly deal with the question of income distribution but rather with the mechanisms which determine its level. Instead he considered in great detail the laws which govern and link consumption, savings, accumulated personal wealth, and productive capital; the arguments expounded are not only refreshing for the modern economist, but provide the foundations for the modern post-Keynesian theory of accumulation of savings and distribution of wealth. A number of equally interesting aspects related to the process of wealth accumulation are reconsidered by Keynes. First he considers the issue of the inequality in income and wealth distribution by stating: 'I believe that there is social and psychological justification for significant inequalities of incomes and wealth, but not for such large disparities as exist today. There are valuable human activities which require the motive of money-making and the environment of private wealth-ownership for their full fruition. Moreover, dangerous human activities can be canalised into comparatively harmless channels by the existence of opportunities for money-making and private wealth, which, if they cannot be satisfied in this way, may find their outlet in cruelty, the reckless pursuit of personal power and authority, and other forms of self-aggrandisement' (Keynes, 1973, p. 374; 1st edn. 1936).

Then Keynes goes on to discuss the well-known case of 'euthanasia of the rentier' which, under different circumstances, will be later resurrected in the context of the Kaldor–Pasinetti–Meade–Samuelson–Modigliani controversy (see Chapter 2 below). For Keynes the 'euthanasia of the rentier' would occur in a situation where the process of accumulation of physical capital would be so rapid as to cause a drastic fall in its marginal efficiency and hence in the interest rates from which rentiers or capitalists draw the totality of their income. Such a situation, according to him, 'would mean the euthanasia of the rentier, and, consequently, the euthanasia of the cumulative oppressive power of the capitalist to exploit the scarcity-value of capital' (Keynes, 1973, p. 376; 1st edn. 1936). Different is the euthanasia of the rentiers or capitalists for the Kaldor–Pasinetti model of distribution and growth; in a condition of steady-state growth the propensity to save of the capitalists must be higher than a given minimum, otherwise all (equilibrium) savings of the system are provided by the other classes, so as to leave no room for a class of 'pure capitalists'.

1.7.6 The role of supply and demand in alternative economic theories

There exists a final important difference between marginalist and most non-marginalist (i.e. classical and post-Keynesian) economic theories which relates to the role of supply and demand in determining the equilibrium conditions. In the marginalist model the interaction between consumption and production units is determined by demand and supply both in the short and long run, and factor prices are determined in terms of this framework on the basis of marginal productivity. This scheme is only partially modified in the case of imperfectly competitive markets.

Quite different is the position shared by classical economists for whom it is possible in the short run only to explain in terms of supply and demand the determination of prices and income distribution. For classical economists, long-run equilibrium values cannot be explained simply in terms of supply and demand, since the former plays a central role in most cases. For instance for Ricardo the level of long-term activity determines the distribution of income and natural prices.

More recently certain authors (Hicks, Hollander, and Casarosa in particular) have put forward an interpretation of Ricardo according to which, contrary to the traditional (i.e. Sraffa–Pasinetti) interpretation, emphasis is given to the forces of both demand and supply in the determination of the wage-rate. The main feature of such a dynamic path is that the wage-rate is, in general, above its natural level and coincides with it only in the stationary state. This approach is based on the conviction that this 'new view' of the Ricardian system allows for an elucidation of all Ricardo's propositions concerning the tendencies of the wage-rate and of the rate of profits during the process of growth (cf., for instance, Casarosa, 1982, and Hicks, 1983, p. 40). This 'new view' of Ricardo is however challenged by the followers of the 'classical' inter-pretation of his work like Pasinetti (1982) who argues that such an interpretation of the Ricardian system simply belongs to a stream of economic thought (which goes back to Marshall) that tries to incorporate the basic propositions of Ricardo into the analytical framework based on the 'mechanical' working of supply and demand. The pre-Sraffa economic literature, as a matter of fact, includes several attempts at reconciling Ricardo with marginal economic theory.

This controversy illustrates the relevance of the issue in the economic literature. Also on this point Marx (quoted in Howard, 1979, p. 4) wrote that:

Classical political economy soon recognised that the change in the relation of demand and supply explained in regard to the price of labour, nothing except its changes, i.e. the oscillations of the market-price above or below a certain mean. If demand and supply balance, the oscillation of prices ceases, all other conditions remaining the same. But then demand and supply cease to explain anything. The price of labour, at the moment when demand and supply are in equilibrium, is its natural price, determined independently of the relation of demand and supply. And how this price is determined is just the question (Marx, 1867, p. 538).

Pasinetti defines the natural wage-rate of the Ricardian systems as follows:

Wages are not related to the contribution of labour to the process of production, as in the modern theories they normally arc. Like all economists of his time, Ricardo relates the level of wages to the physiological necessity of workers and their families to live and reproduce themselves. He is convinced that in any particular state of society there exists a *real* wage-rate (so to speak, a certain *basket of goods*) which can be considered as the 'natural price of labour'. It needs not necessarily be at a strict *subsistence level* (the minimum physiological necessities of life); but at that level which in a given country and in a given state of society, besides allowing workers to live, induces them to perpetuate themselves 'without either increase or diminution' (Pasinetti, 1960, p. 80).

The same position is shared by most non-neoclassical economists. Among post-Keynesian economists there is a general conviction that in order to construct a realistic model of advanced economies, one needs to drop the rigid supply-and-demand framework of the orthodox theory. Indeed, such a framework, with prices as the most important explanatory variable, 'plays the same role in economic analysis that a belief in Divine intervention plays in scientific work in general: it is an extraneous element which obscures the factors actually at work' (Eichner, 1986, p. viii). The conventional supply-and-demand framework, as it is conceived by the marginalist approach, is also rejected by a line of research developed within the Cambridge tradition, which gives particular emphasis to the dynamic of demand composition in relation to income per capita. In this line of research we find *Structural Change and*

Economic Growth of Pasinetti (1981), whose main aim is to study the conditions under which an economic system may maintain full employment and full capacity utilization through time when it is subject to dynamic impulses such as technical progress, a growing population, and changes in consumers' preferences. The latter, according to Engel's Law, depend on income per capita and play an overriding role in determining the structural changes of the economy.

1.7.7 The reconciliation of the two frameworks following our approach to capital accumulation and income distribution

As Pasinetti and Scazzieri (1987a, p. 363) have pointed out, it is not unusual for economists to enquire into a wider domain of economic phenomena by using (sometimes jointly) models that were originally devised to deal with a much narrower range of special issues. The results that have been obtained with this process of generalization are, as was to be expected, mixed. In the case of capital theory for instance, as Pasinetti and Scazzieri further point out, such generalization turned out to be ill-conceived and misleading.[23]

In other cases still the generalization has been fruitful, even in the case in which different types of economic analysis have been combined in order to obtain a more unified system. If we consider, for instance, Pasinetti's long-term structural analysis we observe that it encompasses distinctive classical and Keynesian elements. It may be considered classical because it focuses on the nature and determination of the profit rate and on the distribution of income among factors of production and socio-economic classes; it is Keynesian since it deals also with effective demand and the related conditions which are required for full employment, both on a given steady-state growth path and also along the traverse.

A similar method will be used in the present volume, through an enquiry into accumulation and income distribution by combining two models of analysis (the life-cycle theory and the post-Keynesian income-distribution theory) which have been devised to consider a specific field of analysis. In particular the life-cycle theory was originally put forward to throw additional light on the consumption- and saving-behaviour of individuals and, by aggregation, of the whole private economic system.

---

[23] 'In the case of capital theory, for a long time it has been taken for granted that there is a unique, unambiguous profitability ranking of production techniques in terms of capital intensity as the rate of interest is varied. The discovery that this is not necessarily true has induced many economists to speak of "paradoxes" in the theory of capital. But the roots of apparently paradoxical behaviour are to be found in this case not in the economic phenomena themselves but in the roundabout processes of thought that had led economists to formulate such special "parables" of economic behaviour' (Pasinetti and Scazzieri, 1987a, p. 363).

On the other hand post-Keynesian distribution theory was formulated to explain the macro-economic mechanisms of profit determination and income distribution in a growing system.

Nevertheless these two different theoretical models will be combined on the basis of a precise scheme of interconnection: the post-Keynesian model, which has a macro-economic or social-class basis, stays as the external framework of the unified model, where variables like technology (K/Y), full-employment requirements $(\bar{I} = S)$, and other macro-economic relations define the whole superstructure; while the adjusted version of the life-cycle theory will help to define the structure of the supply of savings, consumption, and bequests on the basis of demographic, behavioural, and institutional parameters. In this way a high degree of compatibility between the two models will be ensured; they will interact within a precise framework, and even if their roots are not common the results will be significant. A more detailed scheme will be provided in the chapters that follow.

1.8 CONCLUSIONS AND PLAN OF THE VOLUME

The issues considered in the previous sections have set out the many problems associated with wealth (and capital) accumulation, income distribution, and profit determination. The main conceptual differences in this area between the major schools of economic analysis, in particular those defined as 'production and distribution' theories and those defined as 'exchange or optimal allocation' theories, have been considered. From this short survey it has emerged that the role of, and the emphasis placed on the process of the accumulation of wealth and, consequently, the distribution of the product, differ according to the methodological approach chosen.

It is the purpose of this volume to enquire into relationships between income distribution and wealth accumulation in a system characterized by the presence of different socio-economic classes. It is divided into two parts: in Part I (Chapters 1–4) consideration is given to the relevance of the topic tackled here with particular reference to the existing literature in the specific area; in Part II an attempt is made to develop an integrated model (incorporating the micro-foundations) of the theory of income distribution and capital accumulation, where a number of issues are examined with different tools. The chapters may be introduced individually as follows.

Chapter 2 considers the most relevant arguments of modern economic theories of income distribution and capital accumulation, with particular reference to the analyses of two or more general class growth models. This will be effected in three successive steps. First, the background of the Two-Cambridges controversies on profit determination will be considered. Secondly, the implications of the well-known Kaldor–Pasinetti and Meade–Samuelson and Modigliani theorems are surveyed and reconsidered. Thirdly, the main criticisms of this approach will be considered, with a survey of the major extensions of the post-Keynesian and neoclassical models.

Chapter 3 develops the argument of wealth accumulation within a long-term framework and establishes its links with price theory and income distribution. In particular the so-called 'reconstruction of political economy' and the revival of interest in classical and neo-Ricardian economics during the last few decades are considered. Three main lines of research seem to emerge here: (*a*) the development of an analysis incorporating the problems of structural dynamics, i.e. the implications of different rates of growth of demand and technical progress on the long-term structure of the economy, in which context the determination of the profit rate, the distribution of income, and the possibility of attaining full employment are discussed; (*b*) the integration of Sraffa's price system (with given physical quantities) with the economic theory that has originated from Keynesian and post-Keynesian analyses: as Pasinetti (1986*b*) has pointed out, the dynamization of Sraffa's static model allows for an exhaustive analysis of the determination of prices, and hence of income distribution, in a system where there is not equiproportional growth of demand and/or of the rate of technical progress in the various industries; and (*c*) the introduction of institutional and micro-economic elements into the traditional post-Keynesian and new-classical models. On this point a summary of the most recent literature on the subject is provided.

Chapter 4 concludes the first part of the volume on the theoretical perspectives of capital accumulation and income distribution by considering the implications of the introduction of a specific micro-economic element into the Cambridge model. (This micro-element is not connected with a theory of the firm—which has already been provided by such Keynesian scholars as Wood (1975) and members of the American school—but may be labelled as a households' accumulation theory.) This specific element is the Brumberg–Ando–Modigliani hypothesis about the life-cycle and consumption-behaviour which has proved to be fruitful during the four decades which have elapsed since it was first put forward. In particular, the compatibility of the life-cycle hypothesis in a post-Keynesian framework is considered, as well as the different role that the rate of interest is bound to play in such a framework. As a matter of fact in a post-Keynesian model the rate of interest, at the macro-level, is determined by the exogenously given overall rate of growth of the system and of the constant propensity to save of the capitalists or entrepreneurs—in other words, by the requirement of the system to grow at a given equilibrium rate or speed. With this rate of profit is associated a unique distribution of income between factors of production and, via saving propensities, among classes. With the introduction of a life-cycle theory the rate of interest comes to fulfil the additional role of allocating income between consumption and savings (both life-cycle and inter-generational) since it represents the reward for postponing consumption; and the requirement for maintaining equilibrium growth is ensured by changes in the level of the rate of interest, both at the macro-level (as required by the post-Keynesian framework) and at the micro-level (as postulated by the life-cycle model). In the second part of the chapter the nature of the inter-generational capital stock and of its significance and relevance in growth models is considered in detail. The various ways in which it may be introduced into the model of accumulation and distribution is also considered. Finally, from a general point of view, the issue of inter-class mobility and that of uncertainty in a pluri-class model is examined.

Part II offers three different analytical models in which the foundations are provided for a micro-economic post-Keynesian growth-model of capital accumulation and income distribution.

In Chapter 5 the analysis begins with a consideration of a simple two-period model which incorporates a modified version of the life-cycle theory and where individuals (i.e. dynasties) have a special bequest utility function. This framework will allow us to define, in explicit terms, the distribution of income (in particular the rate of interest) which maintains in equilibrium the growth of the inter-generational bequests of the economic system. In this way it is possible to focus on the conditions that will ensure a stable growth of each class or, for any given class, the acquisition of a stronger economic relevance through a faster than average accumulation of savings. Once the value of the equilibrium interest rate is derived, one is able to study its properties and to measure the influence on it of the various parameters. Then it will be possible to derive explicitly the analytical value of the other variables of the model and to provide more insight into the distribution of income among classes and the long-term equilibrium properties of the inter-generational/life-cycle stock ratio. The analysis of its long-term properties will show some interesting aspects of the model and the possibility of a long-run equilibrium in which the capital of one class tends to zero, while that of the other classes will proportionally increase.

In the final section of Chapter 5, possibly the most general, the implications of the introduction of a bequest motive for all classes of the model are studied. In this case it will be seen that, under general conditions, classes will maintain the same relative economic strength as long as the 'pure' profit-earners (the entrepreneurs or capitalists) are much more willing than the other classes to leave a financial bequest to their children (a very reasonable assumption indeed). This special case will allow consideration of the implications of the introduction of a different subjective discount rate for the bequest (or for consumption), or of a different rate of return for socio-economic classes, always in order to guarantee a steady-state growth of the system. The results obtained will prove that equilibrium growth will be more easily attained by a given degree of market or behavioural imperfection, which is not incompatible with a post-Keynesian framework.

In Chapter 6 consideration is given to a more articulated two-class continuous-time life-cycle model where an explicit bequest utility function is not introduced (as in the preceding chapter). In this model it is simply assumed that individuals, in the absence of technical progress, plan to leave the same bequest k_o (as they have themselves inherited) to each of their children, so ensuring a steady-state growth of the system in the long term. After spelling out the basic assumptions of the model (which includes a retirement period with a given pension rate) the behaviour of a dynasty of each class is defined; this will make possible a study of the consumption-, saving-, and accumulation-plans of the classes in general. Of course the influence of the various parameters on the behaviour of individuals will be measured and the relative economic interpretation provided. This will be particularly helpful for those cases that are ambiguous or rather paradoxical.

At this point, by aggregating the micro-variables, it will be possible to define the aggregate behaviour of the socio-economic classes. By focusing attention first on the behaviour of the class of 'pure' entrepreneurs, it is shown that, as long as each member of the dynasty inherits the same constant amount of inter-generational bequest (in the case of zero technical progress), the capitalists as a group adjust, whatever the circumstances, their saving so that $s_c = n/r$, which is seen to be a supply function of saving; but in a life-cycle model r (the interest rate) will depend also on all parameters of the model. In this way the equilibrium rate of interest is simultaneously determined by the macro-economic requirements of the post-Keynesian model *and* by the micro-economic behaviour of individuals or dynasties. In the final part of the chapter the implications of the golden rule of accumulation for the process of capital accumulation in this particular model are analysed.

In Chapter 7 an attempt is made to enquire into the role of interest-uncertainty in determining the formation, in the long-run, of different classes (or dynasties) of capital- (or wealth-) owners. More precisely, on the basis of the Merton model, the effects of uncertainty in a life-cycle model with portfolio choice (where individuals have the choice of investing their accumulated savings in risky or safe assets) are considered. Of the various kinds of uncertainty which may be considered in a life-cycle model, such as preference-uncertainty, uncertainty about future technology, income-uncertainty, death-uncertainty, and so on, the focus will be on problems related to interest-uncertainty, where by interest we mean the rate of return on the initial bequest and related life-cycle savings. Since the purpose of this volume is to study the accumulation of wealth in a two-class model (and the sort of reasons that may lead to class distinctions) the consumption- and saving-plan under uncertainty of an individual or dynasty and hence of an entire class are first defined. This will make possible the calculation of the rate of growth of mean wealth for each class, which does not include the variance of risky interest rates since it is based on a large group of people. By studying the behaviour of the rate of growth of mean wealth with respect to the risk-aversion measure (which one may link to the size of the initial wealth), it will be possible to explain, from a historical point of view, the differences among socio-economic classes. As a matter of fact the analysis will show that the variance of risky rates of return has a negative effect on both optimal consumption and rate of growth of mean wealth; on the other hand risk-aversion has a positive effect on consumption and a negative one on the rate of growth of mean wealth.

During the whole analysis the results obtained in this stochastic context will be compared with those obtained in the preceding deterministic models: the effects of a positive interest variance and of risk-aversion will, in this way, be clearly expounded. Additionally, to gain some insight into the quantitative importance of these findings, the value of the variables of the above models for several combinations of economically reasonable values of the parameters will be shown in tables and diagrams.

In the final chapter the main conclusions that can be drawn from the analysis are reconsidered, the methodology employed is evaluated, and some suggestions for further extensions of this line of research are advanced. The coverage of the micro-foundations of post-Keynesian theory concerning the saving supply-side and excluding the theory of production will require further study. Phenomena like savings and wealth accumulation, allocation of resources among consumption, savings, and inter-generational bequests will need much more attention and linkage to the whole macro-economic model. In particular the choice of the utility function may be extended to include a social-utility function, and the relationship between life-cycle savings and inter-generational bequests may be considered with new tools of analysis. One might also consider with more appropriate tools disequilibrium situations where one class emerges as being economically stronger than the others through the acquisition of a higher share of the inter-generational capital stock of the system; in other words disequilibrium growth requires more consideration. The issues outlined in this chapter are important because they attempt to cover a gap in the literature. It should be added that such attempts generally attract severe examination and criticism, especially where the goal is of a double nature, i.e. that of providing a scheme focused on wealth accumulation and income distribution and inquiring into the reasons behind class differences.

2

Wealth Accumulation and Income Distribution in Modern Economic Theories

2.1 THEORIES OF GROWTH AND DISTRIBUTION: A BROAD CLASSIFICATION

Various surveys (for example, Britto, 1973) have made use of the following classification for recent contributions on growth and distribution. The first two groups refer to their saving assumptions, while the remainder refer to other relevant aspects of growth and distribution. We distinguish the following lines of research.

1. Growth and distribution models characterized by a *constant propensity to save* of socio-economic classes. To this group belong the post-Keynesian, Kaleckian, and neo-Ricardian models mainly elaborated in Cambridge, UK. We also find a number of contributions belonging to the neoclassical literature, as those of Meade (1963, 1966*b*), Samuelson and Modigliani (1966*a*, 1966*b*), Sato (1966), Stiglitz (1967), Hahn and Matthews (1971), Furono (1970), Guha (1972), Mückl (1972), Rau (1972), Campa (1975), Balestra and Baranzini (1971), and so on.

2. The models of growth and distribution whose behaviour in regard to saving is determined by *utility maximization*. Individuals allocate their savings, consumption, and bequests in order to maximize their intertemporal utility. These models include both the deterministic and stochastic approaches; and the majority are to be classified within the neoclassical tradition. In general they focus on the existence of a steady-state growth path, the convergence to it, and the possibility for such a path to be dynamically efficient. Among these works and for the sake of our analysis we shall mention those of Arrow (1965), Britto (1968, 1969, 1972), Diamond (1965), Meade (1966*b*), Merton (1969, 1971), Samuelson (1969), Tobin (1967*a*), etc. We note that not all of these works provide a direct answer to the problem of income and wealth distribution (and accumulation), since they often confine themselves to specific points of analysis, mainly at the micro-economic level.

3. The models of growth and distribution which concentrate on the role of *technical progress*. Most of these works have been stimulated by the pioneering contributions of Sir Roy Harrod, Sir John Hicks, and Robert Solow. This wide and complex research programme did receive a new impulse by Kennedy's contribution (1964) who introduced the

concept of 'innovation frontier' (a similar approach was independently developed by von Weizsäcker at about the same time). The Kennedy–Weizsäcker approach deals in particular with the trade-off between two different types of technical progress: labour-augmenting and capital-augmenting; later Samuelson, Drandakis, and Phelps showed that in a traditional neoclassical growth model with a constant saving ratio and a production function with an elasticity of substitution smaller than unity Harrod-neutral technical progress (where the rate of interest and distribution remain unchanged) would take place.

Kaldor (1957, and Kaldor and Mirrlees, 1962) developed a model in which technical progress is deeply linked to capital accumulation ('embodied in new equipment'); Kaldor's approach was of course presented as an alternative to the aggregate production function. Later on, during the 1960s and 1970s, a large number of growth models which embodied technical progress were considered. These include the 'clay-clay' models put forward by Solow, Tobin, Weizsäcker, and Yaari (where there are no possibilities of substitution, *ex ante* as well as *ex post*, of capital for labour) and the 'putty-clay' models of Bliss, Kemp and Thanh, and Bardhan (where the *ex ante* production function is of the general marginalist or neoclassical type). One should finally point out that the empirical literature concerned with the role of technical progress in growth models is very substantial indeed (see Britto, 1973, p. 1350 for a reference list).

4. Growth models of the 'reswitching and capital reversing' debate. Another important debate on 'reswitching and capital reversing' took place in the late 1960s and 1970s, i.e. on the defence or rejection of the statement to the effect that there exists a monotonic relation between the rate of profit and the value of capital per man employed in the production process. As Pasinetti and Scazzieri point out, most of the difficulties of this controversy are associated with the fact that

The idea that there exists an inverse monotonic relation between the rate of interest and the demand for capital was born in the financial sphere. The parallel idea of an inverse monotonic relation between the rate of profit and the 'quantity of capital' employed in the production process is the outcome of a long intellectual process of extensions and generalizations. But the recent debate on capital theory has conclusively proved that such extensions and generalizations are devoid of any foundation (Pasinetti and Scazzieri, 1987a, p. 366).

The controversy was initiated by Joan Robinson who pointed out that in the marginalist one-sector growth model including a smooth production function with diminishing returns to each factor and constant returns to scale, there exists a negative relationship between the capital/labour ratio and the rate of return on capital if this latter equals the marginal productivity of capital. The main contributions in this field are those of Sraffa (1960), Robinson (1956), Pasinetti (1966c), and Morishima on one side, and Bruno, Burmeister and Sheshinski, and Levhari and Samuelson (1966) on the neoclassical side.

5. The models which *incorporate money into real growth models*, on the conviction that the analysis of non-monetary models is worth while only if money is neutral. A first step in this direction was taken by Tobin (1965, 1967b) who suggested that 'if money is in any degree a substitute for material wealth in satisfying the thrift propensities of the population, then it is not neutral' (Tobin, 1967b, p. 72). Actually, as Tobin demonstrates, equilibrium capital intensity is lower *ceteris paribus* in a monetary growth model than in the corresponding real growth model. Later Sidrauski was more explicit, and pointed out that the capital stock for which a monetary economy reaches its steady state is always smaller than the one indicated by the Solow–Swan model. It therefore follows that the golden-rule saving ratio is not any more the one which maximized long-run consumption (Sidrauski, 1967). In earlier models money appears as a costless, alternative store of value, so that 'the link between money and real output via the rate of interest, a fundamental component of Keynesian economics, disappears in the neoclassical world of full employment' (Britto, 1973, p. 1351). Such a link is disturbed by the possible diversion of savings into increased money holdings rather than into the accumulation of physical capital. From a distributive point of view, the introduction of money into growth models raises the following questions: (*a*) does a change in the rate of growth of the money supply alter the steady-state values of the capital/output ratio (in the case of a neoclassical model), the rate of return on capital, and the share of profits in national income? (*b*) how do variations in the level of the money supply affect the accumulation and distribution of wealth? (*c*) under which particular conditions may the money supply be considered as neutral?

Still another approach, in this field of research, is that of Levhari and Patinkin (1968) who consider money as a good that enters directly the utility function of consumers, hence as a consumers' good. They arrive at the conclusion that money is, in general, not neutral in the determination of steady-state values.

6. Growth models which concentrate on *optimal growth*. Within this line of research the analysis is extended to the normative field where one may choose the best path of economic growth among all possible paths of expansion. As Jones states: 'Such a study requires, at a minimum, a *statement of objectives and a statement of constraints*. A statement of *objectives* is clearly necessary for the definition of exactly what is meant by the "optimal" or "best" path of growth—and what is

"best" will depend crucially on the desired objectives' (Jones, 1975, p. 207). Although the foundations of optimal economic growth were provided by the Cambridge philosopher F. P. Ramsey in 1928 and by I. Fisher in 1930, one had to wait until the early 1960s to see a revival of the topic. One of the most important lines of research in this field is the one connected with the Golden Rule of Accumulation with the original contribution of E. S. Phelps (*The Golden Rule of Accumulation: A Fable for Growthmen* published in 1961) and other contributions by Solow, J. Robinson, Koopmans, Pearce, Hamberg, and many others. Basically the Golden Rule of Accumulation consists in finding, amongst all possible paths of balanced growth, the one which maximizes the level of consumption per worker, subject to particular (and varying) conditions. Many other issues have been considered in this field (suffice it to mention the Keynes–Ramsey rule and the role of the time-horizon); we cannot however in this context give more details of this wide research programme which has brought contributions from a large number of important economists.

We return now to the origins of the Two-Cambridges controversies on income distribution, profit determination, and capital theory.

2.2   THE BACKGROUND OF THE TWO-CAMBRIDGES CONTROVERSIES ON INCOME DISTRIBUTION AND CAPITAL THEORY

2.2.1 The general framework: how it all started

When in the late 1930s and in the 1940s the first macro-economic models of economic growth were developed, the theory of income distribution was caught in an impasse, represented by the well-known Harrod–Domar equilibrium condition $s = g(K/Y)$, where s is the aggregate saving ratio, g the natural rate of growth (which can include 'labour-saving' technical progress), and K/Y the capital/output ratio.[1] If these three variables are all constant, then it is unlikely that the Harrod–Domar condition can be satisfied. Hence, in order to have a model in which the possibility of steady growth is assured, it is necessary to relax one or other of the assumptions. The equality between s and $g(K/Y)$ can be obtained by:

1. flexibility in K/Y (also referred to as the technology assumption);
2. flexibility in s (saving assumption);
3. flexibility in g (labour-market and/or labour-supply assumption).

The above cases can, of course, be combined in various ways as, for

[1] On this point see Pasinetti (1974, p. 121).

instance, in Samuelson and Modigliani's (1966) model, where 1 and 2 apply simultaneously.

Solution 1 above was adopted by the neoclassical or marginalist school: 'instead of there being fixed coefficients in production, there may exist a production function offering a continuum of alternative techniques, each involving different capital–labour ratios; ... The consequence is that the capital–output ratio v is adjustable, instead of being fixed, and this provides a way in which s/v and n may be brought into equality' (Hahn and Matthews, 1964, p. 785). But of course the solution of the Harrod–Domar dilemma was just the beginning, for if, on the other hand, it was necessary to provide a device ensuring equilibrium growth, on the other hand, it was necessary to define income distribution in an exhaustive way. Hence, in order to make income distribution determinate, several restrictive assumptions were added, so that in the end the neoclassical economists ended up with a model incorporating a 'well-behaved' constant-returns-to-scale aggregate production function, perfect substitutability between labour and capital, profit-maximizing behaviour, perfect competition in the labour and capital markets—all within a single-commodity framework. In this way, whenever Euler's Theorem applies, both shares are simultaneously determined, and no residual, by definition, can exist. None the less, as the Two-Cambridges (UK versus Mass., USA) controversies on capital theory and on the reswitching of techniques has shown, 'Lower interest rates may bring lower steady-state consumption and lower capital–output ratios, and the transition to such lower interest rates can involve denial of diminishing returns' (Samuelson, 1966, p. 583). Such a statement from a leading representative of the marginalist school would seem to imply that the whole production-function approach is to be reconsidered with great care.

2.2.2 The second answer to the Harrod–Domar dilemma, i.e. the assumption of a flexible aggregate saving ratio[2]

The second answer to the Harrod–Domar dilemma, i.e. the assumption of a flexible aggregate saving ratio, was primarily adopted by the neo-Keynesian or Cambridge school. Of course there are many ways in which one can give flexibility to s; but the one which has played the major role is the hypothesis of a two-class society (namely workers and

---

[2] When we discuss the modern (post-Keynesian or neoclassical) two- or multi-class model of profit determination and income distribution, we shall use the term 'wealth' or 'capital' to denote the amount of real wealth accumulated by the classes of the system. The term 'capital' to indicate the supply side of savings has been widely used in the debate. (Of course specific terms like the 'capital/output ratio' must be interpreted in the traditional sense.)

capitalists), each with different constant marginal propensity to save. In this way there always exists a distribution of income between the two classes which produces precisely that saving ratio that will equal the value $g(K/Y)$, so satisfying the Harrod–Domar equilibrium condition.

The motivations for this approach are to be found in the following considerations which have emerged with the elaboration of successive 'generations' of post-Keynesian models of profit determination and income distribution:

1. The assumption of a uniform rate of saving for the whole economic system ignores all possible differences in saving- and consumption-behaviour among different classes of income-receivers, or categories of income, or even different sectors of the economy.

2. The problem of aggregating savings might give rise to particular and unknown difficulties, so that it may be safer to consider it in a disaggregate way, as the post-Keynesian model precisely does.

3. Thirdly, this assumption also receives empirical support from the observed high rates of saving out of corporate profits and lower rates out of labour income; see, for instance, Burmeister and Taubman (1969), Kaldor (1966), and Murfin (1980).[3]

4. The nature itself of the savings differs from class to class: for instance Kregel (1973, ch. 11) justifies the distinction not so much on considerations of class position in this sense, but on a difference between the form of income as such, that is, between 'quasi-contractual incomes' (like wages, fixed interest, and rent) and 'residual incomes' (like corporate profits). It is worth noting that for Kaldor (1961, pp. 194–5) residual incomes are much more uncertain than contractual incomes and subject to fluctuations.

5. Finally, it may be argued (as Kaldor, 1961, pp. 194–5 has done) that the need to generate internal finance in order to carry out active investment dictates a high saving propensity out of profits. This requirement will be even stronger in a life-cycle model on a steady-state growth

---

[3] By using UK quarterly data for the period 1963–76, Murfin (1980, p. 21) concludes that 'the suggestion appears to be that "workers'" marginal propensity to consume is *circa* 0.85, while that of "capitalists" around a quarter. This latter estimate is almost exactly that obtained by Kalecki for the USA 1929–40 by a very different methodology.' Note that Murfin defines workers as wage-income recipients, and capitalists as non-wage-income recipients, and acknowledges that there might be some overlapping. Kaldor (1966, pp. 312–14) notes that national income accounting procedures typically include in personal saving the saving of unincorporated business enterprises; and when allowance is made for investment by these enterprises, together with personal investment in housing, to obtain a measure of personal saving available for lending to other sectors, the figures show that the latter is about one per cent of personal disposable income, i.e. of workers' income. On the other hand, always for Kaldor, corporate gross saving out of after-tax profits is estimated at some 70 per cent, so that the assumption $s_c > s_w$, crucial for the post-Keynesian model, turns out to be reasonable.

path, where capitalists' saving ratio has to allow for (*a*) life-cycle wealth accumulation and (*b*) gradual accumulation of inter-generational assets in order to let the capitalists' wealth stock grow at the same rate as that of the population. It has been repeatedly pointed out that without this condition (i.e. that the capitalists' propensity to save is higher than that of the workers') the system would not be stable at full employment or near full employment. This does not, of course, directly support the validity of the hypothesis of a differentiated (and constant) saving propensity; but it is, as already pointed out in Chapter 1, an important part of the mechanism through which, in the post-Keynesian model, total saving is brought into line with the exogenously given investment.

As Kaldor (1956, p. 95) points out, the condition that the capitalists' propensity to save is higher than that of the other class(es) is necessary but not sufficient for the stability of the model. Another necessary condition for its stability is that the effect of the change in profit margins on saving exceeds the corresponding effect on investment, otherwise equilibrium would be unstable even if the capitalists' propensity to save were higher than that of the other class(es). This latter condition does not arise in the context of the traditional Kaldor–Pasinetti model, where investment is assumed to be completely autonomous, i.e. of full-employment level; it is however important in all of Kaldor's and Joan Robinson's models, at least where P/Y exerts a positive influence on the level of aggregate demand and hence on investment. Later on it has become more common to restate the requirement as (see e.g. Pasinetti, 1962): $s_w < I/Y$ and $s_c > I/Y$. The first condition ensures that the dynamic equilibrium will not have a null or negative share of profits; while the second one excludes the case of a dynamic equilibrium with a null or negative share of wages. As Pasinetti (1962, p. 269) points out, if the first condition were not satisfied, the system would enter a situation of chronic inflation. 'As a matter of fact the latter limit becomes operative much before s_c even approaches the value I/Y, because there is a minimum level below which the wage-rate cannot be compressed' (Pasinetti, 1962, p. 269).

By commenting upon the properties of his own model Pasinetti (1962, p. 277) concludes that 'in a system where full employment investments are actually carried out, and prices are flexible with respect to wages, the only condition for stability is $s_c > 0$, a condition which is certainly and abundantly satisfied even outside the limits in which the mathematical model has an economic meaning'.

In the late 1950s and early 1970s by considering a full-employment long-run equilibrium growth model with a capitalists' class (whose income is derived entirely from capital) and a workers' class (whose income is derived from wages and accumulated savings), both with constant marginal propensities to save, the Cambridge economists were in a position to (*a*) provide a solution to the Harrod–Domar dilemma (by specifying an aggregate saving ratio *s* which equals $g(K/Y)$, where *g* and K/Y are both exogenously given), (*b*) determine the long-run equilibrium value of the rate of profits, the distribution of income between profits and wages, and the distribution of disposable income between the two classes, (*c*) allow the existence of an income residual, namely wages, consistent with the assumption of a relationship between the savings of that class of individuals (the capitalists) who are in the position to control the process of production and the patterns of capital accumulation, and (*d*) give some insight into the process of accumulation of capital by specifying the equilibrium capital shares of the two classes.

Before moving on to the response of the neoclassical school, we might briefly mention the third answer to the Harrod–Domar dilemma, i.e. that of the flexible rate of growth, which has mainly taken the form of considering an endogenously determined technical progress. (It must be said that most of these analyses have not been prompted by the desire to provide an answer to the Harrod–Domar dilemma.) Clearly the rate of growth of the labour force could, on classical lines, be considered as an endogenous variable instead of a constant as in most modern theories of economic growth. Or, on the other hand, technical progress (included in the rate of growth of population) could be assumed as endogenously determined,[4] as in Eltis (1973, ch. 6) whose approach can be compared to Malthus's theory of population applied to capital accumulation, so that if 'there is too much capital there is not enough demand to feed it. Capital then dies off until it becomes scarce, the rate of profit is driven up, and the birth rate of capital starts rising again' (Kregel, 1974, p. 345). This process however is based on the assumption following which the capital/output ratio, assumed to be infinitely flexible, is an inverse monotonic function of the rate of profits, a marginalistic assumption which gives rise to the impasse mentioned at the end of sect. 2.2.1.

2.2.3 *The reaction of the marginalist school to the Cambridge model of income distribution*

The results obtained by the neo-Keynesian economists did of course attract the attention of the neoclassical economists (primarily Meade, 1963, 1966*a*, and Samuelson and Modigliani, 1966*a*, 1966*b*) who defined

---

[4] Various theoretical representations of endogenous technical progress have appeared in the literature in recent decades. For instance Kaldor's (1957, 1962) technical progress function was presented as an alternative to the neoclassical production function. Kennedy's (1964) and von Weizsäcker's (1966) models were intended to replace the 'classical' production function and to provide a valid alternative theory of distribution (in this sense

the Cambridge equation as a 'paradox'. Their reaction was not surprising, since the Cambridge equation makes the whole 'well-behaved' production-function framework irrelevant. With the main preoccupation of defending the theory of marginal productivity of capital, Meade, Samuelson, and Modigliani set out to find an escape route for which the Cambridge equation ($r = n/s_c$) would be prevented from operating. And they claimed to have found it by arguing that when the workers' propensity to save is exactly equal to that of the capitalists' times the profits share, then the capitalists cannot in equilibrium survive in the system and their propensity to save cannot determine the rate of profits.[5] In such a situation all equilibrium savings of the system would be provided by the workers only, and the two-class system would become a single-class model where the marginalist scheme could be applied again in order to determine income distribution. But what the marginalists did not say (or admit) is that such a situation (*a*) is very unlikely to happen in concrete terms, and more importantly (*b*) does represent a 'knife-edge' solution since in equilibrium it applies only when $s_w = s$. Finally, it may be noted that the marginalists' answer to the Harrod–Domar dilemma, at least within this context, has been to devise another 'knife-edge' solution for which the workers' propensity to save is so high as to guarantee a sufficient saving to the system in equilibrium. The merit of the contribution of Meade–Samuelson and Modigliani has however been that of reinforcing the interest of marginalist and post-Keynesian economists in growth models considering constant propensities to save for different groups or sectors of the economic system. For instance a quite large number of neoclassical economists did take up the issue: apart from the already-quoted Meade (1963, 1966*a*) and Samuelson and Modigliani (1966*a*, 1966*b*) we find, for instance, Meade and Hahn (1965), Sato (1966), Stiglitz (1967), Chang W. W. (1969), Ferguson (1969), Ramser (1969, 1979), Uzawa (1969), Furono

they provide a real alternative answer to the Harrod–Domar dilemma). Arrow's famous 'learning-by-doing' model generated from a quite general dissatisfaction with the conception of exogenous technical improvements. Finally we might mention Eltis's (1973) approach discussed above. On this point see also Jones (1975, pp. 194–206).

[5] We exclude the case $s_w > s_c(P/Y) = I/Y$ for which the economy cannot be in a steady state (and which is outside the scope of this kind of analysis); in this case, in post-Keynesian terms, the economic system would be in a situation in which there is a lack of effective demand and therefore continuing unemployment, which is inconsistent with the assumption of full employment that underlies this analysis. The neoclassical analysis of this particular case (i.e. Meade–Samuelson and Modigliani's marginal productivity results) rests on particular and fairly restrictive assumptions on technology (i.e. that the capital/output ratio is an inverse monotonic function of the rate of profit that goes from zero to near infinity) which we have discussed in Sect. 2.2.1 above. On this point see also Pasinetti (1974, p. 131 n. 12). In Baranzini (1990) it is shown that in the case of $s_c < s_w I/Y$ the system converges towards the 'knife-edge' solution $s_c = s_w I/Y$, via an adjustment of the capital share of the two classes.

(1970), Balestra and Baranzini (1971), Hahn and Matthews (1971), Guha (1972), Rau (1972), Britto (1972), Sheng Cheng Hu (1973), Bevan (1974), Ng (1974), Folkers (1974a, 1974b), Baranzini (1975a), Campa (1975), Schlicht (1975), Blattner (1976), Ramanathan (1976), Mückl (1975, 1979), Brems (1979), Vaughan (1979), Woodfield and McDonald (1979, 1981, 1982), Bombach (1981), Domenghino (1982), Kano (1985), and Fleck and Domenghino (1987) and Samuelson (1990).

Some of these marginalist contributions have taken up (and in certain cases extended) lines of research that had already been explored by post-Keynesian economists, while others have provided interesting insights into the neoclassical theory of distribution of income and wealth. A broad classification of these contributions, along with those of the post-Keynesian and other schools, will be given in the final section of this chapter.

2.2.4 The main criticisms of the Cambridge model of distribution

The most common criticisms of the post-Keynesian income-distribution models (at least of those formulated in the 1950s and early 1960s) generally reflect the main differences that exist among the various streams of economic thought in this field of research. Not surprisingly the main attacks concentrate on those points that have been developed mainly by the marginalist school, and which, for obvious reasons of coherence and general framework, have not been considered by the post-Keynesian school. These criticisms seem to concentrate mainly on:

1. the constancy of the two propensities to save, exogenously given and hence independent of other variables as, for instance, the rate of return on capital and the rate of growth of population;
2. the assumption and identification of individuals who retain their class identity forever, i.e. of classes which are inter-generationally stable;
3. the assumption of equality, in the long run, between the rate of profits which capitalists get from their investments and the rate of interest received by workers on their accumulated savings (and hence lent indirectly to the active capitalists);
4. the assumption of classes which are almost entirely identified with given factors of production.

These criticisms have, at least in part, led to partial answers from the post-Keynesian side (for instance, Pasinetti, 1974, ch. 6, and Baranzini, 1982a and b) and to the development of further research in this field; in the next section we shall expound some of these contributions. Today, after thirty years of uninterrupted research, the post-Keynesian theory of income distribution represents a well-structured and nearly complete answer to the other streams of economic thought in this field (see, for instance, Hamouda and Harcourt, 1988, or Bortis, 1988).

2.3 THE EXTENSIONS OF THE POST-KEYNESIAN TWO-CLASS
MODEL OF KALDOR AND PASINETTI

Since the mid-1950s a large number of neo- or post-Keynesian models of
economic growth and income distribution have appeared, mainly grafted
on the original contributions of Kaldor (1956) and Pasinetti (1962).
Post-Keynesian distribution theory now occupies an undisputed place in
most macro-economic textbooks. These models have been labelled as
post-Keynesian since savings passively adjust to the externally given
full-employment investment, via redistribution of income between wages
and profits and/or among social classes. This contrasts with the pre-
Keynesian or neoclassical framework, where investment is governed by
saving, and where the production function and marginal productivity
theory play a crucial role in determining income distribution. The
post-Keynesian model also differs from the static Keynesian scheme,
where changes in the level, rather than in the distribution, of income
ensure equality between saving and investment. The numerous contributions have branched out in various directions, covering many fields of
research relevant to the general topic of income distribution, profit
determination, and capital accumulation, both from a theoretical and
empirical point of view.

Before identifying the main lines of research opened up by the
Kaldor–Pasinetti distribution model it will be appropriate to mention
briefly the seminal contributions in this field, both in the post-Keynesian
(and neo-Ricardian) and neoclassical side.

1. On the *post-Keynesian* side we find: Kaldor (1956, 1957, 1960c,
1962, 1966, 1970), Champernowne (1958), Kahn (1959), Kaldor's reply
to Tobin and Atsumi (1960), Kaldor and Mirrlees (1962), Robinson
(1962, 1966), Pasinetti (1962, 1965, 1974, ch. 6, 1981), Pasinetti's replies
to Meade (1964b), to Chang (1964a), to Meade and Hahn (1966b), to
Samuelson and Modigliani (1966a), to Nuti (1974b), to Campa (1975),
to Stiglitz (1977), to Fazi and Salvadori (1983), and to Fleck and
Domenghino (1989b).

2. On the *neoclassical or marginalist* side we find: Solow (1956, 1970),
Swan (1956), Tobin (1960), Atsumi (1960), Meade (1963, 1964, 1966a),
Meade and Hahn (1965), Chang (1964), Hahn and Matthews (1965,
1971), Sato (1966), Samuelson and Modigliani (1966a) and their reply to
Pasinetti and Robinson (1966b), Stiglitz (1967), and Uzawa (1969).

Among the most authoritative review articles in this field are those of:
Sen (1963, 1970), Hahn and Matthews (1964, 1971), Frey (1970),
Harcourt and Laing (1971); Harcourt (1969, 1972, 1973, 1985), Kregel
(1971, 1973, 1978), Hahn (1971), Britto (1973), Eichner and Kregel
(1975), Bortis (1978), Brems (1979), Asimakopulos (1980–1), Bombach

(1981), Darity (1981), Schefold (1981), Skott (1981), Marglin (1984), and Hamouda and Harcourt (1988).

At the same time it may be worth mentioning a number of important works or textbooks which consider in detail the Cambridge debate on profit determination and income distribution; in particular we would like to mention, in chronological order, Phelps (1966), Weintraub (1966), Allen (1967), Meade (1968), Ferguson (1969), Morishima (1969), Casarosa (1970), Stiglitz and Uzawa (1969), Burmeister and Dobell (1970), Solow (1970), Bronfenbrenner (1971), Dernburg and Dernburg (1971), Hamberg (1971), Wan (1971), Harcourt (1972), Lombardini and Quadrio Curzio (1972), Krelle (1972), Dobb (1973), Eltis (1973), Sylos Labini (1973), Blaug (1974), Atkinson (1975), Bliss (1975), Jones (1975), Robinson and Eatwell (1976), Harris (1978), Eichner (1979, 1986), Lydall (1979), Howard (1979), Craven (1979), Dougherty (1980), Matyas (1980), Schefold (1981), Marglin (1984), Backhouse (1985), Bortis (1988) and van Ewijk (1989).

Clearly this is not an exhaustive list, since a larger number of essays, volumes, and textbooks dedicate a section to the controversy in the field of income and wealth distribution starting from specific socio-economic classes with constant propensity to save.[6]

At this point let us identify the lines of research which have been stimulated by the Kaldor–Pasinetti original analyses and which are considered below:

1. The introduction of a differentiated interest rate for the classes of the system.
2. The introduction of the monetary sector and of a portfolio choice.
3. The stability analysis and the long-term properties of the model.
4. The introduction of the public sector.
5. The extension of the Kaldor–Pasinetti model to include other kinds of socio-economic classes.
6. The introduction of the life-cycle theory into the model, thus providing a micro-economic framework.
7. The analysis of the long-term distribution of wealth and of the income share of the socio-economic classes.
8. Other general aspects of the Kaldor–Pasinetti model, in particular the applicability of the Meade–Samuelson and Modigliani dual theorem.

These points will now be considered in detail.

1. *The introduction of the hypothesis of a differentiated interest rate for the classes*, i.e. the rejection of the equality, in the long run, between the rate of profits which capitalists get from their investments and the

---

[6] On this point see also Baranzini (1987, 1988).

rate of interest received by the workers on their loans to the capitalists. The assumption that the rate of interest received by workers is equal to the rate of profits generated by the system (and perceived by capitalists) is of course obvious in a neoclassical world where individuals may be different due to their initial endowments, but where equilibrating mechanisms are always at work: in this case the differences between the various rates of return may be explained only in terms of risk differences bound to disappear in the long run if the perfect information context remains valid. But if complete foresight exists as to all possible events in the neoclassical model, as Eichner and Kregel (1975, p. 1309) point out, in the post-Keynesian theory 'only the past is known, the future is uncertain'. In other words, if we abandon the neoclassical approach, it may not be clear which particular mechanisms make the interest rate equal to the rate of profit, even if Pasinetti (1962, pp. 271–2) maintains that '[i]n a long-run equilibrium model, the obvious hypothesis to make is that of a rate of interest equal to the rate of profit'.[7]

One could argue that in post-Keynesian models, as in most classical models, individuals first belong to different classes, with a different function and 'withdrawal power' as has been pointed out in Chapter 1. Even the nature of their income is different, since for the workers wages are of a residual nature. From these points of view consumers and entrepreneurs (or workers and capitalists) have a completely different socio-economic profile, and the difference between profit and rate of interest may not be solely imputed to the risk factor but takes a much wider significance. This point will be taken up in Chapter 3.

The implications of the assumption of a different rate of return for the accumulated savings of the various classes are far-reaching. First of all it affects directly the distribution of income among classes, then the overall saving ratio and the patterns of wealth accumulation. In this way the steady-state solutions of the model are profoundly modified, and a new programme of research has been opened up along these lines. The number of contributions and comments in this field is growing and, chronologically, starts with Laing (1969), followed by Balestra and Baranzini (1971), Harcourt (1972), Sheng Cheng Hu (1973), Moore (1974), Pasinetti (1974, pp. 139–41), Campa (1975) and Pasinetti's reply (1975), Baranzini (1975, 1976), Gupta (1976), Riese (1981), Fazi and

---

[7] As a matter of fact Pasinetti (1974, pp. 139–41) himself developed a post-Keynesian model of growth and distribution in which the assumption of equality, in the long run, between the rate of profits which capitalists get from their investments and the rate of interest perceived by the workers is dropped. Truly this digression was advanced in order to show that in the long run the propensity to save of the workers does not determine the distribution of income between profits and wages, in spite of P/K being different from r (the rate of interest).

Salvadori (1981) and Pasinetti's reply (1983*a*), and Miyazaki (1986). Other authors, as Ramanathan (1976), Dougherty (1980), Marglin (1980), Craven (1982), and Panico (1984, 1985), although not developing a straightforward model, enquire into the implications of the long-run equality between the rate of return on capital and the rate of interest earned on accumulated savings.

The results obtained within this context vary according to the assumptions made and to the framework of analysis adopted, although the basic results may well be obtained in both post-Keynesian and marginalist frameworks: a typical example is the neoclassical model considered in Balestra and Baranzini (1971) and the post-Keynesian counterpart expounded in Gupta (1976). Perhaps the most interesting results are to be found in the implications relative to the process of capital accumulation. In fact a lower than average rate of return on savings, in order to ensure a steady-state growth of the system, requires either a higher propensity to save or a larger share of income of the class under consideration, which has a strong influence on income distribution (which would have to be reallocated in order to maintain such steady growth). The implications of this assumption outside the balanced growth path would be even more far-reaching, since this would, other things being equal, lead to a lower rate of capital accumulation by those classes that benefit from a lower rate of return. In other words this would lead, in the long run, to a polarization of the socio-economic classes of the system, except in the case in which this disparity is counterbalanced by an increase in other kinds of income, like wages or rent.

2. *The introduction of the monetary sector and of a portfolio choice.* Since the early 1970s quite a number of analyses have focused on the introduction of the monetary component into the post-Keynesian distribution model. These works were first motivated by the desire to assess the neutrality or non-neutrality of money in these models of growth and distribution; secondly they were aimed at determining whether the equilibrium rate of interest, in a monetary context, would maintain the same characteristics as in the non-monetary model. In this framework we find the contributions of Davidson (1968), Baranzini (1975), Sheng Cheng Hu (1973), Ramanathan (1976), and Skott (1981); but see also Darity (1981), Kano (1985), and van Ewijk (1989). As Ramanathan points out:

The introduction of a monetary asset that competes with a capital asset substantially alters not only the behavioural characteristics of an economic system but the long-run implications as well. For instance, in the standard two-class model with capitalists (or firms) and workers (or households), the proportion of capital held by each group is endogenously determined. If a monetary asset exists, then firms and households will not only save different proportions of their respective incomes and earn dividend income on capital assets but also have different demands for money (Ramanathan, 1976, p. 389).

The way in which the demand for money is determined and introduced into the real model is hence crucial in this context. But here another problem arises, making the introduction of money even more challenging. To quote Ramanathan again:

The two groups will thus respond differently in terms of money demand to changes in the inflation rate or rate of return to capital. This in turn alters the portfolio composition in a dissimilar way with substantial impacts on capital accumulation and the balanced growth path of real and monetary variables (Ramanathan, 1976, p. 389).

The results of these analyses are quite interesting. In general they confirm the relevance of the monetary sector in growth models, but at the same time, in quite a few cases, they confirm the strength of the results obtained in the real model. This is the case of Baranzini (1975); also Ramanathan (1976) shows that when a monetary sector is added, the condition for the so called Pasinetti theorem is empirically more plausible than that of the Meade–Samuelson and Modigliani dual theorem. Other analyses enquire into the optimal conditions for steady-state growth in the presence of money, while others consider the role of money in a model where individuals, or groups, try to maximize their utility function under given conditions (Sheng Cheng Hu, 1973), or the neutrality of money in a model which considers a different rate of interest for the socio-economic classes (Baranzini, 1971, 1975).

The introduction of the monetary sector, in general, gives a higher flexibility to the Kaldor–Pasinetti model, since it comes to bridge the 'research programme' of the post-Keynesian stream of thought labelled as 'subjectivist' (mainly made up by US economists concerned by monetary issues) and the 'research programme' of the 'objectivist' school of thought which is well established in the UK and continental Europe and is mainly concerned with the real phenomena of economic systems. The difference between the two post-Keynesian schools of thought is expounded by Pasinetti commenting on a recent work by Delli Gatti (1987):

The post-Keynesian 'subjectivist' line of thought gives a central relevance to the investment function, which is characterized by a high level of volatility caused by the uncertainty conditions influencing entrepreneurial decisions. Therefore, in order to undertake any investment program, 'animal spirits' are not sufficient, but one needs a 'financial instrument'. Money is shown to be the instrument necessary to confront these situations characterized by uncertainty, and financial institutions are considered as essential elements of the investment process. They are at the centre of what Delli Gatti (1987) defines as 'financial Keynesianism' of the post-Keynesian 'subjectivist' line of thought.

In this sense the introduction of the monetary factors and of the portfolio choice (where individuals may choose among different assets with different rates of return and variance) has the effect of bringing together the two research programmes, 'objective' and 'subjective' respectively. Moreover, as shown in Baranzini (1976, 1977, 1978, 1982a) and in Chapter 7 of this volume, stochastic models including portfolio choice under general conditions confirm the polarization of different economic classes, with a very different rate of capital accumulation. In this way the original classical hypothesis of different socio-economic classes, with different propensities to save and to consume, is reinforced by the outcomes obtained in monetary models including portfolio choice.

3. *The stability analysis and the long-term properties of the model.* A large number of authors have considered the adjustment-time required for the economy to return to steady-state situations from any initial disturbance, and the stability and instability conditions in general. In this context the conditions under which one group of savers may not be able to hold a positive share of the total capital stock are also analysed and the mechanisms at the basis of capital accumulation are brought into the open. Always within this context various authors (mainly working with neoclassical models, which seem appropriate for deriving complicated analytical results) consider long-term adaptations of wealth distribution between the two classes to their respective saving-supply functions, while at the same time it is postulated that the short-run saving-investment equilibrium is immediately realized.

In this wide field of research we find the following contributions (in chronological order): Moore (1967), Stiglitz (1967), Britto (1968), Kubota (1968), Chang, W. W. (1969), McCallum (1969), Colinsk and Ramanathan (1970), Furono (1970), Champernowne (1971), Dernburg and Dernburg (1971), Darity (1971), Guha (1972), Mückl (1972, 1975, 1978), Steedman (1972), Folkers (1974), Gupta (1977), Marrelli and Salvadori (1979), Vaughan (1979), Fazi and Salvadori (1981), Pasinetti (1983), Franke (1984), Bidard and Franke (1986a, 1986b), Taniguchi (1987), and Miyazaki (1987a, 1988).

As was to be anticipated, the adjustment time which is required to arrive at the steady-state solutions (or to return in the case of initial disturbances) is, in general, quite long. But this is quite understandable, since the Kaldor–Pasinetti steady state (as any other long-term steady-state growth path) exhibits a fairly strong local and global stability, so that an external shock or disturbance will take a long time to work its way through a modification of the distribution of income and wealth. But we should not forget that the scope of comparative-static analysis is not primarily to consider the conditions under which the system may converge towards, or may be deviated from, its long-term steady-state growth path, but to enquire into the mechanisms that under general conditions are bound to influence and determine the distribution of income and wealth. However, the analysis of the long-term properties of these models may still yield interesting insights, since, as Mückl (1975, p. 145) points out, it cannot be disregarded that in any adjustment process most, if not all, parameters of the model affect the distribution of income and wealth. In other words one should be aware of the fact that outside any equilibrium situation all variables and parameters come to play an equally important role in the determination of the evolution of the system.

Taniguchi (1987) has recently shown that, in the specific case of the Kaldor–Pasinetti model, there exists a traverse which from one steady-state equilibrium approaches asymptotically a new long-run equilibrium path, provided the rate of profit is constant in the long run; the conditions of existence of such a traverse also correspond to the stability conditions of the equilibrium situation of the model. If this were to be confirmed, the global stability of the model would be, once again, proved.

4. *The introduction of the public sector*, i.e. of government taxation and expenditure. Yet another line of research has been taken up by several authors who set themselves the task of answering the question: in what way will the post-Keynesian model of income distribution be affected by the introduction of a public sector, with its own propensity to save, to consume, and to run into deficits or surpluses? This question is particularly pertinent in the framework of the post-Keynesian model, since it was Keynes who underlined the necessity of a non-neutral public sector.[8] The contributions in this field are those of Steedman (1972), Domenghino (1982), Fleck and Domenghino (1987), Pasinetti (1989*a*, 1989*b*), Dalziel (1989), Sepehri (1989), Mastromatteo (1989*a*, 1989*b*), and Denicolò and Matteuzzi (1989).

Steedman (1972) considers the case of a perfectly balanced government budget and states that the existence of government expenditure and taxes should not affect the validity of the Kaldor–Pasinetti theorem while, except in quite particular cases, it denies the possibility of the Meade–Samuelson and Modigliani dual theorem.

---

[8] Pasinetti states that: 'It is surprising that the various authors, while trying so many extensions, should have paid so little attention to the role of Government taxation and expenditure, a topic on which Kaldor worked so much in his life' (Pasinetti, 1989*a*, p. 26).

Domenghino (1982) and Fleck and Domenghino (1987) analyse an extension of the Cambridge model which incorporates direct and indirect taxes and government spending, so arriving at a more generalized version of the Cambridge equation according to which the workers' propensity to save determines, inter alia, the steady-state income distribution. Domenghino points out that: 'However Pasinetti's Theorem continues to be valid with government activity if one specific requirement is fulfilled: government must have a balanced budget' (Domenghino, 1982, p. 299). In this case, obviously, the system has many similarities with the Kaldor–Pasinetti original two-class model. In the more general case in which the public sector does not show a balanced-budget situation, according to Fleck and Domenghino, two quite different 'Anti-Pasinetti cases' may arise: (a) where the government underspends a steady ratio of its tax income—here it is proved that the higher the workers' propensity to save, the lower the share of income going to capital, a result in line with the Kaldor–Pasinetti approach, and referred to as the 'well-behaved Anti-Pasinetti case'; or (b) where the public sector constantly overspends a fraction of its tax revenue (and accumulates a national debt at a steady rate)—here the higher the workers' propensity to save, the higher the share of steady-state profits, a result which has been labelled the 'pathological Anti-Pasinetti case'. The point about these results is that in the presence of a non-balanced state budget the workers' propensity to save does determine the distribution of income between profits and wages.

The results obtained by Fleck and Domenghino have been recently challenged by Pasinetti (1989a, 1989b) who considers a corrected version of the two-class model with a central government which levies direct and indirect taxes. For the case of a balanced budget Pasinetti obtains the usual Cambridge equation for which the long-run rate of profits is determined by the natural rate of growth divided by the capitalists' propensity to save, now corrected by the taxation parameter, independently of anything else.

It must also be pointed out that, at this stage already, any symmetry with the Meade–Samuelson–Modigliani case has disappeared. Unless ... the workers' *net* propensities to save out of wages and out of profits coincide, the Meade–Samuelson–Modigliani Dual Theorem no longer holds, as it has been pointed out already by Steedman (1972). The reason is very simple. With the introduction of differentiated taxes on wages and on profits, the workers' *net* saving propensities out of wages and out of profits are different. Therefore, the capital/output ratio is no longer determined independently of the rate of profits (and of the distribution of income) (Pasinetti, 1989a, p. 28).

But also in the case of a government budget deficit or surplus the Cambridge equation maintains its relevance. As a matter of fact for this specific case Pasinetti (1989*a*, p. 30) proves that the equilibrium rate of profits is determined by the natural rate of growth divided by the capitalists' propensity to save, here corrected by the effects *both* of taxation on profits *and* of government deficit spending. According to Pasinetti:

This means that, given the rate of taxation and of deficit spending, an equilibrium rate of profits, and consequently an equilibrium share of profits in income, exist, which are sufficiently high as to leave—net of capitalists' consumption, of profits taxes, and of Government destruction of savings—that amount of savings that are exactly equal to required equilibrium-growth investments. As in the cases earlier considered in the literature, workers' savings do not have any effect on the determination of this equilibrium rate, and share, of profits (Pasinetti, 1989*a*, p. 31).

Other important aspects of the model are hence considered by Pasinetti, with particular reference to the way in which the deficit may be covered (monetary financing or debt financing) and to the links between the Ricardian and Kaldorian theory of distribution. (On this point see also the recent contribution by Denicolò and Matteuzzi, 1989.)

Apart from the above-quoted works, in this area may be mentioned the papers of Masamichi (1987), Noda (1987), and Dougherty (1980, pp. 158–9) who considers the role of fiscal policy in more general terms.

5. *The extension of the Kaldor–Pasinetti model to include other types of socio-economic classes.* Immediately after the publication of Kaldor's (1956) seminal paper appeared a contribution by Tobin (1960) where the model of distribution is generalized to include many subclasses of capitalists and workers. A number of papers followed along the same line (see, for instance, Pasinetti, 1974, pp. 141–2). Another series of articles took up the assumption of mixed classes which have a different propensity to save and to consume according to the type of income earned: here we find the works of Stiglitz (1967), Pettenati (1967), Vaughan (1971), Chiang (1972, 1973), Maneschi (1974), Hattori (1975), Moore (1975), Blattner (1976), Moss (1978), Upadhyay (1978), Craven (1979), Darity (1981), Fazi and Salvadori (1981, 1985), Riese (1981), Skott (1981*a*), Chiodi and Velupillai (1983), Pasinetti (1983*a*), O'Connell (1985, 1987), Oda (1986), Miyazaki (1987*a*, 1987*b*), and also Pasinetti (1989*a*). The results obtained in this framework are quite interesting, since they tend to give a higher flexibility to the model of distribution, and provide additional insights into the mechanisms of capital accumulation with particular reference to the kind of income earned by the classes. Additionally these analyses tend to confirm the validity of the Cambridge equation, as long as the system comprises a subclass of 'pure' capitalists, or 'pure' profit-earners.

Still another line of research has focused on the hypothesis of a three-class society, made up of capitalists (or profit-earners), workers (who derive their income from wages and interest), and rentiers (deriving their income from both rent and interest): see the analyses of Pasinetti (1977b, pp. 57–8), Schianchi (1977), and Baranzini and Scazzieri (1987). The introduction of an additional type of income (i.e. rent) and of savers, had led Pasinetti to stress that: 'If one were to take Ricardo's view that landlords save nothing and are a separate class from capitalists, then the long-run rate of profit would precisely be determined by the "Cambridge equation"' (Pasinetti, 1977b, p. 58). More explicit is the analysis to be found in Baranzini and Scazzieri (1987) who generalize the original two-class model of Kaldor–Pasinetti to include rent as a distinct type of income and rentiers as a distinct class with a positive propensity to save. The analysis of the conditions for equilibrium, full-employment growth shows that three long-run equilibria are possible, one of which (when workers and rentiers alone coexist in the economy) leads to new results for the theory of income distribution and capital accumulation. In this latter case it is shown that steady-state growth is compatible with a unique income distribution between social classes, but with more than one distribution among wages, profits, and rent. Of course one of the solutions confirms the validity of the Cambridge equation.

Finally it is worth noting that two authors (Dougherty, 1980, pp. 159–60) and Mainwaring (1980) consider the case of the external economy in a two-class context.

6. *The introduction of the life-cycle theory into the model, thus providing a micro-economic framework.* As pointed out in Sect. 4.2 the idea of introducing some micro-economic elements into the two-class model of income distribution and capital accumulation came, not surprisingly, from neoclassical economists considering the traditional two-class model; marginalist economists are used to think in terms of micro-foundations, and hence to aggregate in order to arrive at the macro-model. The first step in this direction was provided by Samuelson and Modigliani (1966a, p. 297). Other analyses followed, like those of Britto (1969b, 1972), Hahn and Matthews (1971), Atkinson (1974b), Bevan (1974), and Baranzini (1976, 1981, 1982b). The purpose of these works is not exclusively that of providing some micro-foundations to the model of distribution, but only of providing a framework where the propensities to save of the various classes are not exogenously given, but are a function of the rate of interest and of other economic, demographic, and institutional variables. The results obtained in this particular framework are summarized elsewhere (Chapter 4). The point is that the outcomes obtained depend (a) on the kind of framework of analysis chosen—post-Keynesian, neoclassical, or neo-Ricardian—and (b) on the

profile of the socio-economic classes considered. In quite general terms this line of research has provided us with new insights into the micro-mechanisms of wealth accumulation and inter-generational transmission of wealth. These mechanisms, as will be seen in Chapter 5, may well be integrated both in the original post-Keynesian model of distribution, where there is not perfect substitutability between the factors of production and where the neoclassical production function is not introduced, and in the neoclassical model. In this way the historical aspects of savings and capital accumulation are brought to the forefront. The main contribution of this volume will be along this line of research.

7. *The analysis of the long-term distribution of wealth and of the income share of the socio-economic classes*. Another field of research concerns the determination of the share of income (and wealth) accruing to each class of the system. The aspect is important, since the seminal works focused on the distribution accruing to the factors of production on the basis of the value of the equilibrium rate of profits. The authors who have considered this specific problem are: Chiang A. C. (1972, 1973), Sheng Cheng Hu (1973), Pasinetti (1974, pp. 129–31), Woodfield and McDonald (1979, 1981), Craven (1979), Darity (1979), Miyazaki (1988), and Pasinetti (1989*a*, 1989*b*).

These analyses have in certain cases led to the formulation of models where savings of the classes are determined by the kind of income earned and not by the class status. This of course tends to weaken the assumption of two constant propensities to save related to the existence of homogeneous socio-economic classes, and introduces the possibility of a more flexible approach to the treatment of savings. The extreme step in this direction is the one expounded in point 6 above, where the saving ratio becomes endogenously given and is conditioned by the value of a number of parameters and variables. But once again the analytical solutions obtained will depend on the framework of analysis chosen, i.e. on the assumption or rejection of a neoclassical production function, and on the constancy or flexibility of the capital/output ratio.

8. *Other general aspects of the Kaldor–Pasinetti model, in particular the applicability of the Meade–Samuelson and Modigliani dual theorem*. A large number of contributions have concentrated on aspects of the Kaldor–Pasinetti model of distribution which do not fall under the seven headings treated above. This does not mean that the topics considered are of second order; but they cannot be grouped easily. A given number of these papers concern, in one way or another, the applicability of the Meade and Samuelson–Modigliani dual theorem which, under particular conditions, replaces the Cambridge equation. This list includes: Meade (1963, 1964, 1966*a*), Pasinetti (1965*a*, 1966), Chang P. P. (1964),

Baranzini (1975b, 1982), Craven (1979), Woodfield and McDonald (1979, 1981, 1982), Miyazaki (1988), and Samuelson (1990).

Other general works include: Findlay (1959–60), Frey (1970), Ferguson (1972), Guha (1972), Rau (1972), Näslung (1973), Bevan (1974), Ramser (1969, 1979), Hattori (1975), Morishima (1977), Bortis (1978), Brems (1979), Craven (1979), Weintraub (1979), Dougherty (1980), Mainwaring (1980), Darity (1981), Bombach (1981), Skott (1981a, 1981b), Chiodi and Velupillai (1983), Ahmad (1986), Miyazaki (1987a), Das (1988), Bortis (1988), and Soldatos (1988).

2.4 CONCLUSION

In this chapter we have considered in some detail the way in which the post-Keynesian model, over more than three decades, has been developed and refined in order to include a great number of the issues associated with the distribution of income and wealth and the determination of the profit-rate in a steady-state growth model. The historical, demographic, and institutional aspects of the model have come under close scrutiny and a number of relevant questions have found an adequate answer.

There would be little sense in comparing the results obtained within this framework with those obtained for other schemes of analysis. As pointed out in Chapter 1 the scope and method of analysis of the post-Keynesian and neoclassical (or marginalist) schemes are quite different. In particular the post-Keynesian scheme has a primary objective: the elucidation of the causality links of the process of distribution and accumulation and the study of the historical reasons connected with such a process. The interaction between economic, historical, demographic, and institutional parameters has also been studied in great detail. The 'predictability' of the model is not its focal point of analysis, and even its empirical use does not necessarily dominate, for various reasons, the agenda of the post-Keynesian research programme. On the whole it is our opinion that such a research programme has fulfilled, at least partially, its ambitions.

3
Capital Accumulation and Long-Term Economic Dynamics

3.1 LONG-TERM ECONOMIC DYNAMICS: A FRAMEWORK OF ANALYSIS

The post-Keynesian Kaldor–Pasinetti model belongs to the so-called field of comparative static analysis; the reason for this classification may be found in the fact that this model describes a situation where all variables expand at the same positive rate (equiproportional growth) and where the ratios among variables remain constant, so that, year after year, the relative strength of the socio-economic classes remains the same, both in terms of income and wealth. Within this model the propensities of classes to save and to consume and the technological factor (as expressed by the capital/output ratio, K/Y) remain constant; and the requirements for a steady-state growth from one period to another determine the equilibrium value of the endogenous variables of the model. This does not mean that within this framework the problem of capital accumulation and long-term relationships among classes is not considered, in particular with reference to the saving propensities of classes. However, in general, the model gives more emphasis to the long-term relationships among the variables than to the true dynamic factor.

The framework of analysis of the present volume ought, at first sight, to remain fundamentally the same, since the macro-economic scheme remains unaltered. However, the causality relationships at the interior of the model are modified. These relationships concern the role of the life-cycle model and of the division of the financial capital stock between the inter-generational and life-cycle savings. The tools of analysis which we shall use are typical of a long-term enquiry. Consider, for instance, as already pointed out, the life-cycle approach, which focuses on the whole consumption- and saving-plan of an entire generation, spanning over five decades at least. The same is true for the bequest motive which implies freezing a given share of one's financial means over a long-term horizon. Or consider the assumption of a given rigidity in the composition of classes, which makes more sense in a long-term perspective. Hence the whole argument has clearly a long-term flavour.

But there exists another element which differentiates the Kaldor–

Pasinetti model from our own, i.e. the causality chain at the interior of the system. The rate of interest in a life-cycle model influences directly the saving- and consumption-plans of individuals, since it determines the income from interest on all kinds of accumulated savings; on the other hand the rate of interest must be determined at that precise level which guarantees a rate of accumulation (or growth) compatible with a steady state. This is the double role that the rate of interest must simultaneously fulfil, one through the usual mechanism of determining income from interest, the second through the utility function of individuals who must, in equilibrium, save a given amount in order to ensure the right amount of savings. The dynamics at the interior of the model are hence more complicated than those of the traditional model where the saving propensities are constant and exogenously given. Surely the dynamics of such a model come closer, even if they do not fully meet all the requirements, to the definition of economic dynamics which is given by Sir John Hicks:

The distinction between statics and dynamics is (of course) not originally an economic distinction. It is an echo of a far older distinction in mathematical mechanics; a reference to that older meaning will always be at the back of one's mind. ... In mechanics, statics is concerned with rest, dynamics with motion; but no economic system is ever at rest in anything like the mechanical sense. Production is itself a process; by its very nature it is a process of change. All we can do is to define a static condition as one in which certain key variables (the quantities of commodities that are produced and consumed, and the prices at which they are exchanged) are unchanging. A dynamic condition is then, by inevitable opposition, one in which they are changing; and dynamic theory is the analysis of the processes by which they change (Hicks, 1985, p. 2).

One might argue that in general the study of the processes of accumulation of saving and of financial capital in a capitalistic society[1] is clearly of long-term and dynamic nature. The long-term aspect concerns the fact that certain equilibria require very long periods before they are reached. For instance Furono (1970) and Mückl (1975) have shown that, in the case of an external shock, equilibrium in the Kaldor–Pasinetti model is reached again only after a number of decades. The dynamic aspect of our accumulation model, in Hicks's sense, will be underlined by the analysis of a traverse along which the shares of the inter-generational bequest of the two socio-economic classes change in the long-run. In other words we shall concentrate on the particular mechanisms which are important to determine the relative strength of the various classes and the overall process of capital accumulation and economic growth. It

[1] As Bliss (1975, p. 5 n.) points out, one can use the term capitalistic, which is derived from the term capital, and not from the term capitalism. Hence capitalistic production processes are those which use capital (both in a financial and physical capital sense).

is in this sense that the nature of our analysis may be considered as dynamic.[2] But in order to define the scope and method of the analysis it is necessary to retrace the various steps of modern economic dynamics.

3.2 LONG-TERM ECONOMIC DYNAMICS: RECENT DEVELOPMENTS

In this section we shall discuss briefly the recent developments in long-term economic dynamics models, which may be divided into two broad classes:

1. Non-structural economic dynamics models, characterized by a multi-sectoral economic system where all sectors expand at the same rate and where the economic structure remains unchanged (equiproportional economic growth).
2. Structural economic dynamics models, where the sectors do not expand at the same rate (with some of them expanding faster and others slower or even declining) due to different rates of technical progress and growth of demand. In this case the structure of the system changes continuously.

We shall start by recalling the first type of these models.

3.2.1 Long-term economic dynamics: equiproportional growth models

As pointed out by Pasinetti and Scazzieri (1984, 1987*b*) the problems of long-term dynamics have originated two waves of contributions this century. The first wave was sparked off by the works of von Neumann and Harrod in the late 1930s, and concentrated chiefly on the dynamic properties of a multisectoral economic system on an equiproportional steady-state growth path. The works that followed (for instance, Domar (1946) as well as other studies) concentrated mainly on the long-term relationship between macro-economic variables once the rate of growth of technical progress (neutral and equal for all industries) and of active population has been given. Both the neoclassical and post-Keynesian schools have produced a huge literature in this field, mainly with the aim of providing an answer to the Harrod–Domar dilemma ($K/Y = n/s$, see Sect. 2.2.1 above), by assuming flexibility of the capital/output ratio

[2] The switch from statics to dynamics is illustrated by Hicks as follows: 'The line between statics and dynamics is not a line between abstraction and realism. It may indeed be noticed (as a confirmation) that a similar distinction appears in a wholly realistic field of economic history. One of the standard ways of writing economic history (much practised by political historians in their economic chapters) is to survey the state of the economy under consideration, as it was in various historical periods, comparing one state with another. This is comparative statics. It is when the economic historian tries to throw his work into the form of a narrative that it becomes, in our sense, dynamic' (Hicks, 1985, p. 7).

in the case of the most neoclassical models, and by assuming flexibility of the aggregate saving ratio, via redistribution of income, in the case of post-Keynesian theories.

The long-term nature of post-Keynesian growth models is evinced by one of the first sentences of Pasinetti's seminal paper:

The profit and distribution theory which is common to a number of macro-dynamic models recently elaborated in Cambridge has emerged as a development of the Harrod–Domar model of economic growth. As is well-known, all these models are theories of *long-run equilibrium*. They consider full employment systems where the possibilities of economic growth are externally given by population increase and technical progress. Therefore, the amount of investment—in physical terms—necessary in order to keep full employment through time, is also externally given. The interesting device which has made the analytical formulation of these models so simple and manageable consists in assuming that the externally given possibilities of growth increase at a *steady proportional rate* through time, i.e. according to an exponential function. When this happens, and the corresponding investments are actually carried out, all economic quantities grow in time at the same proportional rate of growth, so that all the ratios among them (investment to income, savings to income, rate of profits, etc.) remain constant. The system expands through keeping all proportions constant (Pasinetti, 1962, pp. 268–9).

All these models did not however explicitly deal with the issue of long-term structural dynamics where the rate of growth of the various sectors of production is not equiproportional and the structure of the economy changes continuously.

3.2.2 Long-term economic dynamics: structural models

The models expounded above concentrate on the long-term equiproportional growth of an expanding system focusing primarily on the distribution of income and profit determination in the long-run. They fail however to deal with long-term structural changes, where the rates of growth of the various sectors of the economy may differ.

Another research programme was initiated in the early 1960s (see Pasinetti, 1965; Spaventa, 1962; Leon, 1967) and later taken up by others (see Pasinetti, 1981). These works tend to give emphasis to these aspects of structural dynamics: (a) continuous technical progress, as a consequence of which income per capita continues to rise, causing profound changes in the composition of private demand (Engel's law); and (b) changes in the composition of demand which are the source of profound changes in the structure of the productive economy, with some industries expanding at a faster rate than others, while others still may decline.

Hence changes in the composition of demand lead to structural changes in the composition of production. These relationships also lead, not surprisingly for a post-Keynesian or post-classical framework, to circularity between households (and consumption composition) on the one hand and industry (and output composition) on the other. As expounded in Pasinetti and Scazzieri (1984, 1987*b*) three sources of economic change may be at work: (*a*) changes in population growth; (*b*) different increases in productivity in each industrial branch; and (*c*) Engel's law. To these we could add the institutional changes that take place in an endogenous manner in quite a number of systems. The following explanations may be useful:

1. Changes in the rate of population growth (both by natural growth or by inward or outward migrations) and changes in the ratio of working to total population (both for males and females) have an impact on both the amount and composition of final demand, as well as on the supply of labour for the various industries according to professional qualifications.

2. The second source of economic change is represented by the different rates of technical progress that are registered in the various sectors of the economy: this causes different increases in productivity in each industrial branch. This process is moreover cumulative and leads to disparities in the payment of productive factors among branches of production.

3. The third element, as Pasinetti and Scazzieri point out, is a

straightforward consequence of Engel's Law. Technical progress brings about a continuous increase in average *per capita* real incomes and thus it brings about increases in the demand for the various goods and services. Such demand increases will generally be different for different goods and services, and, as a consequence, also for different sectors (Pasinetti and Scazzieri, 1987*b*, p. 526).

Note that changes in the composition of demand are not necessarily connected with changes in the composition of population, or tastes, or fashion, but simply with increases in real per capita income.

4. An additional element of economic change, which has not directly been considered by Pasinetti, may be associated with endogenously generated institutional changes taking place in most economies in the long run. This is one of the least-covered areas of the whole post-Keynesian and new-classical analysis, as Pasinetti and Scazzieri point out:

It is with reference to the fundamental relationships that are common to all types of institutional set-ups that it has been possible to derive a pretty complete picture of the structural dynamics of an industrial economy. On the other hand, with reference to specific institutions, the economic analysis is still at the initial and preliminary stage, even though important results have already been achieved (Pasinetti and Scazzieri, 1987*b*, p. 527).

3.3 LONG-TERM ECONOMIC DYNAMICS AND A NEW
FRAMEWORK FOR THE THEORY OF VALUE AND DISTRIBUTION

From the above exposition there emerge two characterizing aspects of the new structural analyses, one linking them directly to classical economists (or at least bridging the gap between them), the other representing a break with all previous schools of thought. The former is represented by a new theory of value (a 'pure' theory of value as it has been defined) and the latter refers to a new version of the productive process, where consumption is no longer completely subordinated to the process of accumulation. We shall briefly consider the two points.

1. *The re-emergence of the 'pure' labour theory of value and distribution.* Pasinetti (1986a, 1988b), following his *Structural Change and Economic Growth: A Theoretical Essay on the Dynamics of the Wealth of Nations* (1981), has put forward a new theory of value based on the analytical device of partitioning an economic system into subsystems (and correspondingly of constructing vertically integrated sectors, as in *Metroeconomica* in 1973). The economic system comes in fact to be partitioned into as many such newly defined subsystems as there are consumption goods; and these newly defined subsystems 'include not only the labour and the means of production for the reproduction of each subsystem, but *also* the labour and the means of production necessary to its *expansion* at its particular rate of growth $(g + r_i)$' (Pasinetti, 1988b, pp. 126–7). Assuming that the rates of growth of the subsystems are different (due to a different rate of growth of technical progress and changes in the level and/or composition of demand) and defining by $l^{(i)}$ the vector (equal for all sectors) of the vertically hyper-integrated labour physical coefficient i Pasinetti (1988b) obtains the specific set of natural prices $p^{(i)} = l^{(i)}w$, where w is the wage-rate. This result is remarkable since, as Pasinetti (1988b, p. 130) points out: 'This is a complete generalization of the pure labour theory of value. Each physical quantity of any consumption good is unambiguously related to a physical quantity of labour; and the two have, in between them, a physically defined self-replacing, and expanding, circular process.'

These results lead Pasinetti to conclude that: 'The general labour theory of value that has emerged from the foregoing elaboration has to be taken as providing a logical frame of reference—a conceptual construction which defines a series, actually a family of series, of ideal *natural* prices, which possess an extraordinary high number of remarkable, analytical and normative, properties' (Pasinetti, 1988b, p. 132).

Pasinetti's analysis proves, among other things, that there is no need for Keynesian dynamic analysis to be carried out exclusively in macro-economic terms. This may of course be done in various directions, according to the particular aims of one's research programme. For Pasinetti, for instance: 'The singling out of the concept of vertically integrated sectors allows the possibility of its complete disaggregation into as many sectors as there are final goods. And this allows the possibility of breaking it down to a complete scheme of structural dynamics' (Pasinetti, 1986*b*, p. 15). Such an approach, as we have seen, leads to the formulation of a price theory and hence to the determination of the distribution of income among factors of production.

In contrast, the ultimate goal of our analysis is that of the identification of the conditions and mechanisms which determine the process of capital accumulation, although in this perspective the long-term distribution of income remains crucial. In this framework the disaggregation into vertically integrated sectors is replaced by the division of society into two or more socio-economic classes. All these attempts respond to the expectations following which Keynesian analysis ought to be developed beyond its macro-economic original conception.

2. *The predominance of consumption over accumulation.* From this particular point of view the new results represent a clear break with the classical and post-Keynesian tradition. For the classical economists (including Marx) emphasis is placed on accumulation and on the various mechanisms through which accumulation influences the distribution of income and the relative strength of the various classes; in a sense consumption is hence secondary to accumulation. For the pure labour theory of value and distribution, which may be easily inserted into the post-Keynesian framework, the emphasis is reversed and consumption is focused upon as the main variable of the model. Thanks to technological progress changes in the level of income per capita alter the composition of demand or consumption so entailing changes in the structure of production. But, at least to a certain extent, technology and the accumulation of capital do not play a major role in the determination of the price structure and the distribution of income. In other words, accumulation is secondary here to the consumption structure, so reversing the classical tradition.

3.4 MACRO- AND MICRO-ECONOMICS AND INSTITUTIONAL FRAMEWORK

As we have just seen one of the major programmes of the post-Keynesian school (see, for instance, Hamouda and Harcourt, 1988) has been that of the dynamization of Sraffa's model. A specific feature of Sraffa's system consists in the facts that the domain of structural analysis solely concerns the determination of the system of relative prices and income distribution with a given set of techniques. Long-term structural dynamics does not play a significant role and even in the case of technical choice emphasis is on comparative statics analysis rather than on the analysis of the actual traverse path. As Pasinetti (1986*b*) points out, the post-Keynesians, in sharp contrast with Sraffa, have concentrated on movements of macro-economic magnitudes, while neglecting the relations at the inter-industry level. This leads Pasinetti to add: 'This situation seems to cry out for a clarification, on the one side, of what has (improperly) been referred to as the micro-foundation of Keynesian analysis and, on the other side, of what is the macro- and dynamic implication of the type of analysis that Sraffa has revived' (Pasinetti, 1986*b*, p. 4). The dynamization of Sraffa's static model put forward by Pasinetti has concentrated on a multi-sectoral growth model of production. For Hamouda and Harcourt Pasinetti's

distinctive contributions are not only his work on the rate of profits and the distribution of income within a growing economy in which investment is constrained to be at levels that are needed to maintain full employment growth over time, but also a major extension to take account of changing patterns of demand as income grows because the demands for individual products grow at different rates over their life-cycles. He also considers the problems of production interdependence, technical advance, exhaustible resources and international considerations from the point of view of maintaining overall balance over time, deriving an intricate and comprehensive set of conditions (Hamouda and Harcourt, 1988, p. 22).

By expanding the argument relative to the micro-foundations of the post-Keynesian model to the supply side of capital (savings and inter-generational bequests) we may now consider some of the elements which are relevant for such a framework. In particular:

1. *The institutional set-up*, within which economic relationships take place. We might consider relevant for the behaviour of consumers and entrepreneurs:

(*a*) *the degree of class distinction*: independently of economic variables. This may be associated with a given class rigidity, or with different resources endowment; this element may also be reinforced by a dissimilar attitude of dynasties concerning the transmission of any type of wealth (human or financial) from one generation to the other.

(*b*) *the presence of market imperfections* which, for instance, may strongly influence the distribution of income among classes. This may concern a different reward for financial savings, according to their size or to the level of risk involved.

(*c*) *the presence of a public sector*, which may levy direct (on income and wealth) or indirect taxes, and may also operate a given redistribution of income and wealth. For instance the way in which the inter-generational transmission of wealth is conditioned by estate duties may be relevant for the determination of the relationship between life-cycle and total savings in defining the whole process of capital accumulation.

(*d*) *the presence of a monetary sector*, an issue which has been often considered in the literature on growth economics. The presence of a monetary sector concerns the neutrality of money in the process of income formation and distribution and hence, indirectly, on the process of accumulation; another point concerns the way in which the rate of profit may be influenced by the monetary policy of the central bank.

2. *The level of disaggregation of the model*. We have already mentioned that the traditional post-Keynesian model of profit determination and income distribution is, to a certain extent, already partially disaggregated since it considers the existence of two (or even more) socio-economic classes characterized by a different propensity to save. However, such a disaggregation may (and needs to be) carried out further, by examining how individual families behave during their life-cycle. Additionally, since generations are quite often linked to one another via the endowment of human or financial capital stock, one may focus on the behaviour of dynasties. (Note that the analysis of the behaviour of the single individual may be different from that of his dynasty since the study of the latter includes aspects that are not necessarily considered by the single individual, as the long-run planning of the inter-generational bequest or consumption- and saving-plans extends over a long period.) Generations do also overlap for quite a while, and they may attach a certain importance to each respective level of consumption (on this point see Meade, 1964). Dynasties may then be aggregated on the basis of a given common economic behaviour (composition of their income, propensities to save, etc.) in order to mould classes. In this sense we may identify the following relationships: individuals or families make up dynasties; dynasties make up classes; and classes define the aggregate supply of (private) savings.

We may at this point anticipate the elements that such an analysis should uncover for the examination of the mechanisms of capital accumulation and income distribution. This list of objectives has been drawn up without taking into consideration the technical and more specific aspects of the model which will be considered in the following chapters. Broadly speaking such a framework should help to define:

(*a*) the aggregate level of consumption and saving of the classes of the system as a function of behavioural, institutional, demographic, technical, and economical factors via the introduction of a modified version of the life-cycle hypothesis;

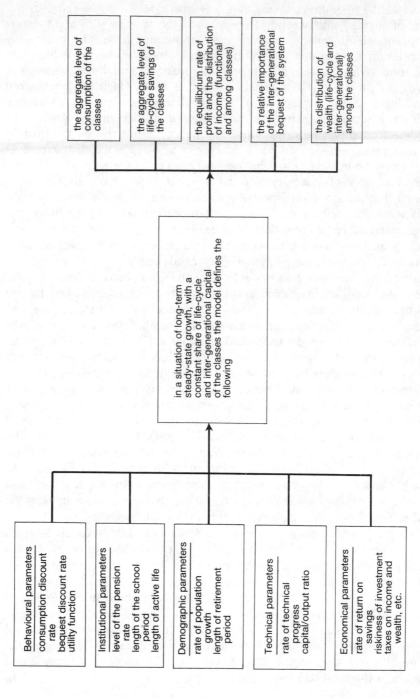

Fig. 3.1 The scheme of causality in a life-cycle model of consumption and accumulation

(*b*) the patterns of accumulation of financial capital, as determined by personal savings, during the life-cycle of individuals;

(*c*) the relevance of the inter-generational bequest for the various classes, i.e. of the inter-generational transmission of financial capital, and the sort of reasons which may lead certain dynasties to accumulate at a faster rate than others;

(*d*) the role played by the rate of interest in connection with equilibrium growth of the system;

(*e*) the distribution of income among factors of production and among the classes of the system in equilibrium; and

(*f*) the share of the global capital stock owned by each class in equilibrium.

In this way a number of institutional factors may be incorporated into the model and their relevance will be checked. We may try to represent in graphic terms the kind of analysis that we intend to carry out.

3.5 CONCLUSION

In the first part of this chapter we have considered the efforts that have been made to provide the Keynesian framework with a long-term structural dynamics analysis, where changes in the composition of demand and other factors are the source of profound modifications in the structure of the productive economy, with some industries expanding at a faster rate than others, while others still may decline. The exact causes and consequences of the dynamics of such a long-term process have been reported, in the same way as the re-emergence of a 'pure' labour theory of value and distribution.

But if the (post-) Keynesian analysis of the productive sectors, of the composition of demand, and of the price-structure may be considered as a fully developed research programme, the supply side of savings (both life-cycle and inter-generational), linked to the behaviour of individuals and families, requires additional attention. In particular a theory is required that explains the mechanisms which lead individuals to allocate in a given way income between consumption and savings *and* to pass on a given amount of their resources to the next generation. More precisely, it is important to assess in what way behavioural, institutional, demographic, technical and economic factors influence the process of saving and accumulation. This 'savings supply-side' of the model should also help in assessing the relevance and dynamics of possible class differences among individuals or dynasties. The general framework of the analysis is provided in Figure 3.1.

4

The Life-Cycle Hypothesis in Models of Income Distribution and Wealth Accumulation

4.1 THE LIFE-CYCLE HYPOTHESIS: A GENERAL PERSPECTIVE

In the traditional comparative-static model aggregate saving is normally postulated as a constant fraction for the whole economy in the case of a one-class model, or as a constant ratio for each group in the case of two- or multi-class society. This assumption, which at least in the recent literature goes back to Keynes's and Kalecki's saving functions, is a simple formulation which can be, from a statistical point of view, estimated with common data: it is hence simple and realistic at the same time.[1]

Since the late 1940s and early 1950s, however, many attempts have been made to formulate more sophisticated theories of saving, with the main objective of providing a link between the micro-economics of rational household behaviour and the macro-economics of the rate of savings. This was done, essentially, by moving from the 'empirical laws' between macro-aggregates of Keynes and Kalecki towards the 'micro-economic' context of household decisions. (It should not be forgotten that this idea may be traced back to Fisher's theory, according to which the rate of interest influences the saving decisions through preference for present goods with respect to future goods; see Fisher, 1907, 1930.)[2]

---

[1] Note that the Keynesian (or Kaleckian, Robinsonian, or Kaldorian) hypothesis is that the saving of both profit- or wage-earners is a function of their income, or composition of income, so that the overall saving/income ratio depends on income distribution. A special case (labelled the 'classical saving function') is to be found when the propensity to save out of wages is zero and out of profits is unity; in this case total savings will be equal to total profits.

[2] The relationship between accumulation of wealth and the time-preference theory of saving has been very early studied by Del Vecchio: 'The accumulation of wealth is taking place for a number of reasons of a social character: the relative position of social strata, general variations of technique, and so on. The economic calculus governs the allocation of the available resources between the various branches of the productive system, it also governs the allocation of the available resources between the various forms of consumption, but it does not determine the distribution of available resources between production and consumption, not even between forms of consumption that take place at different time periods. The rate of interest, that is the expression of economic calculus through time, is not therefore a determining element of accumulation and is, in turn, determined independ-

The original analytical results are mainly due to Modigliani, Brumberg, and Ando who formulated their 'life-cycle hypothesis', one of the best-known versions of the theories of the consumption function.

The fundamental insight of the life-cycle theory (i.e. that aggregate savings are positive in a growing economy because the younger workers who save are more numerous and have higher earnings than the older persons who dissave, even if we do not take into consideration the inter-generational capital stock of the system) was initially put forward by Sir Roy Harrod in the second lecture of his book *Towards a Dynamic Economics* published in 1948. In his Lecture Two on 'The Supply of Saving' Harrod (1948, p. 45) writes that 'in a society in which population and the state of technology are stationary [aggregate humpsaving] should be zero' and then goes on to speculate about the effects of population growth and increasing per capita income. But it was Modigliani, Brumberg, and Ando who developed Harrod's concept of 'hump-saving' into an analytical and quantitative theory and began the process of empirical verification that has made the life-cycle hypothesis a central feature of so many consumption analyses.[3]

The basic idea of the life-cycle theory of optimal consumption- and saving-behaviour is that individuals (or households, or consumption-unities) include future as well as current consumption in their plans: more precisely they make their optimal consumption- and saving-plans in order to maximize the flow of the discounted utilities from consumption. Therefore, to a certain extent, consumption (to which we attach a utility function) determines the optimal saving plan, so that instead of a supply function for saving we end up with a supply function for consumption. Note that this definition might be somewhat mitigated if we were to consider a bequest utility function, or final-consumption utility function, for the case where individuals want to leave a positive bequest to their children.[4] In this way current consumption may be

---

ently of this latter' (Del Vecchio, 1956, pp. 43–4; 1st edn. 1915. As quoted in Baranzini and Scazzieri, 1986, p. 40 n.). It is clear however that if the rate of interest does not directly determine the process of accumulation (as a matter of fact in most modern models of growth the rate of technological progress and of population growth are exogenously given), it does determine the distribution of income and savings among individuals or socio-economic classes. The point made by Del Vecchio may no longer hold in a situation where the rate of accumulation is endogenously determined. This aspect will be reconsidered in the second part of this volume. (On the notion of capital in Fisher see, e.g., the contribution by Meacci, 1989.)

[3] An excellent survey of the life-cycle hypothesis of saving and consumption behaviour is given in Modigliani (1975, 1986) with a detailed reference list; an interesting empirical verification is given in Tobin (1967a).

[4] Note that the introduction of the bequest into the model does not interfere with the life-cycle accumulation of savings; it simply adds an inter-generational qualification to the model and allows for the study of the relative importance of life-cycle/inter-generational

expressed as a function of one's individual present and future resources (like the expected wage-rate and the expected rate of return on the eventual initial bequest) and of the rate of return on life-cycle savings.

These considerations allow us to draw the following conclusions. While in the traditional post-Keynesian or neo-Ricardian macro-economic model (where consumption is a linear function of disposable income) individuals' consumption behaviour is related to their income in that specific period, the life-cycle model views individuals (or classes) instead as planning their consumption and saving behaviour over longer periods, with the aim of allocating their consumption in a satisfactory way over their lifetimes. Savings, and hence the accumulation of savings (or eventually dissavings), will hence be a residual. In other words the life-cycle hypothesis considers savings as resulting mainly from individuals' desire to provide for consumption in old age or even for future generations if inter-generational accumulation is permitted. It is well known that the main point about this approach is to suggest that current consumption depends on a broader measure of income than the traditional post-Keynesian model, as well as on other economic variables of an institutional, demographic, and economic nature.

It has been pointed out that following the life-cycle hypothesis in the long run the consumption/income ratio, in normal circumstances, is quite stable, although in the short run it can fluctuate quite sharply; and the short-run marginal propensity to consume appears to be smaller than the long-run one. Individuals prefer to maintain a smooth profile of consumption even if their lifetime income profile is expected to be uneven, thus emphasizing the role of accumulated savings in the consumption function (or the role of permanent or relative income in the case of the permanent- and relative-income theories of consumption).

At a later stage many attempts have been made to extend these models.[5] One, for instance, is the attempt by Cass and Yaari (1967) to incorporate the Brumberg–Modigliani–Ando saving theory into Solow's growth model in order to study how the life-cycle saving patterns fit into the economy-wide growth trend. As will be pointed out in Chapter 5, one drawback of this analysis is that it does not consider the existence of inter-generational assets, which may seem rather unrealistic from an empirical point of view.

wealth in a model of economic growth. The patterns of life-cycle accumulation of savings may in any case be studied with the same efficacy, even in the presence of the inter-generational bequest.

[5] Note that in most of these models the saving propensities differ by class rather than by type of income; moreover it is assumed that classes are inter-generationally stable. These aspects will be reconsidered later.

4.2 THE LIFE-CYCLE HYPOTHESIS: ITS MAIN CONTRIBUTIONS IN A TWO-CLASS CONTEXT

The main features of the post-Keynesian, neo-Ricardian, and marginalist growth models elaborated since the mid-1950s and which consider a class of 'pure' capitalists (or rentiers) whose income is derived entirely (or mainly in certain cases) from capital, and a class of workers whose income is derived from both work and accumulated savings, are: (*a*) the saving ratio of the classes is exogenously given and hence independent, for instance, of the interest rate;[6] (*b*) little attempt is made to explain the 'historical' importance of the inter-generational bequest of the system; and (*c*) they rest upon an important assumption, namely the equality in the long-run equilibrium between the rate of profit earned by the entrepreneurs and the rates of interest earned by the other classes on their accumulated savings.

The general purpose of this volume is that of studying, essentially from a dynamic and historical point of view, the patterns of accumulation of capital in a two- or multi-class model incorporating the basic ingredients of the life-cycle theory, the possibility of the existence of an inter-generational bequest, and, at some stages, the existence of an imperfect capital market.

The basic contribution to this analysis, namely the introduction of the life-cycle hypothesis into the traditional two-class growth model, was originally suggested to us by Samuelson and Modigliani (1966*a*, p. 297) who, concluding their masterly essay 'The Pasinetti Paradox in Neoclassical and More General Models', admitted their uneasiness with the assumption of permanent classes of capitalists and workers ('pure profit and mixed-income receivers' in their words) with given and unchanging saving propensities on which most neo-Ricardian and post-Keynesian models are based. To quote the two MIT economists:

This assumption completely disregards the life-cycle and its effects on saving and worker behavior. In the first place with a large portion of saving known to occur in some phases of the life-cycle in order to finance dissaving in other phases, it is

---

[6] An alternative explanation that differs in detail, but shares entirely the spirit of the life-cycle approach, is the permanent-income theory of consumption, due to Milton Friedman (1957). This theory argues that people link their consumption behaviour to their permanent or long-term consumption opportunities, but not to their current level of income. Another influential theory along much the same lines is the relative-income hypothesis put forward by James Duesenberry (1952) who argued that current consumption depends not only on current income but also on the history of income (and hence indirectly of expenditure). More precisely, individuals build up consumption standards that are adjusted to their maximum income levels. If income declines relatively to past income, then individuals do not at once reduce the consumption standard adopted. Asymmetrically, an increase in income relative to past peaks leads to higher consumption levels.

unrealistic to posit values for s_c and s_w [the propensities to save of the two classes] which are independent of n [the rate of growth of the system] (Samuelson and Modigliani, 1966a, p. 297).[7]

The essential contributions that the life-cycle theory can contribute in a society characterized by the presence of socio-economic classes with different income structures and different consumption and saving propensities, are the following:

1. More insight into the determination of the distribution of income among classes (at least when they all own a positive share of the capital stock) and determining the equilibrium variables of the model.

2. An understanding of the sort of reasons that may lead to historical class differences, to a different accumulation of capital (both life-cycle and inter-generational), and to the particular conditions under which a class may start accumulating inter-generational assets.

3. An elucidation of the applicability of the Meade–Samuelson and Modigliani condition (following which the capitalists' capital share vanishes in the long run) or of the opposite condition (following which the workers' inter-generational capital share tends to zero). This should allow us to determine when the equilibrium interest rate is the same for all classes of the system and when there exists the possibility of a multiple equilibrium.

4. Assessment of the relative strength of the life-cycle versus the inter-generational capital stock and the conditions which favour one or the other of the capital stocks.

These are, briefly, the issues we shall tackle in the present analysis. To these we shall add the following two questions:

5. What are, in this context, the consequences of the introduction (both in a deterministic and stochastic context) of the hypothesis of an imperfect capital market, which is rather appealing in a two-class or multi-class context?

6. What are the consequences of the introduction of uncertainty (relative to the rate of return on accumulated savings) on the optimal consumption and accumulation rates of two classes; and how relevant is uncertainty in generating differences among classes, i.e. classes with a higher propensity to save (or to accumulate) than average? Additionally, in what way will classes react, according to their risk-aversion, to the

---

[7] Samuelson and Modigliani (1966a, p. 297) conclude their analysis by stating that 'this shortcoming is probably not too serious and could be handled without changing our results drastically'. In the course of this analysis, it will be shown that this is not necessarily true, and that the results obtained are much more complicated and ambiguous than it would seem at first sight.

existence of different investment possibilities, with different rates of return and different expectations?

There is of course no pretence that all relevant aspects of a life-cycle growth model with fixed technology and different classes have been mentioned or will be analysed. The purpose of our analysis is simply to extend our knowledge a little further, as well as our intuition concerning important aspects of economic growth, wealth accumulation, and class distinction in a particular socio-economic and theoretical framework.

4.3 THE LIFE-CYCLE HYPOTHESIS AND ITS COMPATIBILITY IN A MODERN MACRO-ECONOMIC THEORY OF DISTRIBUTION AND ACCUMULATION

4.3.1 Investment, savings, and propensities to save and distribution of income in post-Keynesian growth models

It may be worth recalling that the Cambridge distribution theories (in particular those of Kaldor, Robinson, and Pasinetti, as well as those of Kalecki) are based on the assumption of full employment. As a matter of fact they can be defined as long-run, full-employment equilibrium-growth models. Surely full employment was regarded by Keynes as a feature of a particular period, but—at least in the quarter of a century following the Second World War—it seemed to be almost normal in the economic systems of the industrialized world. Not surprisingly it became the focus of attention of most theoretical frameworks, including the marginalist theory. However, full employment in the marginalist model is the natural outcome of the assumption that factor input prices are equal to their marginal productivities, so making it an inherent feature of the model, and that adjustments take place via the flexibility of these prices. Contrary to the marginalist approach, the assumption of full employment is grafted onto the Cambridge models of economic growth and income distribution; it is exogenously given (by assuming that the level of desired investment ensures full employment of the production factors).

Another important feature of all Cambridge models consists in the fact that savings adjust themselves passively to the exogenously given level of investment (which, as stated above, ensures full employment). This again contrasts with the adjustment mechanism of the marginalist school for which investment is determined by saving in general. Within the post-Keynesian framework the mechanism which ought to ensure, in all cases, the equality of planned saving and investment consists of movements in the level of prices relative to money wages whenever aggregate demand differs from aggregate supply or, conversely, planned investment differs from planned savings. Hence with full employment, which is assumed throughout this argument, an excess of investment over savings *ex ante* implies an excess aggregate demand which will cause an increase in prices and profit margins, so boosting the profits/output ratio (P/Y). And since the propensity to save of the entrepreneurs (s_c) is greater than that of the workers (s_w) the redistribution of income which results in favour of profits will depress aggregate demand and eventually increase aggregate real savings. Conversely a shortfall in investment relative to total aggregate savings lowers the level of aggregate demand, leading entrepreneurs to lower certain prices (at least relatively to money wages), so reducing the profits/output ratio, P/Y; in this case since the propensity to save of the 'pure' profit-earners is higher than that of the other classes the redistribution of income which results will determine a fall in total real savings, establishing the equality investment equals savings. In this way the condition $s_c > s_w$[8] is the stability condition and, quoting Kaldor (1956, p. 95), 'assuming flexible prices (or rather flexible profit margins) the system is thus stable at full employment'.

Hence in the Kaldor–Pasinetti distributive model, where the propensity to save of the two social classes is constant and exogenously given, the long-run equilibrium interest rate (equal to the overall profit rate) and the profit share P/Y correspond to that precise distribution of income ensuring equality between full-employment investment, determined by the 'animal spirits' of the entrepreneurs, and *ex-post* total savings of the system.

4.3.2 Towards an integrated model of income distribution

The topic of this paragraph considers and expands the arguments already treated in the two preceding chapters. Back in 1972 Kregel wrote that one of the least-refined areas of post-Keynesian economics was that of its micro-foundations (Kregel, 1972, p. 346). However, as

---

[8] This assumption, as already pointed out, receives empirical support from the observed high rates of saving out of corporate profits and lower rates out of labour income (see e.g. Kaldor, 1966, pp. 312–14; Pasinetti, 1966a, p. 304; Murfin, 1980). By using UK quarterly data for the period 1963–76 Murfin (1980, p. 21) concludes that 'the suggestion appears to be that "workers"' marginal propensity to consume is *circa* 0.85 while that of "capitalists" [is] around a quarter. This latter estimate is almost exactly that obtained by Kalecki for the USA 1929–40 by a very different methodology.' Note that Murfin defines workers as wage-income recipients, and capitalists as non-wage-income recipients, and acknowledges that there will be some overlap. Kaldor (1966, p. 314) indicates a realistic value of s_w of, say, 0.01–0.03, and a realistic value of $s_c = 0.7$ so that 'the Kaldor–Pasinetti type of model is safe enough on empirical grounds—even allowing for the "Kuh–Meyer" effects, the validity of which is in any case highly questionable.' A clear distinction between the two propensities to save is also admitted by Samuelson and Modigliani (1966a, p. 274), although on their estimate Pasinetti (1966a, p. 304) strongly disagrees.

we have seen, in the last two decades a great deal of effort has been spent in extending it in this direction.

One important question may be raised at this stage. Is it right to expand Keynesian analysis to the micro-economic level, or should it be confined to the aggregate or semi-aggregate level as was the case with its first scholars? To quote once again one of the most prominent post-Keynesians:

> there is no need for Keynesian dynamic analysis to be carried out only in macro-economic terms. The singling out of the concepts of vertically integrated sectors allows the possibility of its complete disaggregation into as many sectors as there are final goods. And this allows the possibility of breaking it down to a complete scheme of structural dynamics. ... It has become commonplace by now that Keynesian analysis must be developed beyond its macro-economic original conception (Pasinetti, 1986b, p. 15).[9]

If the necessity for a disaggregation of post-Keynesian production and price theory is felt so strongly, then in a symmetrical way this argument must apply to the saving and consumer theory of the same framework, where the allocation of income to consumption and savings is determined by the behaviour of socio-economic classes. The macro-foundations of this analysis have already been exhaustively examined, and these foundations will have to be retained in any extension of the analysis. In other words the micro-analysis has to be carried out by taking into account the most important requirements of the macro-model, i.e. the original model, connected with the necessity to ensure full employment and to ensure a given constant rate of growth of the system.

4.4 A POSSIBLE FRAMEWORK OF ENQUIRY

An extension of the post-Keynesian model of distribution to its micro-foundations will necessarily have to focus on the steady-state or equilibrium values of the model, as in the case of the original framework. It is also clear that the various elements which make up the inter-generational transfer of wealth may combine differently outside equilibrium situations than on the steady state and hence require an adjustment of the distribution of the capital stock in order to reach equilibrium values (a sort of 'traverse').

The advantages of considering a macro-model with two or three classes are evident: the share of the capital stock (or revenue) of a class may be expressed as a function of a reduced number of variables in a

---

[9] In a similar way Pasinetti views the generalization of Keynes's theory to the long-run; see Pasinetti (1984/5, p. 246).

simple scheme of causality; a micro-economic approach will not allow for such a simple examination—except for individualistic and hence non-macro-economic considerations. On this point Craven writes that: 'The life cycle theory of savings is attractive at the microeconomic level, but it is not much use in an attempt to construct a simplified macroeconomic theory of distribution. We need some sort of approximation to the way in which individual decisions to save and borrow will balance out to give an overall view of the role of savings' (Craven, 1979, p. 68).

Yet it is clear that most macro-economic models mentioned above were formulated and developed in the thirty years after the Second World War, a period which was not only characterized by a sustained rate of growth, but also by a fairly stable relationship among economic variables and relatively reduced movements in wealth distribution. In such a situation priority is given to the study of the conditions under which this steady state may be maintained. In general the analysis is of a macro-economic nature; and in the case of the post-Keynesian scheme it is (partly) disaggregated to the class level, where different groups (namely entrepreneurs and workers) are identified with a given propensity to consume and to save. The consumption and saving propensities become in this way crucial; they come to determine, among other things, the equilibrium rate of profits and the distribution of income (among factors of production and classes) and of capital.

By introducing a given form of life-cycle theory (or indeed any other theory or scheme which may help to explain the consumption and saving behaviour of individuals, and their desire to hold and transfer inter-generational wealth) into the model one may reach a much higher flexibility and provide more comprehensive answers to the theory of distribution and accumulation, including the analysis of the properties of a simple version of a 'traverse', i.e. of a change in the distribution of wealth among dynasties and classes.

In the next section we consider the general framework of four particular aspects of the life-cycle model connected with our objectives, i.e. the significance of the inter-generational bequest, the assumption of an imperfect capital market, the problems of interest-uncertainty, and the relevance of the time-horizon considered.

4.5   THE RELEVANCE OF THE DISTINCTION BETWEEN INTER-GENERATIONAL AND LIFE-CYCLE CAPITAL STOCKS IN DISTRIBUTION MODELS

4.5.1 *Introductory remarks*

The assumption of a two-class society within the post-Keynesian theory and the neoclassical models of Meade–Samuelson and Modigliani considered above goes back to the classical economists' scheme of distribution, in particular Ricardo. The distinctive feature of these models is that there exists a group of individuals (the capitalists, with permanent membership) who derive their income entirely from their dynastic and life-cycle capital stock, and another group of individuals (the workers, also with permanent membership) who derive their income both from wages and accumulated savings.

This conception lies realistically between the two propositions of Kalecki and Cass and Yaari (1967). More precisely while Kalecki's view was that the capitalists play the key role in the growth of the economy since they alone save (which is also in a certain sense Kaldor's original view), Cass and Yaari show how capital accumulation is made in an economy where everyone is first of all a worker and where there are no inter-generational assets.

From a more general point of view we may say that the distinction between life-cycle savings and inter-generational transfers in the process of the distribution of income and wealth and the accumulation of capital is relevant for a number of issues in economic modelling. Relevant new results have been obtained in the context of growth models that incorporate bequest motives or inter-generational transfers, often considered as a 'final consumption' of the individual's life-cycle. These new results concern the incidence of direct and indirect taxes, the perpetuation of inequality in the distribution of income and wealth, the continuity or discontinuity in the standard of living through generations, the optimal structure of taxes and public expenditure in order to promote growth, and other aspects of redistribution of income and wealth mainly through social security. On some of these issues see, for instance, the seminal works of Meade (1966*b*, 1968, 1973), Diamond (1970), Atkinson (1971), Feldstein (1970, 1973), Mirrlees (1965, 1967), and Bevan (1974, 1979).

On more specific issues concerning our analysis, i.e. on the process of wealth accumulation, Kotlikoff and Summers (1981) present evidence which seems to rule out the life-cycle or 'hump' savings as the major determinant of wealth accumulation in the US economy, while inter-generational transfers appear to be the major element in determining such accumulation. In other words the findings of Kotlikoff and Summers seem to show that: 'life-cycle savings cannot explain the capital stock in an accounting sense and that in the absence of inter-generational transfers the US capital stock would be substantially smaller' (Kotlikoff and Summers, 1981, p. 707).[10]

---

[10] Modigliani (1986, pp. 305–6) suggests that the proportion of bequeathed wealth is only 20–25% in the US and UK: these figures are much lower than the majority of estimates in this field (see e.g. Bevan, 1974, who gives figures between 50 and

As a matter of fact, as the two authors point out, the use of more accurate longitudinal age–earnings and age–consumption profiles shows that they are too flat to generate substantial life-cycle savings: 'Life-cycle models of savings that emphasize savings for retirement as a dominant form of capital accumulation should give way to models that illuminate the determinants of intergenerational transfers' (Kotlikoff and Summers, 1981, p. 706). This conclusion seems to have two implications for our analysis. First of all it shows the importance of including in our two-class life-cycle model a bequest motive, i.e. the possibility of transferring from one generation to the other a part of the capital stock; secondly it comes to reinforce the validity of the assumption that a class of individuals draws most of its earnings from accumulated savings since they may be passed through generations.

A further argument in favour of the above statements comes also from the observation that the elderly either continue to save in retirement or decumulate much more slowly than would be predicted by the simplest life-cycle model without bequest motive in a deterministic context. Recently Mirer (1979) has found that for a number of cohorts the mean net worth of American couples continues to rise in retirement. Taking into account secular growth, as well as an increase in the number of retired people, this would seem to imply the growing importance of bequeathed wealth.

In the context of a two-class life-cycle model we are faced with the following choice. Do we have to consider the capital of the workers' class simply as an accumulation of life-cycle savings, or do we have to introduce the possibility of workers' inter-generational bequests? For sake of generality we shall consider both cases. And while the first possibility, i.e. where the capitalists only may hold bequeathed capital, does not present difficult problems, the second, where both classes hold a share of bequeathed capital, becomes more complicated and requires further assumptions. This is due to the fact that along a long-term steady-state growth path the solutions are easier to find when the constraints are imposed only on one class (as in the case of the Kaldor–Pasinetti model). As a matter of fact in the case in which both classes are allowed to hold inter-generational assets they are fitted into the same balanced growth path only when (*a*) we assume that the two classes differ in their willingness to make bequests, or when (*b*) we introduce the hypothesis of an imperfect capital market.

66%). Clearly for other countries like France, Switzerland, and Germany the share of bequeathed wealth must be much higher, due to the higher concentration of income and to the historical aspects of capital accumulation. But even taking into account Modigliani's low estimates the role of inter-generational capital needs attention.

But, as in any growth model, it would be wrong to assume that a steady state in which capitalists or both classes own a positive inter-generational bequest is always possible; the analysis of the equilibrium properties of the various models will confirm or reject that hypothesis.

4.5.2 *The nature of the inter-generational bequest*

A few hints about the nature of bequeathed capital or inter-generational bequests may be useful. There are various points relating to the existence of the inter-generational capital stock which are of relevance for the study of the patterns of capital accumulation. Broadly speaking we may say that there exist three kinds of bequest that the older generation passes on to the next generation:[11] (*a*) the educational endowment, or human capital stock; (*b*) material wealth, in the form of physical or financial assets (note that this kind of bequest cannot normally be negative); and (*c*) at the macro-level, a share of the national or public debt.

In this analysis we shall confine ourselves to the consideration of the second point above, since it is the only one which is directly related to micro-economic decisions, excluding the case of private education. In order to be in a better position to frame the issue within a rigorous economic framework, we may at this point consider the reasons for which parents often consider leaving a positive bequest to their children. According to Olson and Bailey:

---

[11] According to Meade (1973) there exist four broad forms of endowment that individuals might receive from parents and that will directly influence the amount of income and wealth that they will enjoy during their life-time as well as the wealth that they will transmit to their children. First, individuals are endowed with a given genetic make-up, like intelligence, which in most cases is bound to affect the earning capacity. The genetic make-up, according to Meade, might also include bodily strength and health, or special talents since: 'A certain streak of ruthlessness and aggression may be helpful to the accumulation of wealth without being in any basic ethical or aesthetic sense good or desirable qualities in and for themselves' (Meade, 1973, p. 4). Secondly, individuals may inherit financial or real wealth from their parents, income earning in most cases. Thirdly, individuals do inherit a human capital acquired through education and training. In a strictly *laissez-faire* society education and training is provided by the parents; but in mixed societies it is increasingly provided by the state. Meade (1973, p. 5) takes education as 'covering practically all the environment influences which affect the development of an individual's knowledge, character and motivation'. Education may hence be fairly broadly defined. Finally social setting and contacts, much affected by the social background in which individuals are brought up, represent a precious endowment. Social contacts may provide someone with a favourable occupational and investment opportunity.

To these four elements determined by his family background Meade (1973) adds a fifth one, unconnected with the family background, and represented by the many elements of good and bad luck that an individual will encounter in the course of his professional career or wealth accumulation. This stochastic element may bring important distortions in the process of earning and wealth accumulation. (On some of these points we shall return in the concluding chapter where we consider the links between personal and functional distribution of wealth and income.)

What a married couple during the course of life gives to its children and what it bequeaths to them has a capital value equal to the discounted future value of the consumption (and later bequests) it is expected to provide. In the minds of the givers this bequest must have a prospective value or utility at least equal to the utility forgone by not consuming it themselves.... A household with the faith that it will have a continuing line of descendants with the same regard for their children as it has for its own will act as if it had an indefinitely large or infinite time horizon, even if it gives such a long time horizon no explicit attention (Olson and Bailey, 1981, pp. 16–17).

The reasons for making endowments may be traced back to the following:

1. The *precautionary motive*. Total net saving over the lifetime might well be positive since individuals do not know for certain when they will die and therefore find it impossible to plan their savings in such a way that they will be zero at the moment of their death (and this applies in both cases of a positive or nil initial endowment). The fear of having to live part of their last days without financial means—and so having to rely completely on their heirs or on leaving debts—leads people to overestimate their needs during their retirement period. It is doubtful whether improvements in social security for the elderly will completely eliminate this precautionary motive.[12]

2. The *altruism motive*. Individuals are often altruistic towards one's children and one's grandchildren and so on. The altruism may be based on historical considerations (the desire to leave to one's own children the wealth inherited from the previous generations) in order to have a certain continuity of wealth endowment for the dynasty. Or, in the case in which no material wealth has been inherited from the previous generations one might decide to start building an inter-generational bequest by positively endowing one's own children. The altruism motive may concern both consumption and wealth endowment of the future generation(s), maybe by allowing them to enjoy at the beginning of their life-cycle a higher standard of living than is usual for young couples. In this case the term 'altruism' simply means that the continuity of consumption through the life-cycle is extended to the next generation, avoiding unpalatable breaks, especially if generations overlap for a while (as is usually the case).

3. This brings us to the third reason that one may find behind the act of bequeathing—that related to the overlapping of generations. It may be argued that if the next generation realizes that it will inherit no wealth at all, it might impose upon the previous generation a sort of 'punishment' or 'blackmail' by denying it adequate assistance in old age.

[12] On this point see Modigliani (1986, pp. 305–6).

In this sense the evidence and promise of a positive financial bequest may be interpreted as a safeguard against ill-treatment in the final part of the life-cycle.

4. A fourth factor leading families to bequeath some of their children financial wealth may be to compensate for the inadequate educational background they have received as compared with other siblings. Parents may feel, for instance, that one or other of their children (often their daughter or daughters) has not gone to university as the others have, and therefore deserves better treatment in financial terms at their death or at some stage of their old age. It is also not unusual in certain countries to bequeath to daughters a financial endowment on marriage: this is clearly a way of transmitting wealth inter-generationally.

5. There is another reason for leaving a financial bequest at the end of one's life-cycle which may apply to high-income and wealthy classes. For certain individuals the last years of their life do not necessarily lead to high levels of consumption or expense, especially in those countries where most of health and social welfare are free. Old people, especially those who have had hard times in their youth and quite independently of their consumption discount rate and of their inter-generational concerns, simply accumulate their excess income which most probably will end up in the hands of their heirs. It is relevant to note that this behaviour has more to do with aversion towards present consumption in general (often associated with waste or futility) than with a firm and clear desire of bequeathing to future generations.

6. One last motive explaining endowment has been indirectly put forward by Collard (1978, p. 165) who maintains that 'the altruistic generation will presumably take a different attitude towards conservation and the environment than will a selfish generation'. The desire to conserve non-reproducible resources might then lead to a reduction of the level of present consumption and consequent faster accumulation of wealth.

These are some of the most important motives leading to inter-generational transmission of wealth. We shall now consider further aspects of the inter-generational bequest.

4.5.3 The asymmetry between positive and negative bequests

As Bevan (1979, pp. 381–2) points out, the transmission of material wealth (as opposed to human wealth, which represents a separate issue) exhibits a special asymmetry between positive and negative bequests. This is due to the following factors (the first and the last being mentioned by Bevan himself):

1. First of all while a positive bequest may be considered as a final

act of consumption for the individual bequeathing to his children (so that it does not necessarily require an evaluation of the heirs' consumption discount rate and preferences), a negative bequest requires 'the active agreement of his children', and 'in this case it is the preferences of the children that matter and in particular the weighting that they attach to the consumption of the parents' (Bevan, 1979, p. 382). This leads Bevan to state that the distribution of bequests of material wealth around zero may not be normal.

2. The second point concerns the nature of the bequest itself, which in the case of a negative bequest may be refused. The fact that it may be refused means that financial creditors (other than the heirs themselves) may restrict or may not even allow negative bequests in ordinary cases.

3. There is a third point, which is related to the high level of uncertainty connected with the planning of consumption and saving during retirement. Most individuals do not have sufficient information to assess their financial expenditure during the later part of their lives, and tend to prefer plans which allow for a positive bequest by trying to reduce the chances that debts may be left due to a long retirement.

4. Finally, as Bevan also points out, there exists a limit to the size of a possible negative bequest. 'It is inconceivable, for example, that any individual could make a negative bequest in excess of the expected lifetime earnings of his children, however fondly they regarded him' (Bevan, 1979, p. 382).

It may be added that an example of a negative financial bequest at the macro-level is to be found in the public debt, which represents a transfer of a negative inter-generational financial bequest from one community to its heirs. We shall return to this below.

4.5.4 Positive and negative bequests and redistribution of income and wealth

It should be noted that the inter-generational transmission of wealth implies the following:

1. First, private transmission of wealth, which exists in both financial and human terms. This is normally effected within a given 'dynasty'. Although it is an important element in income and wealth distribution, it does not have a clear redistributive effect in itself.

2. Secondly, transmission of public wealth—quite different in its nature—in the form of positive capital endowment often associated with the national or public debt. The impact of the national debt is well known both for (*a*) the way in which taxes are collected in order to pay for it and the interest on it; and (*b*) in a more direct way, the

redistributive effect of the payment of this interest.

The way in which the financing and payment of the national debt take place can have a strong impact on the determination and distribution of income, especially in those countries where the debt (both internal and external) reaches a significant fraction, or even a multiple, of the annual national income. For suppose that the top 20 per cent of income- and wealth-earners pay 50 per cent of all direct and indirect taxes but own 70 per cent of the national debt; in this case the payment of the interest on the national debt might represent a significant element of redistribution from the less well-off classes to the richest ones; and this would be even more relevant in cases where, due to a high national debt or to other reasons, the interest rate is quite high.

The difference between private and public transmission of wealth is hence relevant, since the former (leaving aside the argument relative to the way in which the fiscal structure may interfere with it) is not a primary source of income and wealth redistribution, while the latter has often a strong redistributive effect which may partially offset Keynesian policies of income and wealth redistribution pursued by the public sector since the end of the Second World War.

The implications of this element are far-reaching. As a matter of fact a number of Western countries have introduced, or are planning to introduce, fiscal policies aimed at reducing or setting an upper limit to the level of inequality of wealth (and income) distribution. Provided that these policies have a sufficiently strong impact, and that the private inter-generational transmission of wealth (which according to a number of writers accounts for about half of total wealth in the UK and one-third in the USA; Bevan, 1972) among rich families is slowed down, this may lead to one or more of the following outcomes: (*a*) a higher rate of wealth transmission among lower-income groups; (*b*) an overall lower rate of wealth transmission for the society as a whole; (*c*) a higher rate of wealth transmission by the public authority, often associated with a high level of national debt.

While point (*a*) seems unlikely to be fully met, point (*b*) would have serious implications, since it would probably mean a lower aggregate rate of accumulation of wealth for some time. It is however likely that point (*c*) has often been the case, i.e. that, at least to a certain extent, public authorities have increased the level of infrastructure building through new public programmes of construction and rearmament that have characterized post-war decades. This has led quite often to a proportional increase in the level of public debt, the redistributive effect of which we have already seen. Hence the possible shift from private to public transfer of wealth may yet generate new problems; on this point see also Pasinetti (1989*a*, sect. VI).

4.5.5 Bequests, inter-generational transfer of wealth, and public debt

It is obvious that the introduction of a bequest function into a life-cycle consumption model leads to new perspectives and dimensions in the two-class consumption, saving, and accumulation model. The bequest represents a link of partial continuity, in economic terms, between generations, which may lead to a higher or lower wealth accumulation compared with the case where individuals leave no bequest or where individuals can live forever (or secure a smooth transition from one generation to another). King points out that:

If the utility of an individual is defined over the utility level of his heirs, then he belongs to an infinite chain of families. This means that there can be no inter-generational externalities and the existence and size of government debt and social security, where funded or pay-as-you-go, has no real effect (Barro, 1974, 1978). This is because individuals can alter their bequests so as exactly to offset the inter-generational redistribution implied by policy and to attain the original optimum (although taxes may lead to additional efficiency losses). In this way, private transfers will offset the public transfers implied by debt or social security policy (King, 1985, p. 282).

The point of this latter argument concerns, of course, the way in which inter-generational transfers and public-debt securities are distributed among social classes. It is doubtful whether such a process is neutral in its effects since it is very unlikely that there is perfect identity between the recipients of inter-generational transfers and the taxpayer who will bear the burden of paying the interest on the national debt and its eventual reimbursement.

4.5.6 The rationale behind attitudes to bequests by social classes

At this point it may be worth considering the conditions imposed on the bequest's utility function of a given socio-economic class to ensure a steady-state growth of the system, i.e. a path of development of the system along which the relative strength of each class remains the same. Outside such an equilibrium (or 'knife-edge') the strength of one class would increase through growing shares of income and wealth, while that of the other class(es) would diminish through shrinking shares of both income and wealth. It may be that in the short- or middle-term a disequilibrium growth of the economy might take place, and that the relationships between the classes would be upset (both of an external or internal nature) so determining an alternative system of income and wealth distribution. But we are not especially concerned here with the final state(s) of this hypothethical process of disequilibrium—which may well have been considered by authors mainly interested in special instances of the polarization of economic power—but instead with the specific mechanisms which may be the basis of such potential evolution. In other words we are looking for those factors whose existence ensures (or conversely cannot ensure) a sort of economic status quo among the social classes in the long run, in terms of both income and wealth distribution. These conditions, as our analysis will point out, may be one of the following:

1. A higher than average propensity to bequeath in financial terms to the next generation of the entrepreneurial class, and a lower than average one for labour-income-earners.
2. A two-assets capital market, where the entrepreneurial class has a mean rate of return higher than that earned by the labour-income-earners (other things being equal).
3. A higher human/financial capital ratio for workers, and a lower one for entrepreneurs, other things being equal. Note that this requirement for stable growth is implicit in the basic assumptions of the model, where we assume that the 'pure' capitalist or entrepreneur draws capital income alone.

The steady-state growth of the model may of course be guaranteed by a combination of the above elements. Points 1 and 2 will be recalled repeatedly throughout our analysis, the latter in particular being considered in sect. 5.9.3 below, and again in Chapter 7 where the implications of a two-assets capital market are considered in detail. Here let us look briefly at the arguments for the hypothesis of different rates of bequest discount for the classes. What are the particular reasons for assuming that capitalists should have a higher propensity to leave assets to their children than other socio-economic classes? Support for the assumption of a stronger bequest motive among more affluent classes and of a much weaker or non-existent one among the least affluent classes comes from King and Dick-Mireaux who, at the end of their analysis, state:

We have found that there is evidence that wealth declines after retirement once we control for differences in permanent income. . . . But the rate at which wealth declines after retirement is less than would be predicted by a life-cycle model with neither bequests nor uncertainty about date of death. Our evidence is consistent, therefore, with either a significant bequest motive or uncertainty about date of death. There is a tendency in the literature to identify the behaviour of all households with a single model. Our evidence suggests that different motives are likely to exist side by side. The estimated 'life-cycle' model accounts for only 50% of the variance of the ratio of wealth to permanent income, it is likely that there is a distribution of motives for saving in the population. The observation that the wealth holdings of a majority of the population appear explicable in terms of a life-cycle model is perfectly consistent with the evidence that a certain fraction of the population does not, for whatever reason, save adequate resources for retirement. Indeed, the evidence in our data set suggests that there is such a group—although we cannot rule out the possibility that households with little wealth plan to finance retirement consumption almost entirely out of indexed social security (King and Dick-Mireaux, 1982, pp. 265–6).

This evidence seems to confirm that there exists a different attitude among social classes *vis-à-vis* the amount of capital that individuals plan to hold at the end of their life; moreover, according to King and Dick-Mireaux, the results obtained apply to net worth, excluding the value of rights to future payments of pensions and social security. Obviously if an individual does not plan to save adequate resources for retirement, then he is even less motivated to bequeath to his own children in financial terms.

4.5.7 The incorporation of the bequest in a model of distribution

Having considered various aspects of inter-generational bequests, let us consider now the ways open to us to incorporate a bequest motive in a life-cycle model and retain this for the analysis of the following chapters.

1. *The bequest utility function*. In this case individuals (or dynasties or classes) are assigned, besides a consumption utility function, a bequest utility function, according to which they will choose to leave to their children a share (lower, equal, or higher than unity) of their inherited bequest. One might also consider the case of a dynasty which, though starting off with no inter-generational wealth, at a given time starts to accumulate long-term wealth. The bequest is here considered as a final (or terminal) consumption by attaching to it the same utility function adopted for the consumption stream. The same approach may be found in numerous other analyses, like Merton (1969, 1971), Samuelson (1969), and Atkinson (1974). In this framework we shall study the value of the variables for which the per capita inter-generational capital stock of the capitalists (and later of all classes) remains constant, so maintaining the system in equilibrium. Moreover we shall study the conditions under which the two classes can coexist in equilibrium. Our analysis will show that when the workers do not have inter-generational capital stock (but life-cycle savings only), for reasonable values of the parameters the 'pure' capitalists exist and own a positive share of the total capital stock. On the other hand when wage-earners are allowed to hold inter-generational bequests in addition to their life-cycle savings, and no allowance is made for a double capital market (where capitalists would earn a higher than average rate of interest on financial capital) the capitalists may exist, in equilibrium, when they exhibit a higher propensity to leave assets to their children than the workers, a rather reasonable assumption.

2. The second possibility is to assume, as in Chapter 6 below, that individuals, in the absence of technical progress, plan to leave to each of their children the same bequest that they have themselves inherited from their parents. Note that this can be done without introducing a bequest utility function and that in the presence of a positive rate of technical progress, m, the bequest left to the next generation ought to include an addition in order to let capital per capita grow at rate m. In this framework the bequest that each individual inherits when he is born is exogenously given and determines with all other parameters the equilibrium value of the variables of the model, like rate of interest, wage-rate, and capital per capita.

3. *The Meade case*. We shall consider this particular case in Sect. 6.4 below. Meade (1966b, 1968, ch. 13) considers the cases of perfect altruism and perfect selfishness, to which we shall add that of super-altruism. Except for the case of perfect selfishness (where individuals write off any bequest at the end of their life) the two other cases establish a precise relationship between a positive bequest and some of the equilibrium variables such as the interest rate. In the case of perfect altruism it is supposed that the children start with the same standard of living as their parents and plan to ensure to their children the same standard of living that they will enjoy during their retirement; in other words the same standard of living continues through the generations, and this is made possible by adjustments to the inter-generational bequest. In a growth model, in a situation of steady growth, we shall demonstrate that the parents' attitude towards the next generation (via the bequest) directly determines the level of the rate of interest and hence of the other variables of the model.

In the course of our analysis we shall assume a caste system where classes remain inter-generationally stable: this hypothesis has the merit of making our analysis much easier. Stiglitz (1967) and Bevan (1974), for instance, assume a random process ('towards the mean' in Bevan) following which dynasties become unstable as the generations pass.

4.6   THE ISSUES OF INTER-CLASS MOBILITY

This issue of inter-class mobility in income distribution and wealth accumulation has often been raised in the appropriate literature; see, for instance, Bliss (1975, ch. 6), Meade (1964, 1973), Vaughan (1979), Stiglitz (1967), etc. Clearly if on the long-term steady-state growth path inter-class mobility takes place in a non-neutral way, most results of the classical two-class model (both post-Keynesian or neoclassical) are bound to be inaccurate. By non-neutral we mean here a process of inter-class transfer of income and wealth that directly influences the equilibrium rate of profit and the wage-rate. It should be noted that, as Vaughan (1979) has shown, at least from a theoretical point of view, even in the case of low class mobility the two-class model with fixed propensities to save retains its traditional solutions (and in particular the validity of the Cambridge equation).

The factors influencing inter-class mobility

Inter-class mobility (or immobility) may be caused by various factors which may act independently or jointly. Among these we may find:

1. the socio-economic framework, which in case of rigidity may preclude movements from one class to another;
2. the dynamic of the economic structure, which in the case of relevant changes may influence the structure of wages and incomes in general, leading to changes in the relative strength of given categories;
3. the impact of the fiscal and redistributive policies of the public sector, leading to alterations in the disposable income generated by market forces;
4. the structure of the inter-generational transmission of inequality by taking into account the relevance of estate duty;
5. the mechanisms at the basis of the actual distribution of income and wealth on past and present generations;
6. the way in which human capital is transferred to the next generation.

Clearly other factors may come into play at any time. From a theoretical point of view the presence, or absence, of a certain degree of inter-class mobility will of course have implications for the study of the role of inter-generational and life-cycle accumulation of wealth in a model based on the coexistence of stable socio-economic classes.

We shall not in our analysis allow for changes in the socio-economic framework of a given economic society (which in any case may be assumed as exogenously given), nor significant changes of the structural framework,[13] nor of the fiscal and redistributive policies of the public sector. In other words we shall consider the socio-institutional setting as given. More important, from this point of view, are the mechanisms related to the inter-generational transmission of inequality or to the past distribution of capital and wealth which have to do with the general problem of distribution, accumulation, and profit determination.

Two particular issues are relevant in the context of inter-class mobility

---

[13] These issues are considered in Baranzini and Scazzieri (1990, ch. 9).

via the inter-generational transmission of inequality; these problems have been considered by Bevan (1979) among others. First of all it may be argued that inequality may be a result of the transfer of human wealth (genetic or educational) as well as of transfers of a material kind (physical or financial capital in particular, but in the shape of social relations as well). These two mechanisms may of course be interrelated, leading to a cumulative effect. And within this framework the question is then to measure how sensitive wealth distribution is to different degrees of mobility of inter-generational earnings.

The second point concerns the asymmetry between positive and negative bequests, which is relevant in the context of inter-class mobility. A negative bequest may arise when (*a*) the parents enjoy a much lower income than that (expected) of their children, *and* (*b*) a certain degree of consumption equalization through generations is considered. This situation has been labelled by Meade (1964) as 'perfect inter-generational altruism'. In this case the optimal inter-generational allocation of income would imply a transfer from the children to their parents, i.e. a negative bequest. This may be done only with the direct consent of the children but, as Bevan points out, 'in this case it is the preferences of the children that matter and in particular the weighting they attach to the consumption of the parents. Hence there is likely to be a discontinuity in the bequest distribution at zero bequest' (Bevan, 1979, p. 382).

The same author considers in great detail the question of inheritance and wealth distribution by developing a model combining inheritance with various degrees of mobility of inter-generational earnings. The model is also capable of generating a distribution of inheritances that—if combined with life-cycle components—fits the observed wealth distribution rather well. At the end of his analysis Bevan states that:

First, the relationship between inherited wealth and earnings that emerges from a standard statistical analysis (e.g. R^2) is weak, even when earnings continuities are strong. Second, the average bequest is extremely sensitive to variations in the equilibrium rate of interest. Third, the existence of bequests may either raise or lower consumption inequality. Fourth, an increase in the fluidity of society may leave the distribution of wealth unaffected, even though it reduces consumption inequality (Bevan, 1979, p. 401).

The second result obtained by Bevan, i.e. that the average bequest is extremely sensitive to changes in the equilibrium rate of interest, reinforces the post-Keynesian income and wealth distribution theory following which inter-class distribution of both income and wealth is directly connected with the equilibrium value of the rate of interest.

The issue has also been studied by Menchik (1979) who maintains that the issue of mobility of wealth is clearly distinct from the issue of equality in general:

For any degree of inequality we can have a relatively static society in which children always assume their parents' position, or a highly mobile society in which the position of the child is unrelated to that of his parents. The degree of inter-generational mobility is determined by market, institutional and genetic factors, among others. The systems that provide education and care for children, distribute public expenditures and transmit material inheritance all influence mobility across generations (Menchik, 1979, p. 349).

Menchik provides empirical estimates of the relationship between material wealth held by parents and that held by their children in the USA from a quite large sample. He concludes that wealthy parents do indeed have wealthy children, although most of the children are not quite as wealthy as their parents were. He also notes that the child–parent comparison is strictly linked with the family size: in one-child families children tend to hold more wealth than their parents, as opposed to families with three or more children where wealth tends to be more diluted. Menchik concludes that:

If however the elasticity between parental resources and bequests to children is 'high' (i.e. bequests are luxury goods), it is not only possible but likely that wealth immobility across a generation is substantially greater than earnings immobility. There remains, of course, the question as to whether such immobility is desirable (Menchik, 1979, p. 360).

According to these results inter-class mobility seems to be fairly weak, especially in Western societies where the rate of population growth is relatively low or even nil. In general terms, inter-class mobility is connected not only with the distribution of the factors of production (such as financial and human wealth), but also with their income. For these reasons it would seem reasonable to leave this issue somewhat in the background of the general models of distribution and profit determination. This is not to deny that in the long term inter-class mobility retains all its relevance, and that an exhaustive examination of the distribution of wealth and income should not omit this aspect. On the other hand profit determination and income distribution at the macro-level seem, according to the above results, to be more important than the personal concentration of wealth which seems to exhibit a high level of rigidity.

4.7   THE PROBLEMS OF UNCERTAINTY IN A LIFE-CYCLE MODEL WITH TWO OR MORE SOCIO-ECONOMIC CLASSES

The original life-cycle models were based on the explicit assumption of perfect subjective foresight regarding the value of all variables (both economic and extra-economic) like labour income, rate of returns on savings, length of the life-cycle, and demographic and institutional parameters as the length of the retirements. These models ignored all problems resulting from uncertainty about these important variables. Since the late 1960s, however, a growing number of analyses have been carried out in order to incorporate uncertainty into the deterministic life-cycle model: seminal papers are those by Merton (1969, 1971), Samuelson (1969), Champernowne (1969), Sandmo (1979), and Drèze and Modigliani (1972). The scope of these models, due to the analytical difficulties associated with uncertainty, is of course fairly restricted and attention is focused on the choice that individuals have between consumption and saving (the latter defining the accumulation process) and alternative types of assets in order to maximize the expected utility of the consumption flow (over an infinite horizon in the case of a consumption flow covering more than one generation). Because of the stochastic nature of one or more variables of the optimal consumption- and accumulation-plans[14] the flow of future consumption which will result is of course a stochastic variable; and the same aspect applies to the process of savings accumulation.

Different approaches have been used to tackle several aspects of these issues; in general, in order to arrive at unambiguous analytical results, most authors have been forced to impose quite restrictive assumptions, in particular about (*a*) the nature of the utility function, (*b*) the length of the life-cycle (often fitted into an infinite time-horizon which enormously simplifies the mathematics), and (*c*) the definition of the bequest function. In particular the cardinal utility function has been assumed to be 'additive' and often of the logarithmic form. In this way the analytical results have been simple and unambiguous.

In order to link the original deterministic life-cycle model with these stochastic analyses it is useful to quote Modigliani who stresses that:

The only additive cardinal utility function that satisfies the Modigliani–Brumberg

---

[14] It may be worth recalling that the stochastic variables which have been more often focused upon in this context are: (*a*) the rate of return on the various kinds of assets, both inter-generational or life-cycle savings; (*b*) the flow of future labour income (or rate of return on human capital); (*c*) the length of the active and retirement period, and (*d*) the level of technology. The effect of uncertainty about the future upon present consumption and saving is, generally speaking, ambiguous, and depends very much on the assumptions made. For instance uncertainty over the length of life leads to a conflict between the desire to save more for a possibly longer life-cycle and the desire for certain consumption in the present: see Yaari (1965), Champernowne (1969), Levhari and Mirman (1977), and Davies (1982). The same conclusions seem to apply to future earnings (cf. Hall, 1978; Eden and Pakes, 1981) and to the rate of return on accumulated savings and inherited capital (see Merton, 1969, 1971; Samuelson, 1969; Champernowne, 1969; Sandmo, 1970; Drèze and Modigliani, 1972; and Levhari and Mirman, 1977, already quoted above).

homogeneity postulate is the power form $U(C) = AC\mu$ (including as a limiting case the logarithmic form), which implies a constant relative risk aversion $1 - \mu$ (with $\mu < 1$ to ensure risk aversion). It has been shown ... that with this utility function, and with standard assumptions about the stochastic nature of returns on assets, the basic Modigliani–Brumberg result, that the rate of consumption at given age to life resources is independent of the level of resources, continues to hold (at least as long as income is not itself stochastic). The ratio does, however, depend not only on the sure rate but also on the parameters of the joint probability distribution of return on assets (Modigliani, 1975, p. 5).

It is not the purpose of our volume to provide here a systematic review of developments in this field; a few more specific links with the relevant literature will be provided when our analysis is developed in the final chapter. However, in order to illustrate the importance of uncertainty in a life-cycle context we would like to report some reflections of Champernowne (1969, pp. 42–3) for whom the effects of uncertainty may be more easily observed on the saving ratio of rational individuals.

After pointing out that apparently slight variations in the choice of assumptions may lead to striking modifications in the conclusions reached, Champernowne points out that:

Under fairly general conditions, any risk that lowers the expected marginal utility to be gained at future dates from savings made today is likely to discourage savings, and any risk that raises the expected marginal utility is likely to encourage savings; but even this platitudinous pronouncement has to be interpreted very cautiously. Risk can influence the future marginal utility of today's savings, both through effects on the rate of profit earned on the savings and through other effects on the total future income; and these latter effects will react on the marginal utility of (future) consumption. Risks lowering the profitability of invested savings discourage saving today, but at the same time (by lowering the expected value of future u-levels) they may raise the expected marginal utility of future consumption and thereby encourage present saving. It is the balancing of these two opposed effects that makes it so difficult to see in one's head just what should be the effects of any particular change in expectations on the rational inducement to save today (Champernowne, 1969, pp. 42–3).

From the above two excerpts it is clear that uncertainty does have an important impact on the consumption- and saving-behaviour of individuals, so affecting directly their life-cycle behaviour and process of capital accumulation. For this reason we shall consider a stochastic model in Chapter 7. Of the various kinds of uncertainty which may be considered in a life-cycle model, and which we have mentioned above, we shall focus on the one related to interest uncertainty, i.e. on the rate of return on the inter-generational bequest and life-cycle savings. As a matter of fact it may be argued that within the context of a model which considers the existence of different socio-economic classes or dynasties, interest uncertainty plays a relevant role, since the rate of return on wealth (or capital) determines directly the level of savings and hence the patterns of wealth accumulation. The analysis of the stochastic framework will allow us to observe the implications of the introduction of an imperfect capital market where individuals may choose to invest in safe or risky assets. Under particular conditions such a hypothesis will throw additional light on the mechanisms which lead to a different accumulation of wealth and class differences. Since the purpose of our analysis is to study the different patterns of wealth accumulation, this approach is particularly appropriate as it shows that the introduction of interest uncertainty may be relevant in explaining in general circumstances the existence of a two-class society.

4.8 CONCLUSION

In this chapter we have enquired into various aspects associated with the accumulation of savings and the inter-generational transmission of wealth in modern society, both in a deterministic and stochastic context. In particular we have focused on the contribution of the life-cycle theory of consumption and savings in explaining the way in which individuals and dynasties may allocate their disposable income. We have seen that this approach may help us to consider the following issues in a two-class model: (*a*) the determination of the distribution of income among classes; (*b*) the sort of reasons that may lead to the formation of different historical classes, to different paths of accumulation of capital; and (*c*) the assessment of the relative strength of life-cycle versus inter-generational capital stock and the conditions under which one or other of the two assets may acquire a greater relevance.

In the second part of this chapter we enquired into the significance and relevance of the inter-generational transmission of wealth. One must say that this issue has not drawn the necessary attention in growth and distribution models, and its relevance, as pointed out by a number of scholars, requires more careful consideration. For this reason we have considered various theoretical perspectives associated with the transmission of wealth. In particular we have analysed the links between life-cycle savings and bequests; the nature of bequests and the sort of reasons for which parents decide (or come) to transmit wealth to their heirs; the 'asymmetry' between positive and negative bequests; and finally the effect of bequests on the distribution of income and wealth. This has allowed us to formulate two different ways to incorporate bequests into the model of distribution and accumulation that we shall consider in Part II. Finally we have also considered the issue of inter-class mobility and its implications in the context of growth models.

PART II

An Essay on the Micro-Foundations of the Macro-Economic Model of Distribution and Accumulation

5

Income Distribution, Capital Accumulation, and Inter-Generational Transfers in a Discrete-Time Model

5.1 INTRODUCTION

As pointed out in the previous chapter the idea of the introduction of some micro-foundations (as the life-cycle hypothesis) in the traditional two-class model of distribution is somewhat recent and has drawn increasing but scattered attention in the literature. Britto (1972), in a short note, has confined his analysis to demonstrating that in a two-class life-cycle growth model, in equilibrium, the saving/income ratio of the 'pure rentiers' is always greater than the saving/income ratio of the workers, who derive their income from work and accumulated life-cycle savings. (This outcome will, *inter alia*, be confirmed by our analysis.) The first part of Bevan's unpublished work (1974) is surely much more appealing and comprehensive, although the main purpose of his analysis falls outside the traditional two-class framework since he focuses on the case where the caste assumption is relaxed. In our view it has, however, at least three shortcomings: (*a*) it considers an infinite time-horizon for the bequest discount rate;[1] (*b*) it considers the two classes separately without closing the aggregate model; and (*c*) it does not consider the possibility of market imperfections (like the case of a double capital market). Still other hints at this issue may be found, as pointed out in Sect. 2.3 above, in Samuelson and Modigliani (1966*a*, p. 297), Hahn and Matthews (1971), Atkinson (1974), and Baranzini (1976, 1981, 1982*b*).[2]

---

[1] In a deterministic model the assumption that the mortal consumer discounts his utility at a constant rate over an infinite horizon has been characterized as 'hardly acceptable' by Flemming (1969, p. 63). Note that this assumption, for the sake of simplicity, is often postulated in stochastic models.

[2] Still other economists do not find the idea of a constant propensity to save attractive: for instance, Bliss (1975, p. 138) asks why the saving propensities of the two classes should not be 'influenced by the growth rate, or the rate of interest, or the price of champagne?'; and Atkinson (1975, p. 179): 'The capitalists' class may possibly accumulate without regard to the return, but if working-class saving is interpreted in life-cycle terms, then it is very likely to be influenced by the rate of interest.' Even Harcourt (1972, p. 217) writes that 'Pasinetti's assumption that all classes receive the same rate of return on their savings has not been much commented on in the literature (but see Chang, 1964, and Laing, 1969).' The point is that most of the literature on this topic appeared after Harcourt's volume.

Plan of the Chapter. After considering the significance and implications of the inter-generational bequest and of the two-period analysis, we start by examining (Sects. 5.2–5.8) the case where the workers own no inter-generational assets, but only life-cycle savings (the 'pure' workers' case). In Sect. 5.3 the basic assumptions of the model are specified, followed, in Sect. 5.4, by an analysis of equilibrium growth and the existence of balanced growth paths. In Sect. 5.5 we define aggregate capital accumulation in equilibrium for both classes; while in the next section we provide some numerical results in order to gain additional insight into the quantitative relevance of our findings. In Sect. 5.7 we analyse the properties of the two propensities to save of the two classes; the following section considers the implications of a particular case in which the two-class society, in the long run, ends up with one class only. The assumption that workers can inherit and bequeath assets is considered in Sect. 5.9 with all its implications, including the case of a different rate of return on capital and of a different subjective discount rate for bequests; the long-term properties of the model are also considered in detail. Section 5.10 assesses the significance of the results obtained.

5.2   INTER-GENERATIONAL BEQUEST AND TWO-PERIOD ANALYSIS: A GENERAL FRAMEWORK

Before spelling out the basic assumptions of the model a specification of the bequest motive of the classes may be worth while. In all traditional two-class models (except for Kaldor's original model) both classes own a capital stock as long as their propensity to save is positive; more precisely we find a 'pure' capitalist or entrepreneurial class whose income is derived entirely (or predominantly) from capital, and a workers' or consumers' class deriving its income from both wages and return on accumulated savings.[3] If we introduce, at the micro-level, the Ando–Brumberg–Modigliani hypothesis on life-cycle savings into a two- (or multi-) class model, we are faced with the following problem: whether to consider the capital stock of the workers' class simply as life-cycle capital, or as a capital stock which is the sum of life-cycle savings *and* a durable inter-generational asset? (Britto, 1972, for instance has considered it as a simple life-cycle savings capital stock.)

---

[3] Through Chapters 5–7 the term 'capital' will be used also to indicate the amount of real wealth accumulated by individuals, dynasties, or classes. The term capital, instead of wealth, has been widely used in the literature of this area. Here it will indicate the inter-generational and life-cycle savings accumulated by individuals, dynasties, or classes (and for which we shall use, with the same sense, the terms capital, or wealth, or even assets).

In order to give more generality to our approach we shall consider the two cases, by analysing first a simple model where the workers do not hold inter-generational assets, and secondly one in which they do. It seems to us that this last proposition has the advantage of being more in line with the welfare theories elaborated in recent decades, so allowing us to consider the accumulation of capital in a two-class economy with more generality; in this way our results will be reached without imposing particular restrictions on the behaviour of one class or the other. For the sake of simplicity the analysis will be carried out within the framework of the familiar two-period model of optimal consumption and invest-ment, since it will allow us to derive, in more simple terms than otherwise, the value of the equilibrium variables of the model. It may be worth noting that this approach entails little loss of generality, since it has been shown (see, for instance, Fama, 1968) that, under general conditions, most of the empirically observable implications derived from a multi-period model of saving and consumption are indistinguishable from those implied by a simple two-period model.[4] In Chapter 6 we shall analyse a more complete two-class model in a continuous-time framework.

5.3 INCOME DISTRIBUTION AND CAPITAL ACCUMULATION IN A TWO-CLASS LIFE-CYCLE MODEL WITH 'PURE' CAPITALISTS AND 'PURE' WORKERS

In this section we shall consider a one-sector growth model with two classes, one whose income is derived entirely from capital (the capitalists or entrepreneurs) and a second one which derives its income from both wages and interest on accumulated life-cycle savings (the workers or consumers).

The basic assumptions of the model
Let us consider a simple two-period model with just one capitalist and one worker, with the following features:

---

[4] Sir John Hicks, in his *Method of Dynamic Economics*, by describing the single-period analysis (for him a sort of prelude to the continuous treatment) states that: 'In the discontinuous treatment we begin the working of the model in a unit period (week, or month, or year); then we proceed to a sequence of such periods. There is of course a sense in which we do the same thing in statics; only in statics the periods are exactly alike, so one will serve for all. In dynamics the single periods (as we shall call them) will not be alike, or not exactly alike; but they will still have some common features, so that much of the analysis can be made repetitive. Much of the work can be done on a *representative* single period: this single period analysis is always a first step. But it is never the only step in a dynamic theory; some means of linkage between successive single periods must also be provided' (Hicks, 1985, p. 24).

1. *Demographic assumptions*: individuals live two periods (of equal length) and there is no uncertainty about the date of retirement (which concludes the first and 'active' period) and of death (at the end of the second period). At the end of the first period each person has $1 + g$ children, so that population grows at the exogenously given rate g.

2. *Income*: the worker born at the end of the period $t - 1$ receives during the first period (t) a wage-rate equal to W_t; the capitalist on his side will have a disposable income equal to rB_{t-1}, where B_{t-1} is the bequest that he has inherited at the end of period $t - 1$ when he was born. For the sake of simplicity, but without loss of generality, retired persons earn no pension. These variables are, under general conditions, constant and known to everybody.

3. *Consumption and accumulation plans*: both individuals make their consumption- and saving-plans in order to maximize the discounted value of their two consumptions $C_t^{c,w}$ and $C_{t+1}^{c,w}$, to which the capitalist (but not the worker in this section) will add the utility that he will derive from leaving an endowment to his children (of the value B_t). Since, by definition, the worker inherits and leaves no assets, the capital stock of the economy will be made up by the inter-generational bequest of the capitalists *and* by the life-cycle savings of both classes.

4. *Utility functions*: we assume a constant elasticity utility-function of the form $U(C_t) = (1/a)(C_t)^a$. Although most of the results are valid for a lower than unity, for the sake of simplicity we focus on the case $a = 0$, i.e. on the widely used logarithmic utility function. The same *u*-function will be assumed for the bequest motive; this assumption is not new in the literature (see, for instance, Merton, 1969, 1971; Atkinson, 1974; and Samuelson, 1969) and assumes that the bequest is a final consumption. We assume an independent rate of utility discount for the bequest, b.

Saving- and consumption-plans

1. *The capitalists' class*: each capitalist, at time t, or more precisely at the end of his first period, will maximize the following *u*-function which incorporates a bequest motive (note that the bequest is set aside at the end of the first period of the donor's life):

$$\text{Max } U(C_t^c, C_{t+1}^c, B_t) = \text{Max } \frac{1}{a}\left[(C_t^c)^a + \frac{(C_{t+1}^c)^a}{1 + \delta} + \frac{1 + g}{1 + b} B_t^a\right]$$

(5.1)

$$\text{s.t. } (1 + r)B_{t-1} = C_t^c + (C_{t+1}^c)/(1 + r) + (1 + g)B_t,$$

where a is the (constant) elasticity of the *u*-function; δ is the rate of utility discount for consumption (or pure time-preference); b is the subjective discount rate for the bequest; B_t is the bequest left to each child at the end of the period t; the superscripts (for variables) and subscripts (for parameters) c and w are for capitalists and workers respectively. As pointed out, the u-function is separable and additive; it applies to consumption and bequest motive (the final consumption).

2. *The workers' class*: workers are in the labour force for the whole of the first period of their lives and receive a uniform wage W_t. They consume C_t^w and save the rest for the second period of their lives. They seek to maximize:

$$\text{Max } U(C_t^w, C_{t+1}^w) = \frac{1}{a} [(C_t^w)^a + (C_{t+1}^w)^a/(1 + \delta)] \tag{5.2}$$

s.t. $W_t = C_t^w + C_{t+1}^w/(1 + r)$.

We can now write the two Lagrangeans, the first concerning the capitalist's and the second the worker's consumption-plan:

$$L_c = \frac{1}{a} \left[(C_t^c)^a + \frac{(C_{t+1}^c)^a}{1 + \delta} + \frac{1 + g}{1 + b} B_t^a \right]$$

$$+ \lambda \left[(1 + r)B_{t-1} - C_t^c - \frac{C_{t+1}^c}{1 + r} - (1 + g)B_t \right] \tag{5.3}$$

$$L_w = \frac{1}{a} \left[(C_t^w)^a + \frac{(C_{t+1}^w)^a}{1 + \delta} \right] + \lambda(W_t - C_t^w - (C_{t+1}^w)/(1 + r)), \tag{5.4}$$

from which we obtain:

$$C_{t+1}^{c,w} = C_t^{c,w}(1 + r)^{1/1-a}(1 + \delta)^{1/a-1}, \tag{5.5}$$

$$B_t = C_t^c(1 + b)^{1/a-1}, \tag{5.6}$$

$$C_{t+1}^c = B_t(1 + b)^{1/1-a}(1 + r)^{1/1-a}(1 + \delta)^{1/a-1}. \tag{5.7}$$

We note immediately that the relationship between the two consumption-rates of the capitalist class given in relation (5.5) is independent of b, the bequest discount rate; moreover the bequest does not depend upon the interest rate (cf. (5.6)). We are now in a position to rewrite the budget constraints in terms of $C_t^{c,w}$:

$$(1 + r)B_{t-1} = C_t^c[1 + (1 + r)^{a/1-a}(1 + \delta)^{1/a-1}$$

$$+ (1 + g)(1 + b)^{1/a-1}], \tag{5.8}$$

$$W_t = C_t^w[1 + (1 + r)^{a/1-a}(1 + \delta)^{1/a-1}], \tag{5.9}$$

from which it is easy to obtain the whole consumption- and saving-plans for both classes.

5.4   EQUILIBRIUM GROWTH AND EXISTENCE OF BALANCED GROWTH PATHS

We now focus on the steady-state behaviour of the model. The question we are interested in is the existence (and eventually the uniqueness) of balanced growth paths. It is easy to see that, in the case where the workers have no inter-generational assets, if there exists a balanced growth path with both classes represented in the system it is unique, since the equilibrium condition can be imposed on the capitalist class alone, being the only class that can inherit and transfer wealth.

We shall start by assuming that the capitalist class exists in equilibrium in order to derive the necessary basic results, enabling us to complete the convergence analysis; the conditions under which the capitalists cannot exist in equilibrium are discussed in a separate section below. In the absence of technical progress, when the two classes exist in equilibrium we may write:

$$\dot{k}_c = \dot{k}_w = \dot{k} = 0, \tag{5.10}$$

which implies that in equilibrium capital per capita grows at rate zero. How do we introduce this relationship into our model? From (5.9) it is easy to see that the consumption and saving of the workers depend, *inter alia*, on W_t, r, and hence on B_{t-1}, the capitalists' bequest. Therefore we first define the equilibrium value of r, the interest rate, which (a) maximizes the capitalists' utility and, at the same time, (b) assures an equilibrium growth of the capital stock of the same class. For this purpose let us rewrite the capitalists' budget constraint in terms of the bequest only; from relations (5.6) and (5.8) we can write:

$$(1 + r)B_{t-1} = B_t((1 + b)^{1/1-a}$$
$$+ (1 + b)^{1/1-a}(1 + r)^{a/1-a}(1 + \delta)^{1/a-1} + 1 + g).$$

$$\tag{5.11a}$$

It is clear that for relation (5.10) to be valid, B_{t-1} must be equal to B_t: in this way the capital per capita of the capitalists grows at rate zero. Hence we write, noting that for equilibrium values of the bequest B_t^* we omit the subscript t where there is no possibility of confusion:

$$B_{t-1} = B_t = B^*, \text{ in equilibrium.} \tag{5.12}$$

Hence the two bequests of relation (5.11a), in a state of steady growth, are equivalent. When a, the elasticity of the utility function, is assumed non-positive (not an unusual assumption) clearly the right-hand side of (5.11a) is a monotonically decreasing function of the rate of interest, r.

Therefore since the left-hand side of the same relation is a (monotonic-ally) increasing function of r, we can conclude that there exists a unique equilibrium value of r which solves (5.11a). Always setting $B_{t-1} = B_t$ we may rewrite (5.11a) as:

$$r = g + (1 + b)^{1/1-a} + (1 + b)^{a/1-a}(1 + r)^{a/1-a}(1 + \delta)^{1/a-1}.$$

(5.11b)

We proceed now to solve (5.11b) with respect to r in order to obtain the explicit value of the equilibrium interest rate. As pointed out in Sect. 5.3, while most of the results of this chapter are valid under more general conditions, we shall assume, for the sake of mathematical simplicity, a logarithmic utility function (i.e. $a = 0$). As pointed out at the beginning of this chapter this function has been widely used in the literature. It is clear why the logarithmic case is much easier, as demonstrated by relation (5.13) below: and this is surely a good reason for concentrating on it. When possible we shall try to be more general. In this case we obtain the following result:[5]

$$r^* = g + (1 + b)\frac{2 + \delta}{1 + \delta}.$$

(5.13)

Relation (5.13) gives us the unique value of the interest rate which keeps the system on a steady-state growth path. It is a function of g (the natural rate of growth), of δ and b (the subjective discount rate for consumption and bequest respectively). We note, moreover, that r^* is independent of technology (i.e. of the form of the production function in the case of a neoclassical model) and that, by definition, it is determined by the behaviour of the 'pure' entrepreneurial class only; this aspect will be reconsidered below.

To study the influence of the parameters on r^* we may differentiate it partially with respect to the individual parameters:

$$\partial r^*/\partial g = 1.$$

(5.14)

---

[5] Note that in the more general case $a \neq 0$, where we assume, for simplicity, $(1 + r)^{a/(1-a)} \cong 1 + a/(1 - a) . r$, we obtain:

$$r^* \cong \frac{g + (1 + b)^{1/1-a}(1 + (1 + \delta)^{1/a-1})}{1 - \dfrac{a}{1 - a}(1 + b)^{1/1-a}(1 + \delta)^{1/a-1}}.$$

(5.13a)

In this case, however, the approximation postulated may be somewhat misleading since in a two-period life-cycle model r may be rather large. For this reason we retain solution (5.13) only.

$$\partial r^*/\partial b = \frac{2 + \delta}{1 + \delta} > 0. \tag{5.15}$$

$$\partial r^*/\partial \delta = -\frac{1 + b}{(1 + \delta)^2} < 0. \tag{5.16}$$

Hence an increase in the natural rate of growth g and in the bequest discount rate have a positive effect on the optimal interest rate, while the opposite applies with respect to δ, the pure time-preference or consumption discount rate. The sign of (5.14) is not surprising and is to be found in most growth models; the same result applies for the more general solution given in (5.13a).

Relations (5.15) may be interpreted in the following way. If the parameter b were to increase, meaning more bequest-discounting, the 'pure' capitalist class will have a propensity to make smaller bequests to their children than required in the steady state. Steady-state growth will be restored only when the rate of interest is increased, meaning a higher share of income for the capitalists who with their high propensity to save during the life-cycle will make up with the lost saving. In this way, according to the post-Keynesian argument, the rate of interest brings about that redistribution of income which is necessary to ensure steady-state savings. (From a marginalistic point of view (5.15) may be interpreted as follows: as the subjective discount rate for the bequest increases thrift is discouraged, so causing an increase in the marginal productivity of capital equal to the interest rate.)

Let us consider now the implications of (5.16). An increase in δ, other things being equal, will discourage life-cycle savings by proportionally increasing initial consumption and also the propensity to leave assets to the next generation. Since on the steady state B_t (the bequest left to each child) must be equal to B_{t-1}, this will be obtained again when the rate of interest is proportionally reduced, so decreasing the disposable income of the class which transfers inter-generational wealth. One should also not forget the redistributive effects of a variation in the rate of interest, which in the case of an increase would imply a transfer of income from the non-capitalist class to the capitalists. It may be worth comparing these results with the equilibrium profit rate of the traditional Meade–Samuelson and Modigliani and Kaldor–Pasinetti model, where $P/K = r = g/s_c$, and where an increase in the propensity to save of the capitalist class depresses the level of the rate of interest. But, as we shall later point out, the two results differ substantially since in our model the rate of interest expresses also an optimality condition (i.e. of maximization of individuals' utility) and not simply an equilibrium condition as in the case of the traditional neoclassical and post-Keynesian two-class model. Moreover the steady-state requirement does not fall uniquely on the interest rate, but also on the value of the inter-generational bequest via the interaction of the two parameters δ and b, the consumption and bequest discount rates respectively. The traditional two-class model does not consider a bequest motive.

At this point the following general remarks are relevant.

1. The optimal equilibrium interest rate r^* does not depend on the form of the production function nor on the value of the capital/labour ratio. It depends only on the rate of growth of the economy and on the behavioural parameters of the life-cycle model. In a certain sense the simplicity of the Meade–Samuelson and Modigliani and Kaldor–Pasinetti theorems is repeated. Additionally, the fact that r^* does not depend on the form of the production function seems to confirm the validity of the Kaldor–Pasinetti theorem.

2. It is interesting to note that r^*, the equilibrium rate of interest (supposed to be equal to the rate of profits in this case) is greater than the natural rate of growth of the population, g. In our model this outcome is particularly important since it guarantees the existence, in equilibrium, of the entrepreneurial class, which on the one hand has an income equal to rB_t and on the other side is expected to leave to the next generation an amount equal to gB_t. Hence, in order to ensure a steady-state growth and to enjoy a positive consumption during their life-cycle, the entrepreneurs must receive on their capital an interest rate higher than the rate of growth of population. If this were not the case, a lower capital accumulation would take place, and/or a lower demographic rate of growth of the class.

3. The third point concerns the maximization of consumption per capita. In a state of balanced growth consumption per capita is maximized when the profit rate, r^*, is equal to the rate of growth, g. In our model, consumption per capita can be maximized in the usual way (i.e. $r^* = g$) only when $b = -1$ and/or $\delta = -2$, which imply a very strong desire to leave a bequest to the next generation and/or a negative subjective discount rate (the latter very unlikely to happen in the real world). It should be noted that throughout this analysis we shall assume, in general, positive values of b and δ only.

4. It may be noted again that we have postulated for both classes (entrepreneurs or pure profit-earners and workers) the same identical behavioural parameters. Had we assumed that they are different, then the equilibrium interest rate would not depend on the behavioural parameters of the working class at all.

It must again be stressed that the above results are valid when the 'pure' capitalist class can exist in equilibrium; this question will be reconsidered in Sects. 5.7 and 5.8 below.

5.5 AGGREGATE CAPITAL ACCUMULATION IN EQUILIBRIUM

Once the equilibrium interest rate, r^*, is determined, the various relationships among the equilibrium variables of the model are also determined. Hence we solve the model by first defining, in equilibrium, the accumulation of capital of both classes. The total capital stock of this two-class life-cycle economy consists of three components. First there is the total bequest of the capitalist class (which in equilibrium grows at rate g), then there are the two aggregate life-cycle savings (S_t^c and S_t^w) of the capitalists and workers.

We could have postulated that the two life-cycle savings belong to the retired capitalists and workers. We retain however the assumption set out above since it allows us to write, even outside the steady-state situation, the interest rate at time t, (r_t), and the wage-rate at time t, (W_t), as functions of the aggregate capital stock also at time t, (K_t). This assumption, which does not imply any loss of generality, would be helpful for the analysis of the convergence.[6] Remembering that the total capital stock in the economy at time t is determined, *inter alia*, by the bequest left at the end of period $t - 1$, we may write, always in equilibrium:

$$K_t = B_{t-1} + S_t^c + S_t^w, \tag{5.17}$$

where S_t^c, the aggregate saving of the capitalist class, includes gB_{t-1}, the saving required in equilibrium in order to leave a bequest to each child equal to the amount of capital that every parent has inherited. In the absence of technical progress this ensures that capital per capita grows at rate zero.

We can write now the equilibrium life-cycle savings of both classes; from relations (5.5)–(5.9), in the case of a logarithmic u-function ($a = 0$), assuming for the sake of simplicity that the number of active capitalists and workers is equal to unity ($L_c = L_w = 1$), and recalling that in equilibrium $B^* = B_t = B_{t-1}$:

$$S_t^c = rB_{t-1} - C_t^c = B_{t-1}(r^* - 1 - b) \tag{5.18}$$

since, in equilibrium $(1 + b)B^* = C_t^c$ (cf. relation (5.6)). Now, since in equilibrium from (5.13)

$$r^* = g + (1 + b) \frac{2 + \delta}{1 + \delta},$$

we can write:

---

[6] It has been provided for the neoclassical version of the model in Baranzini (1976).

$$S_t^c = B^*\left(g + (1 + b)\frac{2 + \delta}{1 + \delta} - 1 - b\right) = B^*\left(g + \frac{1 + b}{1 + \delta}\right). \quad (5.19)$$

From relation (5.9), in equilibrium, the capital stock of the workers' class may be defined as follows (we assume $K_t^w = S_t^w$ since the workers' class by definition has no inter-generational assets):

$$K_t^w = S_t^w = W_t - C_t^w = W_t(1 - [1 + (1 + \delta)^{-1}]^{-1}) = W_t(2 + \delta)^{-1}. \quad (5.20)$$

We note immediately that, W_t excluded, the saving plan of the workers' class is independent of the rate of interest. This is due to the fact that in the case of a logarithmic u-function the proportion of labour income saved turns out to be partially independent of the interest rate (but not the whole consumption-plan, surely more important than the interest rate in a life-cycle model). We say partially since the disposable income of both classes is always determined, *inter alia*, by the interest rate via income distribution. Recalling the original assumptions where $Y = W + P$ or $W_t = Y - P$ we may rewrite (5.20) as follows:

$$K_t^w = S_t^w = \frac{Y - P}{2 + \delta} = K_t(Y/K_t - P/K_t)(2 + \delta)^{-1}, \quad (5.21a)$$

and from (5.13), since $P/K = r^*$:

$$K_t^w = S_t^w = K_t \frac{Y/K - g - (1 + b)\dfrac{2 + \delta}{1 + \delta}}{2 + \delta}$$

$$= K_t\left(\frac{Y/K - g}{2 + \delta} - \frac{1 + b}{1 + \delta}\right). \quad (5.21b)$$

We are now in a position to rewrite the total capital stock:

$$K_t^* = B^*(r^* - b) + K_t\left(\frac{Y}{K} - r^*\right)(2 + \delta)^{-1}; \quad (5.22a)$$

and the equilibrium bequest/total capital ratio (or the ratio between inter-generational and total capital stock):

$$(B/K)^* = \left(1 + \frac{r^* + Y/K}{2 + \delta}\right)\frac{1}{r^* - b}, \quad (5.22b)$$

which is positive as long as $r^* - b$ is greater than zero. Since in a two-period life-cycle model $r^* = P/K$ can be quite high, it is realistic to assume that $(B/K)^*$ is normally positive. Let us now consider the partial derivatives of $(B/K)^*$, which will allow us to draw some hints on the relevance of the inter-generational bequest in the total capital stock (the residual being made up by life-cycle savings):

$$\partial B/K/\partial Y/K = \frac{1}{2 + \delta} \frac{1}{r^* - b} > 0 \tag{5.22c}$$

$$\partial B/K/\partial g = -\frac{2 + \delta + b + Y/K}{(2 + \delta)(r^* - b)^2} < 0 \tag{5.22d}$$

$$\partial B/K/\partial b = \frac{g(1 + \delta) - Y/K}{(2 + \delta)(1 + \delta)(r^* - b)^2} \tag{5.22e}$$

$$\partial B/K/\partial \delta = \left[(b + g) \frac{g + Y/K}{2 + \delta} - \frac{1 + b}{1 + \delta} (\delta Y/K - 2g) \right](2 + \delta)^{-1} \tag{5.22f}$$

$$\partial B/K/\partial r^* = -(r^* - b)^{-2} \left(1 + \frac{b + Y/K}{2 + \delta}\right) < 0. \tag{5.22g}$$

Relation (5.22c) shows that the partial derivative of B/K with respect to the capital/output ratio is negative; in other words an increase in the level of capital intensity has a depressing effect on the share of the long-term or inter-generational capital stock and a positive one on the share of the life-cycle savings of the system in equilibrium. One must remember (see relation (5.13)) that the equilibrium interest rate is independent of technology, i.e. of the capital/output ratio, so that the capital/output ratio does not directly affect the rate of profits. Of course the extra saving required by the growth in capital intensity would have to be found in the life-cycle savings of the two classes.

Relation (5.22d) shows that the share of long-term capital in the total capital stock is negatively associated with the rate of population growth; in other words, the higher the rate of growth, the lower the relative importance of the inter-generational bequest. This result, which is due to the fact that g is positively associated with r^* (see relation (5.22b)), may be interpreted in the following way: in equilibrium an increase in the number of children to be endowed with the same capital $B_{t-1} = B_t = B_{t+1}$ does represent a great burden on the capitalists' finances and life-style, so that only a reduction of the B/K ratio may be compatible with steady-state growth.

The sign of (5.22e) is less clear-cut, and depends on whether $g(1 + \delta) - Y/K$ is greater or smaller than zero. In a two-period life-cycle model the ratio Y/K can be rather high, probably higher than $g(1 + \delta)$: in this case an increase in the bequest discount rate, b, would lead to a lower B/K ratio, i.e. to a lower share of long-term capital in the total capital stock. This result would be easy to explain, since a higher b means less willingness to bequeath the children financial capital. However, if g and δ are particularly high, and the inverse of the capital/output ratio is particularly low, it may well be the partial derivative of B/K with respect to the subjective discount rate for the bequest becomes positive; in this case an increase in the bequest discount rate (i.e. a lower willingness to leave assets to the children) would paradoxically lead to a higher proportion of inter-generational capital in the total capital stock. In this latter case the impact of a high g and K/Y is clearly overriding (see discussion above).

Relation (5.22*f*) yields also an ambiguous result. One would expect that an increase in δ, the consumption discount rate, meaning a lower willingness to accumulate life-cycle savings, ought to lead to a higher proportion of inter-generational capital in the total capital stock of the system. Although this may well be the general case (see relation (5.22*f*)), it is possible that in specific circumstances the opposite result applies.

We consider finally relation (5.22*g*) which measures the response of the share of inter-generational assets in the total capital stock to changes in the level of the equilibrium interest rate r^*. The sign of the right-hand side of the derivative is clearly negative, which means that an increase in the level of the equilibrium interest rate has a negative effect on the inter-generational capital stock and, conversely, a positive one on the size of the life-cycle savings of the system. This rather surprising result may be explained by the fact that, according to relation (5.15), an increase in the bequest discount rate has a positive effect on the rate of interest. And since a higher b implies a lower desire to leave assets at the end of the lifetime, a higher rate of interest may be associated with a lower B/K, i.e. the incidence of inter-generational assets in the total capital. At this point we can write the following ratios of the model, which will be useful for the numerical example below:

$$(K_c/K)^* = (K - K_w)/K = 1 + \frac{r^* - Y/K}{2 + \delta}, \qquad (5.23a)$$

$$(K_w/K)^* = (Y/K - r^*)/(2 + \delta), \qquad (5.23b)$$

where the equilibrium value of

$$r^* = g + (1 + b)\frac{2 + \delta}{1 + \delta}$$

is given in relation (5.13), and where K_c^* and $K_w^* = S^w$ are the total capital stocks of the two classes. In Sect. 5.8 we shall reconsider some implications of the above relations and determine when the two classes exist in equilibrium and what capital share they hold.

The ratio $(B_t/K_t^c)^*$, i.e. the share of the bequest in the total capital stock of the capitalists, is easily derived from (5.19):

$$(B_t/K_t^c)^* = \frac{1 + g}{b + r^*} \qquad (5.22c)$$

which is always positive, but lower than unity.

5.6   SOME NUMERICAL RESULTS

To gain some insight into the quantitative relevance of our findings, a numerical computation will be provided. We may immediately stress that the results obtained must be interpreted with due care since we are considering a simplified two-period model where the working period has the same length as the retirement period and which considers one generation only.

Since the original feature of this model is the bequest function (and since, as King (1985, p. 285) has pointed out, little is known about bequest motives) we shall try to identify the equilibrium value of b (the bequest discount rate) for several combinations of realistic values of the parameters g and δ and of the variable (here considered as a constant) r^*. This approach is also due to the fact that, from an empirical point of view, we know more about the interest rate than about the subjective rate of discount for the bequest. We shall also give the equilibrium value of the capital share of the two classes.

Since we are considering a two-period model we shall divide the active and retirement period into twenty-five subperiods, or years, and the value of the parameters (b included) will be given on a yearly basis. In all cases we assume a capital/output ratio $(K/Y)^* = 4$.

Of course, as pointed out above, the extreme simplicity of the model which has been necessary to derive the equilibrium variables explicitly, will cause some distortions; nevertheless the results obtained are interesting. Note finally that these computations are based on the assumption that the workers' class is not allowed to inherit and bequeath assets: this restrictive assumption will be lifted in Sect. 5.9 below.

The results obtained in Table 5.1 may be interpreted as follows. First of all it may be stressed that the value of b (the capitalists' bequest discount rate) hovers around 1–4 per cent (yearly) and is not very sensitive in absolute terms to changes in r (the equilibrium interest rate), g (the rate of population growth), and δ (the consumption discount rate of both classes). Additionally the value of b obtained shows that for an active and retirement period of twenty-five years each (this point will be reconsidered below), a rational dynasty of capitalists will accumulate inter-generational capital at the equilibrium rate g for a

Table 5.1 Equilibrium value of b and other equilibrium ratios[1] for different combinations of the parameters and r (parameters in percentages)

Parameter values (yearly basis)				Equilibrium values			
r	g	δ	b	K_w/K	K_c/K	B_t/K_c	B_t/K
5	1	2	1.3	1.000	0.000	0.000	0.000
5	1	3	1.6	1.000	0.000	0.000	0.000
5	1	5	2.2	0.837	0.163	0.399	0.065
5	1	7	2.5	0.557	0.443	0.383	0.170
5	1	9	2.8	0.358	0.642	0.366	0.235
5	1	11	2.9	0.226	0.774	0.361	0.273
4	1	9	1.0	0.432	0.568	0.641	0.364
5	1	9	2.8	0.358	0.642	0.366	0.235
6	1	9	4.2	0.264	0.736	0.241	0.177
5	0.8	9	2.9	0.358	0.642	0.344	0.221
5	1	9	2.8	0.358	0.642	0.366	0.235
5	1.2	9	2.6	0.358	0.642	0.396	0.255

1. Where r is the interest rate (annual average rate per cent compounded continuously like g, b, and δ);
  g is the (yearly) rate of growth of population;
  δ is the (yearly) discount rate for consumption;
  b is the bequest discount rate (it applies to the capitalist class only);
  K_c, K_w are the total capital stocks of the capitalists and workers respectively;
  K is the total capital stock of the system;
  B_t is the inter-generational bequest of the capitalist class.

rather low value of the bequest discount rate; this means a rather strong desire to leave a bequest to the next generation.

The second column for the equilibrium values gives us the K_w/K ratio, i.e. the proportion of the workers' savings in the total capital stock of the system. We note that as δ, the pure time-preference, is increased the ratio K_w/K decreases from unity to smaller values (for $\delta = 0.11$ it is equal to just less than one-quarter). In other words for low values of the consumption discount rate (which means a strong desire to postpone present consumption) the workers' class will accumulate, in a situation of equilibrium, a greater amount of life-cycle savings, so leaving less space for the capitalists' life-cycle and inter-generational savings. The case corresponds, for very low values of the consumption discount rate (below 4 per cent in Table 5.1), to the Meade–Samuelson and Modigliani dual theorem in which the fraction of the capital stock per man owned by the capitalist class becomes zero (see Sect. 5.8 below). As stated, as the consumption discount rate increases, K_w/K decreases making room for the aggregate K_c/K ratio (always in equilibrium).

But what value of δ is more likely to reflect the realities of the economy? As pointed out above, one of the most important features of this model is the equal length of the active and retirement period: a ratio of three or four to one is perhaps more plausible. This would of course be reflected in the pure time-preference which should be increased in order to shift some consumption from the retirement to the active period. (This means that for a more realistic active-retirement period the share of the inter-generational bequest would be, other things being equal, higher.)

The last two columns give us the share of the inter-generational bequest (which here belongs entirely to the capitalist class) in the capitalists' and aggregate capital stock respectively. Again we note that for low values of the consumption discount rate the ratio B_t/K is equal to zero as the entire equilibrium capital stock is represented by the workers' life-cycle savings. For more plausible values of the consumption discount rate (8–10 per cent) we obtain a value of B_t/K (i.e. the share of the inter-generational bequest in the total capital stock) around one-quarter to one-third. These figures may be compared with Farrell's (1970) calculations based on 1962 US data, which show that the average bequest is equivalent to 1.4 times the average earnings and which imply, given a profit share of one-quarter and a capital/output ratio of three, that just one-third of total capital stock consists of inter-generational transfer. Bevan (1974, p. 27), commenting on a similar estimate, states that 'For the UK with a more concentrated distribution of wealth, one-half might be appropriate.' Modigliani (1986) instead quotes figures between one-fifth and one-quarter, although, as we have pointed out in Part I, they must be clearly understated for most countries of Western Europe.

We note finally that the values for B_t/K that we obtain in Table 5.1 are clearly biased downwards since (*a*) the life-cycle savings of the two classes, due to an equal length of the active and retirement periods, are overestimated, and (*b*) we are not considering workers' inter-generational assets; this assumption will be relaxed in Sect. 5.9 below.

5.7   THE SAVING PROPENSITIES AND THE RATE OF PROFIT

At this point it may be interesting to consider the saving propensities of the two classes which we denote by s_c and s_w respectively. From relations (5.18)–(5.20), in equilibrium:

$$s_c = S_t^c/r^*B_{t-1} = 1 - \frac{1+b}{r^*}, \tag{5.24a}$$

i.e. from (5.13)

$$s_c = \left(g + \frac{1+b}{1+\delta}\right)\Big/\left[g + (1+b)\frac{2+\delta}{1+\delta}\right]. \tag{5.24b}$$

For the workers' class:

$$s_w = S_t^w/W_t = \frac{1}{2+\delta}. \tag{5.25}$$

As already pointed out, we note that s_c depends directly on the rate of interest, r, while s_w does not. (Note that all other relations among the equilibrium variables depend on the interest rate.) This latter result is due to the fact that we are considering a logarithmic utility-function; had we retained the more general power u-function where $a < 1$, we would have obtained:

$$s_w = 1 - [1 + (1+r)^{a/1-a}(1+\delta)^{1/a-1}]^{-1}. \tag{5.25'}$$

However, for the sake of mathematical simplicity and without much loss of generality, we retain relation (5.25) for the discussion. We are now in a position to determine:

1. whether (and when) the saving/income ratio of the workers' class is less than that of the capitalist class, and
2. whether (and when) in this life-cycle model s_w is smaller or greater than $s_c(P/K)(K/Y) = s_c P/Y$; this relates to one of the Two-Cambridges controversies on the theory of capital and income distribution and determines whether we are in Pasinetti's or Meade–Samuelson and Modigliani's régime, as pointed out in the Introduction.

These are the questions we seek to answer in the present section.

1. *The relationship between the two propensities to save*
From relations (5.24) and (5.25) we may derive the following relationships:[7]

$$s_c > s_w \qquad\qquad \text{for } g > 0, \tag{5.26}$$

$$s_c = s_w = \frac{1}{2+\delta} \qquad \text{for } g = 0, \tag{5.27}$$

$$s_c < s_w \qquad\qquad \text{for } g < 0. \tag{5.28}$$

---

[7] Throughout this analysis, as already pointed out elsewhere, we retain the (very reasonable) assumption that the consumption discount rate, δ, is non-negative and that the bequest discount rate, b, is positive (and never equal to zero). Of course B, the bequest per capita, is supposed to be positive.

The interpretation of the above results is straightforward. When g, the rate of growth of population, is positive the capitalists' saving includes, besides life-cycle saving for the retirement period, saving necessary for maintaining the same capital per capita for the dynasty. When g is equal to zero every capitalist bequeaths exactly the same amount of capital inherited: therefore no extra saving is required for equilibrium growth and the proportion of life-cycle saving equals that of the workers. Finally when the rate of growth of the population is negative the capitalists can dissave from their bequests and hence $s_c < s_w$. These results confirm the relevance of the rate of growth of population in the long-term models of income and wealth distribution.

Since in a growing economy g should be positive we may conclude that s_c is always greater than s_w. This result, obtained in the framework of a life-cycle model, confirms the assumption widely postulated (and accepted) in the literature on economic growth, following which the propensity to save of the capitalists (or profit-earners) is greater than the propensity to save of the workers (or wage-earners).

2. *The relationship between* s_w *and* $s_c \cdot (P/K)(K/Y) = s_c \cdot P/Y$.
In Sect. 2.3 we discussed the relevance of the inequality $s_w > s_c \cdot P/Y$ which was at the centre of a long controversy between Kaldor and Pasinetti on one side, and Meade, Samuelson, and Modigliani on the other. The purpose of the present analysis is to determine whether this inequality holds in the context of our life-cycle model. From relations (5.24) and (5.25) we obtain:

$$s_w < s_c \cdot \frac{P}{Y} \text{ when } g > \frac{Y/K}{2+\delta} - \frac{1+b}{1+\delta} \quad \text{and} \tag{5.29}$$

$$s_w > s_c \cdot \frac{P}{Y} \text{ when } g < \frac{Y/K}{2+\delta} - \frac{1+b}{1+\delta}. \tag{5.30}$$

The condition for the existence of Pasinetti's golden age in our model may hence be translated in the following relationship:

$$g > \frac{Y/K(1+\delta) - (1+b)(2+\delta)}{(2+\delta)(1+\delta)}, \tag{5.31}$$

while we would be in the Meade–Samuelson and Modigliani dual theorem for lower values of g. As a matter of fact condition (5.31) seems to be largely satisfied, except for very low values of the rate of growth g: in Table 5.1 above relation (5.31) is satisfied in all cases (even for quite low values of the rate of growth).

Note finally that this analysis provides only an appraisal of such an inequality and does not determine in which conditions the capitalist class can exist in equilibrium in the system; this will be considered in the following section.

5.8 THE 'LIFE-CYCLE VERSION' OF THE SINGLE-CLASS HARROD–DOMAR–SOLOW MODEL, I.E. WHEN THE CAPITALISTS CANNOT EXIST

In this section we consider the case in which a 'pure' capitalist class cannot exist in equilibrium. If we were to compare our model with the traditional two-class model with constant propensities to save, this particular section should be related to the Meade–Samuelson and Modigliani's dual theorem, for which just one class of savers can provide a sufficient amount of saving to keep the system on the equilibrium growth path.

The dual theorem is characterized by the existence of the workers' class only, who are at the same time wage-earners and profit-earners (on their accumulated savings). One has, of course, to rule out the possibility of the existence of the capitalist class only, since this would imply that the share of wages in national income is zero, since the capitalists are supposed to be 'pure profit-earners'.

In order to define the conditions for the non-existence of the capitalist class we shall not set the value K_t^c equal to zero, since it is a function, *inter alia*, of the inter-generational bequest B_t, and it is precisely B_t which will vanish when the capitalist class cannot survive in equilibrium. For this reason we shall enquire into the conditions for which the workers' capital stock is equal to unity (which implies that the capital stock of the other classes is necessarily zero). From relation (5.9), and not necessarily inside the equilibrium conditions, we get (always assuming a log utility function):

$$K_t^w/K_t = S_t^w/K_t = \frac{Y/K - P/K}{2 + \delta} = \frac{Y/K - r}{2 + \delta}. \tag{5.32}$$

Outside the equilibrium conditions (in particular where (5.13) does not apply), when

$$Y/K - r = 2 + \delta, \tag{5.33}$$

there will exist no 'pure' capitalist class, since all the savings will be provided by the workers' class out of both income from work and from profits on their accumulated savings. Clearly the value of r of relation (5.33) cannot be replaced with the equilibrium value obtained in (5.13), since the latter is valid only for the case in which both classes (that of

the capitalists in particular) exist in the model. At this point by solving
(5.33) with respect to r we obtain the equilibrium interest rate r^{**} which
is valid in our one-class model (of workers only, and without inter-
generational bequests):

$$r^{**} = \frac{Y}{K} - 2 - \delta. \tag{5.34}$$

When (5.34) applies the steady state is the 'life-cycle' version of the
classical Harrod–Domar–Solow type with a single class of savers receiv-
ing income from both work and accumulated savings. At first sight the
value of r^{**} might seem negative, since in a normal model the inverse
of the capital/output ratio is well below unity (K/Y being normally
between $2\frac{1}{2}$ and 5). However in our two-period model (where the two
periods correspond to the active and retirement life-cycle phases respectively) the ratio Y/K is computed over a number of years and may well
reach values between 5 and 10; the same note is true for r^{**}, which is
computed over the same period as well. Additionally we note that r^{**} is
a function of both the technology of the system (i.e. the inverse of the
exogenously given capital/output ratio) and of the subjective rate of
discount for consumption. The partial derivatives with respect to K/Y
and δ are both negative. Their interpretation is straightforward: a higher
capital intensity is in this case associated with a lower rate of profit;
similarly an increase in δ, the consumption discount rate, also depresses
the rate of profit (the latter result corresponds to that found for the
more general interest rate expressed in (5.13)).

We note finally that relation (5.34) yields a simple solution for the
equilibrium rate of profits in a life-cycle model with one class of savers
only *and* without inter-generational bequests. To a certain extent the
life-cycle model considered here makes the Two-Cambridges controversies on profit determination and income distribution obsolete. For
relation (5.34) overcomes the Harrod–Domar dilemma which requires
the introduction of the flexibility of the propensity to save (the post-
Keynesian case) or the flexibility of the capital/output ratio (the
marginalist solution). As a matter of fact (5.34) establishes a direct link
between the inverse of the capital/output ratio and the consumption
discount rate *with* the equilibrium rate of profits. These two variables
are exogenously given in the post-Keynesian model of income distribution so that the interest rate is determinate.

It is worth noting that for the more general case of a utility function
with $a \neq 0$ we obtain the following results:

$$r[1 + (1 + r)^{a/(1-a)}(1 + \delta)^{a/(a-1)}] = \frac{Y}{K},$$

from which, by setting

$$(1 + r)^{a/(1-a)} \cong 1 + \frac{a}{1 - a},$$

we get:

$$r^2 \frac{a}{1 - a} (1 + \delta)^{a/(a-1)} + r[1 + (1 + \delta)^{a/(a-1)}] - \frac{Y}{K} = 0,$$

i.e. $r^{**} =$

$$\frac{-1 - (1 + \delta)^{a/a-1} \pm \sqrt{\left\{[1 + (1 + \delta)^{a/(a-1)}]^2 + 4\frac{Y}{K} \frac{a}{1 - a} (1 + \delta)^{a/a-1}\right\}}}{\frac{2a}{1 - a} (1 + \delta)^{a/(a-1)}}.$$

$$(2.34a)$$

Note that in order to obtain a positive value for r^{**} we shall retain the positive sign in front of the square root for values of a lower than unity and higher than zero; for negative values of a two solutions seem to be possible. The point is that for this general case the equilibrium rate of profits is a function of three exogenous variables of the model, i.e. the elasticity of the utility function, the consumption discount rate, and the capital/output ratio. In this case the conclusions drawn from relation (2.34) apply in general terms.

   Had we tackled the question from a marginalist point of view as done in Baranzini (1976, pp. 24–73) we would have obtained the following solution for the equilibrium rate of profits:

$$r^{**} = (2 + \delta) \frac{P/Y}{1 - P/Y}, \qquad\qquad (2.34')$$

where P/Y is the share of capital in national income, and which cannot be determined independently of r^{**} in the framework of the margina-list theory. From this point of view we may underline that the post-Keynesian framework yields a much more satisfactory answer to the question of profit determination, income distribution, and capital accumulation. Of course this solution has, among others, the drawback of not allowing the existence of an inter-generational bequest. Although the exercise may still be worth considering, to rely entirely on the savings provided by the present generation for the accumulation process seems to be rather restrictive. For this reason we turn now to the analysis of the model which allows all classes to accumulate and own an inter-generational capital stock.

5.9 TOWARDS A MORE GENERAL MODEL: BOTH CLASSES HOLD AN INTER-GENERATIONAL CAPITAL STOCK

By making the rather restrictive assumption that the workers have no bequest motive (i.e. no inter-generational transfer), we have seen that the two-class life-cycle model has a unique equilibrium rate of profit which is determined solely by the behaviour of the 'pure' capitalist class and is independent of the form of the production function and of the behaviour of the workers' class—at least as long as the 'pure' capitalist class exists. These results rest upon a crucial assumption, namely the fact that the workers inherit and leave no financial assets: the savings accumulated during the active period of their lives are entirely consumed during the retirement time.

It is thus natural to ask what happens when this assumption is relaxed and we allow all classes to inherit and to make a final bequest, quite independently of the nature of their income. It has been said that certain classes give higher priority to the education of their children, and a smaller one to the financial bequest. This, of course, does not rule out the possibility of bequeathing to future generations in two different ways. Furthermore the purpose of this analysis is to study, starting from possibly fairly general conditions, the different patterns of accumulation of capital in an economy of two or more classes as well as to understand the sort of reasons that may lead to (perpetual) class distinction. From this point of view then the generalization of the model ought to represent a step forward.

5.9.1 Reformulating the model

If workers are allowed to inherit and leave a financial bequest B_t^w, at the end of period t, relation (5.2), which now incorporates a bequest motive, may be rewritten as:

$$\text{Max } U(C_t^w, C_{t+1}^w, B_t^w) = \text{Max} \frac{1}{a} \left[(C_t^w)^a + \frac{(C_{t+1}^w)^a}{1+\delta} + \frac{1+g}{1+b_w}(B_t^w)^a \right],$$

$$(5.35)$$

$$\text{s.t. } W_t + (1+r)B_{t-1}^w = C_t^w + \frac{C_{t+1}^w}{1+r} + (1+g)B_t^w,$$

which yields the Lagrangean for the 'impure' workers' case:

$$\mathcal{L}_w = \frac{1}{a}(C_t^w)^a + \frac{(C_{t+1}^w)^a}{1+\delta} + \frac{1+g}{1+b_w}(B_t^w)^a$$

$$+ \lambda \left[W_t + (1+r)B_{t-1}^w - C_t^w - \frac{C_{t+1}^w}{1+r} - (1+g)B_t^w \right], (5.36)$$

from which we obtain:

$$C_{t+1}^w = C_t^w (1 + r)^{1/1-a}(1 + \delta)^{1/a-1}, \tag{5.37}$$

$$B_t^w = C_t^w (1 + b_w)^{1/a-1}, \tag{5.38}$$

where

W_t is the wage-rate;

B_t^w is the bequest left to each child at the end of time t;

b_w is the bequest discount rate of the workers' class;

r is the interest rate (earned on accumulated savings);

a is the (constant) elasticity of the utility function (smaller than unity);

g is the rate of growth of population (no technical progress);

δ is the consumption time-preference.

Relations (5.37) and (5.38) are similar to relations (5.5) and (5.6) which apply to the 'pure' capitalist class in the previous model. We may now rewrite the budget constraint as:

$$W_t + (1 + r)B_{t-1}^w = C_t^w \Big[1 + (1 + r)^{a/1-a}(1 + \delta)^{1/a-1}$$

$$+ (1 + g)(1 + b_w)^{1/a-1} \Big]. \tag{5.38a}$$

The same kind of argument expounded in the preceding model shows that for $\dot{k}_w = (\dot{k}_c = \dot{k} =) 0$, which in equilibrium implies $B_{t-1}^w = B_t^w = (B^w)^*$, we may rewrite (5.38a) as:

$$W_t + (1 + r)B_{t-1}^w = B_{t-1}^w(1 + b_w)^{1/1-a}[1 + (1 + r)^{a/1-a}(1 + \delta)^{1/a-1}$$

$$+ (1 + g)(1 + b_w)^{1/a-1}]. \tag{5.39}$$

We focus now on the logarithmic case of the utility-function and we obtain the equilibrium value (r_w^*) of the interest rate valid for a society in which there exist 'impure' workers only:

$$r_w^* = \frac{Y/K - B^w/K\left(g + (1 + b_w)\dfrac{2 + \delta}{1 + \delta}\right)}{1 - B^w/K}, \tag{5.40}$$

which is to be compared with the corresponding r_c^* root of relation (5.13) determined by the behaviour of the capitalist class:

$$r_c^* = g + (1 + b_c)\frac{2 + \delta}{1 + \delta}, \tag{5.13)–(5.41}$$

where b_c is the bequest discount rate of the capitalists. A close examination of solution (5.40) shows that in the extreme case where B^w is zero, the optimal interest rate for the workers' class would be equal to Y/K, i.e. the inverse of the capital/output ratio. This outcome shows that in this extreme case only a drastic reduction of the wage-income of the workers' class would, in equilibrium, mean the vanishing of their inter-generational bequest. There exists then a strong correlation between the income from work of the workers and their inter-generational bequest.

We note immediately that the two optimal roots r_w^* and r_c^* are not identical. This means that, in principle, the rates of interest which maximize the total utility of both classes and, at the same time, ensure an equilibrium growth of their inter-generational capital, are not equal. In other words, in order to maintain an optimal plan of consumption and saving, the two classes might eventually accumulate at a different rate; and the class which accumulates at the fastest rate will eventually end up with the entire capital stock of the economy. In order to fit the classes into the same balanced growth path (assuming that both can exist in equilibrium, with a positive share of the inter-generational bequest) we may postulate the following frameworks:[8]

1. The hypothesis of a *different subjective bequest discount rate*, meaning that the two classes may have a different attitude towards leaving assets to their children, i.e. $b_w \neq b_c$. The exact relationship between the two discount rates will allow us to speculate on the inter-generational behaviour of the classes, and to determine in which conditions the model may grow in equilibrium.

2. The hypothesis of a *different rate of return on capital* for the two classes, i.e. of differentiated interest rate. In this case the equilibrium interest rate of the model would be a weighted average of the two; and their relationship would be determined by the particular situation of the economy, where the payment of savings may be imputed in part to market imperfections (see below). As pointed out in Chapter 2, the assumption of a different rate of interest in two-class models has been considered, among others, by Laing (1969), Balestra and Baranzini (1971), Sheng Cheng Hu (1973), Moore (1974), Pasinetti (1974, pp. 139–41), Campa (1975), Baranzini (1975, 1976), Gupta (1976), Riese

---

[8] We do not consider the cases (*a*) of a differentiated consumption discount rate or (*b*) of a different rate of growth of population for the two classes, since this would introduce into the model a too rigid differentiation between the classes. Of course these cases might be considered in different frameworks, as we shall do in Chapter 8 by considering the relationships between personal and functional distribution of wealth and income. We should also recall that one of the main objectives of our research is to endogenize instead of exogenize the differences between socio-economic groups.

(1981), Fazi and Salvadori (1981) and Pasinetti's reply (1983a), and Miyazaki (1986).

Of course the two different hypotheses may apply simultaneously and the model may incorporate both a differentiated discount rate for the bequest *and* a differentiated interest rate, in such a way as to guarantee an overall equilibrium growth of the system. In this context the hypothesis of a different bequest discount rate seems to be the most interesting case, especially since it allows us to get more insight into the different patterns of accumulation of capital of the two (or eventually more) classes and the reasons that may lead to a lasting difference between classes.

We shall consider points 1 and 2 above in detail in the following paragraphs.

5.9.2 The case of a differentiated subjective discount rate for the bequest (with a unique rate of interest)

The question we are interested in, in this context, is the existence and uniqueness of the equilibrium interest rate r^*. This will be possible when (we shall consider the conditions for the existence of both classes below):

$$r_c^* = r_w^* = r^*, \tag{5.42}$$

which implies, according to relations (5.13) and (5.40):

$$g + (1 + b_c) \frac{2 + \delta}{1 + \delta} = \frac{Y/K}{1 - B^w/K}$$

$$- \frac{B^w/K \left(g + (1 + b_w) \dfrac{2 + \delta}{1 + \delta} \right)}{1 - B^w/K} \tag{5.42'}$$

which yields

$$b_c = - b_w \frac{B^w/K}{1 - B^w/K} - \frac{1 - \left(\dfrac{Y}{K} - g \right) \dfrac{1 + \delta}{2 + \delta}}{1 - B^w/K}. \tag{5.43}$$

Relation (5.43) yields the value of b_c, the capitalists' bequest discount rate, for which the two rates of interest are equal. It is a function of all parameters of the model (the rate of growth, g, the capital output/ratio, K/Y, and the consumption discount rate, δ), of the workers' share of the inter-generational bequest in the total capital stock (B^w/K) and of the workers' bequest discount rate b_w.

In order to discuss the relationship between the two bequest discount rates we solve (5.43) with respect to B^w/K and we get the value, in equilibrium, of the workers' inter-generational capital stock:

$$(B^w/K)^* = \frac{(Y/K - g)\dfrac{1 + \delta}{2 + \delta} - (1 + b_c)}{b_w - b_c}. \tag{5.44}$$

Relation (5.44) shows that if we assume $b_w > b_c$, i.e. that the workers show a smaller propensity to leave assets to their children than the capitalists, then the workers will be able to hold a positive share of the inter-generational bequest only when

$$b_c < (Y/K - g)\,\frac{1 + \delta}{2 + \delta} - 1 = A^* \,(< b_w), \tag{5.45}$$

where $(Y/K - g)$ can be set equal to C/Y. At the same time it implies that b_w has to be higher than the right-hand side of (5.45). This means that if we retain the assumption following which the 'pure' capitalist class has a 'natural', stronger disposition to leave assets to their children (after all it is the only way to ensure a strong purchasing power to the dynasty and to ensure its survival through the generations), this disposition must be fairly strong in order to ensure equilibrium growth of the system and, at the same time, the existence of both classes in the system with a positive share of the inter-generational capital stock. How strong the capitalists' desire to leave assets to their children must be is shown in relation (5.45). If (5.45) is not fulfilled, and at the same time b_w remains greater than b_c, then the inter-generational bequest of the workers vanishes and the only class which can hold inter-generational assets are the capitalists. One of the conclusions that one can draw from this result is that, in order to coexist in the same model in equilibrium, the bequest discount rates of the two classes *must* exhibit a sharp difference; if the difference between the two discount rates is not so sharp there is a possibility that one or the other of the classes might not hold any share of the inter-generational bequest.

A particular case arises when (always in the context $b_w > b_c$) the workers show a particularly strong desire to make bequests to their children, so that b_w becomes lower than the value $(Y/K - g)$ $(1 + \delta)/(2 + \delta) - 1$. In this case, even if the capitalists are quite willing to maintain an inter-generational asset for the survival of their classes, the ratio B^w/K is higher than unity, meaning, in economic terms, that the workers will hold *all* inter-generational assets, so squeezing the capitalists out of the system. Again we find that for the two classes to coexist in the system their bequest discount rates must be quite different, otherwise the workers come to own a larger and larger share of the inter-generational as well as life-cycle capital of the system. In other words the capitalists may survive only if they accumulate and are willing to endow their future generation at a much higher rate than the other classes which can enjoy income out of labour and other means. Up to a certain extent one could expect a result like this; however the fact that, in order to survive, the 'pure' capitalists must show *a much higher* willingness to accumulate than the other classes is rather surprising. The introduction of a log utility-function may play a certain role in the determination of these results; however the log u-function has the merit of giving a certain degree of neutrality to the absolute size of the capital stock and of the income from work and wealth; and since the empirical results obtained in this field are not unambiguous we may conclude that the results reached with a log u-function allow us to draw much more general conclusions.

Conversely if we assume that the workers have a stronger desire to leave financial assets to their children than the capitalists (which implies b_w smaller than b_c), relation (5.44) shows that in this case the share of the workers' inter-generational capital stock can be positive only if the capitalists' bequest discount rate is higher than the constant $(Y/K - g)(1 + \delta)/(2 + \delta) - 1$, i.e. if the difference between the two discount rates for bequests is clear-cut. In the case in which this condition is not fulfilled (even if the inequality between b_w and b_c is still valid) the workers are not able to hold a positive share of inter-generational bequests in an equilibrium condition. These results are graphically summarized in Figure 5.1.

A second particular case arises when (always for $b_w < b_c$, i.e. when the capitalists are less willing to leave assets to their children than the workers) both classes show a weak desire to make bequests to their children, so that both bequest discount rates are higher than the value $A = (Y/K - g)(1 + \delta)/(2 + \delta) - 1$. In this case (which we may label as one of 'capitalists' euthanasia') only the workers will be able to hold inter-generational assets, and the capitalists withdraw from the model. The existence of workers' inter-generational capital, in spite of the low desire to bequeath to the next generation, is ensured by the presence of a non-capital income, i.e. of a wage-rate. This case is, of course, asymmetrical to that encountered when b_w is greater than b_c (the latter being more realistic): the capitalists and the workers can both hold an inter-generational asset if the workers show a *clearly higher* desire to endow their children with a financial bequest. When, instead, both classes show both a high willingness to leave assets to the next generation, or a lower one, then just one class can hold inter-generational assets.

All these results are summarized in Figure 5.1, in which we have

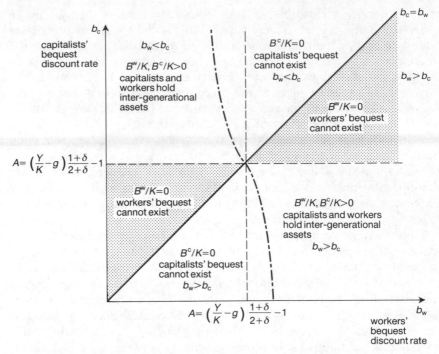

*For a unique equilibrium rate of profit $r_c^* = r_w^* = r$ (cf. relations (5.40)–(5.41)). A higher b_w or b_c means less willingness to leave a bequest to the next generation. The values of B^w/K and B^c/K, i.e. the proportion of the inter-generational bequest of the workers' class and capitalists' class respectively, have been derived from relation (5.44).

Fig. 5.1 The value of the two classes' inter-generational bequest as a function of the bequest discount rates of the two classes in equilibrium

slightly extended (with a dotted line) the area for which $B^w/K = 1$, i.e. the case in which the workers hold the whole of the bequest. This is due to the fact that even if the workers' bequests have not reached the total capital stock, the remainder may be made up by the workers' life-cycle savings, leaving no space, in equilibrium, for a 'pure' capitalists' class. The exact importance of this special case will be considered in the following sections.

A third and final case concerns that for which $b_w = b_c$, i.e. in which both classes have the same desire to leave assets to their children, i.e. the same bequest discount rate. Here both classes are allowed to hold an inter-generational bequest, from relations (5.13) and (5.40), and of course by setting $r^* = r_w^* = r_c^*$ since we are assuming a unique rate of return for both classes, we get:

$$b^* = b_w^* = b_c^* = (Y/K - g)\frac{1+\delta}{2+\delta} - 1, \tag{5.46}$$

which means that in the case of a unique rate of interest (equal for both classes) there is a *unique* value for which the bequest discount rates of the classes (or individuals) can be equal. However, in this extreme case, as relation (5.44) shows, the share of the inter-generational bequest of the workers' class is zero. This allows us to conclude that under equilibrium conditions the two classes cannot hold a positive share of the inter-generational bequest except in the case of a differentiated (strongly differentiated) rate of bequest discount, as discussed above.

The significance of the B^w/K value in equilibrium. Relation (5.44) gives us the value of the workers' inter-generational bequest in equilibrium (when both classes may hold inter-generational assets). The preceding analysis has defined the conditions under which B^w/K is positive, i.e. the conditions for the workers' class to possess both life-cycle saving and an inter-generational bequest. The partial derivatives of B^w/K with respect to the single parameters are:

$$\partial(B^w/K)^*/\partial Y/K = (b_w - b_c)\frac{1 + \delta}{2 + \delta} \ (> 0) \tag{5.44a}$$

$$\partial(B^w/K)^*/\partial g = -(b_w - b_c)\frac{1 + \delta}{2 + \delta} \ (< 0) \tag{5.44b}$$

$$\partial(B^w/K)^*/\partial b_c = \frac{(Y/K - g)\dfrac{1 + \delta}{2 + \delta} - 1 - b_w}{(b_w - b_c)^2} \ (< 0) \tag{5.44c}$$

$$\partial(B^w/K)^*/\partial b_w = \frac{1 + b_c - (Y/K - g)\dfrac{1 + \delta}{2 + \delta}}{(b_w - b_c)^2} \ (> 0) \tag{5.44d}$$

$$\partial(B^w/K)^*/\partial \delta = (2 + \delta)^{-2}\frac{Y/K - g}{b_w - b_c} \ (> 0). \tag{5.44e}$$

The interpretation of the results obtained depends, *inter alia*, on the values of the two bequest discount rates b_w and b_c. First relation (5.44a): it shows that an increase of the capital/output ratio (the inverse of Y/K) has a negative effect on the share of the inter-generational bequest held by the workers if we assume that the latter class has a smaller desire than the capitalists to bequeath financial assets to their children. The opposite result applies for $b_w < b_c$. This means that the class which attaches more importance to the inter-generational capital stock will be favoured by an increase in the capital/output ratio.

The same result applies with respect to the rate of growth of population: an increase in g will reduce the B^w/K ratio as long as b_w is greater than b_c. But if the workers have a stronger desire to hold inter-generational assets (than the other classes) their share will eventually be increased.

Considering now (5.44e) we note that B^w/K is positively affected by an increase in the general rate of discount for consumption (δ), which reduces total life-cycle saving: but for this result to apply b_w must be greater than b_c.

Finally we might consider (5.44c and d). In relation (5.45) we have already defined the value $A^* = (Y/K - g)(1 + \delta)/(2 + \delta) - 1$. Suppose now that b_w is greater than b_c (meaning more bequest discounting for the workers): in this case b_c must be smaller than A^* in order to ensure that B^w is positive (with, of course, b_w greater than A^*). Under these conditions an increase in b_c, the capitalists' bequest discount rate, has a negative effect on the B^w/K ratio; while an increase in b_w yields a positive effect on the same ratio. This confirms the validity of the results obtained at the beginning of this paragraph, i.e. that in order to maintain a positive B^w/K the two discount rates for the bequest must be well differentiated. If their value is too close, the workers may not be able to hold inter-generational assets. The same argument applies for the case $b_w < b_c$, for which, of course, the sign of the derivatives is the opposite of the case just discussed.

The distribution of wealth for a different rate of discount of the bequest of the two classes (i.e. $b_w \neq b_c$). At this point we may try to define the distribution of capital among the classes, including both inter-generational and life-cycle assets. To study the relevance of the capitalists' capital stock, and to define when it exists in equilibrium, we seek the value of the share of the capital stock owned by the other class, which is easier to obtain. From the fundamental relations (5.37)–(5.39) we may write the capital stock of the workers' class as the sum of their life-cycle and inter-generational assets:

$$K_w^* = B^w + S^w = B^w + rB^w + W - C^w$$

$$= B^w + rB^w + W - (W + (1 + r)B^w)$$

$$\times \frac{1 + b_w + (1 + g)(1 + \delta)}{(1 + b_w)(2 + \delta) + (1 + g)(1 + \delta)}$$

$$= (W + (1 + r)B^w) \frac{1 + b_w + (1 + g)(1 + \delta)}{(1 + b_w)(2 + \delta) + (1 + g)(1 + \delta)}. \quad (5.45)$$

Since in a post-Keynesian world $W/K = Y/K - P/K = Y/K - r$, and by recalling (5.44), in equilibrium we get:

$$K_w/K = \left((1+r) \frac{(Y/K - g)\frac{1+\delta}{2+\delta} - (1+b_c)}{b_w - b_c} + \frac{Y}{K} - r \right)$$

$$\times \frac{1 + b_w + (1+g)(1+\delta)}{(1+b_w)(2+\delta) + (1+g)(1+\delta)}. \tag{5.46}$$

Clearly the capital share of the capitalist class (K_c/K) will be positive when the right-hand side of the above relation is less than unity. Always recalling (5.41), which gives us the equilibrium value of the interest rate in terms of the parameters g, δ, and the capitalists' bequest discount rate, we find that the share of capital of the capitalists is positive when:

$$b_c >$$

$$(1+\delta)\frac{(Y/K - g)[1 + b_w + (1+g)(1+\delta)] - (1+b_w)(2+\delta)}{(2+\delta)[1 + b_w + g(1+\delta)]}$$

$$- 1 = A^*. \tag{5.47}$$

The right-hand side of (5.47) is, under general conditions, negative. Hence when (5.47) applies $K_c/K > 0$ and the capitalists can exist in equilibrium with a positive share of the total inter-generational bequest (since the condition *sine qua non* for their presence in the system is the existence of a capitalists' bequest from which they derive their entire income).

At this point it may be of some importance to enquire into the state of the economy when (5.47) does not apply and the entire capital stock is owned by the workers' class; in such a situation the workers will hold a positive inter-generational bequest when life-cycle savings out of wages are smaller than the total capital stock.

In the case in which the capitalists do not exist (since (5.47) is not satisfied) relation (5.40), i.e. $r^* = r_w^*$ applies; additionally from (5.45):

$$(K^w)^{**} = K^{**} = [(1+r)B^w + W]$$

$$\times \frac{(1+\delta)(1+b_w)}{(2+\delta)(1+b_w) + (1+g)(1+\delta)}, \tag{5.45'}$$

which, in a post-Keynesian world where $W/K = Y/K - P/K = Y/K - r$ becomes:

$$(K^w/K)^{**}$$

$$= K^{**} = \left[\frac{B^w}{K} + \frac{Y}{K} + r\left(\frac{B^w}{K} - 1\right) \right] \frac{1 + b_w + (1+g)(1+\delta)}{(2+\delta)(1+b_w) + (1+g)(1+\delta)}.$$

Recalling (5.40), and solving with respect to $B^w = B$, the total inter-generational bequest of the system (since by definition there are no capitalists) we obtain:

$$(B^w/K)^{**} = (B/K)^{**} = \frac{1 + \delta}{1 + b_w + (1 + g)(1 + \delta)}, \tag{5.48}$$

which shows that the equilibrium inter-generational capital stock (which in this case belongs to the workers only) is always positive and smaller than the total capital stock of the system, leaving space for a given amount of life-cycle capital. We note immediately that in this case an increase in b_w, the workers' bequest discount rate, has a negative effect on the share of the inter-generational bequest in the total capital stock, so increasing the share of the life-cycle savings. The interpretation of this result is quite simple, since an increase in b_w means that the workers attach a smaller importance to their bequest, so depressing directly its share in the total capital stock. The same effect would have an increase in g (the rate of growth of population), since in this case there would be a relatively higher accumulation of life-cycle savings and lower accumulation of inter-generational financial capital. We finally consider the impact of a variation in the consumption discount rate δ; the partial derivative of (5.48) with respect to this parameter is equal to $(1 + b_w)[1 + b_w + (1 + g)(1 + \delta)]^{-1}$, which is positive; hence an increase in the consumption discount rate, which discourages the life-cycle accumulation of savings, has a positive effect on the share of the inter-generational capital stock of the system, at least in equilibrium. These results are to be compared with the similar outcomes obtained for the other models, where the inter-generational capital stock is owned jointly by both classes or uniquely by the capitalist class.

We note finally that in this case the bequest/total capital ratio is independent of the form of the production function, i.e. of the capital/output ratio.

5.9.3 *The case of a differentiated rate of interest for the two classes (with a unique rate of bequest discount* $b_w = b_c = b$)

In order to fit the two classes into the same balanced growth path, as-suming that they both can hold a positive share of the inter-generational assets as well as life-cycle savings, we may alternatively postulate a different rate of interest. The two rates of interest would be that of relation (5.40) for the workers and of relations (5.13)–(5.41) for the capitalists respectively. The overall rate of interest of the system would of course be a weighted average of the two, according to the relative importance of the capital stock owned by the two classes. In the first instance it is simpler to consider the general case for which the bequest discount rate is equal for the two classes. From relations (5.40) and

(5.41) we can prove that the optimal rate of return of the capitalist class is higher than that of the workers' class when:

$$b > \left(\frac{Y}{K} - g\right) \frac{1 + \delta}{2 + \delta} - 1. \tag{5.50}$$

This means that in the case in which both classes exhibit a normal or fairly weak willingness to leave assets to their children the rate of interest which maximizes the capitalists' total utility is *higher* than the corresponding optimal rate of interest of the workers' class. We have already seen (see Figure 5.1) that this is the most interesting case, since it offers the possibility of both classes holding a positive share of the total inter-generational capital stock (although within a slightly different framework).

If, on the contrary, relation (5.50) is not satisfied and both classes have a particularly strong desire to leave assets to their children (as a matter of fact a lower *b* means quite a high altruistic attitude towards the next generation) the optimal rate of interest of the capitalist class will be *lower* than that of the workers. It is, however, quite unlikely that both classes have such a high desire to bequeath to their children. A final case might arise when $b_w = b_c = (Y/K - g)(1 + \delta)/(2 + \delta) - 1$. In this exceptional case the two optimal rates of interest would coincide, and the share of the inter-generational bequest of the workers would be zero as pointed out in the preceding paragraph. We do not, however, attach too much importance to this remote possibility.

If relation (5.50) is satisfied, the optimal rate of interest which maximizes the utility of the capitalists will be higher than that of the workers' class. This case has already been considered widely in the economic literature on two-class growth models, as pointed out above; but there is one important difference: here the inequality appears as an outcome of a model based on optimality, whereas in the other models it is an initial condition or assumption. The overall rate of profit of the system would however be included between the two rates of interest, according to the distribution of wealth which we shall define shortly.

But why should the two interest rates be different, apart from the optimality conditions which we have described in the model above? Several reasons may be adduced in support of a differentiated interest rate in a two- or multi-class model. Property rights are fundamental determinants of distribution in post-Keynesian, as well as classical and neo-Ricardian, theories where the production process implicitly or explicitly requires some form of co-operation from individuals having powers of 'withdrawing' (or at least 'conditioning') certain essential inputs. As in most classical theories, social classes remain crucial for post-Keynesian theories, and their distinctive feature is given by saving-, consumption-, and investment-behaviour. In more sophisticated theories

Table 5.2 The relevance of the inter-generational bequest

	Capitalists own all inter-generational capital by definition	Both capitalists and workers own inter-generational capital stock	Workers own all inter-generational capital stock
Equilibrium rate(s) of profit	$r^* = g + (1+b_c)\dfrac{2+\delta}{1+\delta}$	$r_c^* = g + (1+b_c)\dfrac{2+\delta}{1+\delta}$ $r_w^* = \dfrac{Y/K - B^w/K\left(g+(1+b_w)\dfrac{2+\delta}{1+\delta}\right)}{1-B^w/K}$	$r^{**} = \dfrac{Y/K - B^w/K\left(g+(1+b_w)\dfrac{2+\delta}{1+\delta}\right)^1}{1-B^w/K}$
Equilibrium rates of profit: Specifications	unique equilibrium interest rate	Two equilibrium interest rates. Unique if (a) different rate of return, or (b) different bequest discount rate	unique equilibrium interest rate
Value of B/K (total bequest to total capital ratio)	$\dfrac{B}{K} = \left(1 + \dfrac{r + Y/K}{2+\delta}\right)\dfrac{1}{r-b} \quad {}^2$	$B^w/K = \dfrac{(Y/K - g)\dfrac{1+\delta}{2+\delta} - (1+b_c)}{b_w - b_c}$ $B^c/K = \dfrac{1 + b_w - (Y/K - g)\dfrac{1+\delta}{2+\delta}}{b_w - b_c}$	$\left(\dfrac{B}{K}\right)^{**} = \dfrac{1+\delta}{1 + b_w + (1+g)(1+\delta)}$

Table 5.2 (*Cont.*)

$\partial B/K/\partial \delta$	ambiguous (negative)	ambiguous	positive
$\partial B/K/\partial b$	negative	ambiguous	negative
$\partial B/K/\partial g$	positive	(B^w/K: negative)(B^c/K: positive)	negative
$\partial B/K/\partial Y/K$		(B^w/K: positive)(B^c/K: negative)	zero

A unique rate of interest independent of technology and of the behavioural parameters of the workers' class

There exists the possibility of a unique interest rate in equilibrium if: (*a*) one considers the hypothesis of a different rate of return for the classes; (*b*) and/or a different rate of bequest discount for the classes

A unique rate of interest in equilibrium since there exists one class only. It depends on the capital/output ratio and on all parameters of the model (cf. relation below)

[1] i.e. $r^{**} = Y/K\left(1 + \dfrac{1+\delta}{1 + b_\text{w} + g(1+\delta)}\right) - 1 - \dfrac{(1+b_\text{w})(1+\delta)}{1 + b_\text{w} - g(1+\delta)}$.

[2] i.e. $\dfrac{B}{K} = \dfrac{(2+\delta)\left(1 + \dfrac{1+b}{1+\delta}\right) + g + Y/K}{(2+\delta)\left(g + (1+b)\dfrac{2+\delta}{1+\delta} - b\right)}$.

(like that of Pasinetti and the one which we are considering here) the assumption of 'separate appropriation' of each production factor is no longer as drastic as in other models, but it is maintained in the background, even if workers' income is made up by wages and interest on accumulated savings. As a matter of fact interest on accumulated savings may be linked only indirectly to the profit rate, as in the case of deposit and savings accounts which have a predetermined rate of interest (which is not necessarily linked to the overall rate of profits of the economy). Of course in a general sense in post-Keynesian theories different rates of saving are associated with different economic and social classes. And the distribution of saving among classes will be such as to yield an overall saving equal to the desired level of full employment. In this way a differentiated interest rate may further redistribute income among the classes of the system: for this reason its analysis constitutes a key element in the determination of the overall equilibrium interest rate.

Considering specific points we might say that (cf., for instance, Balestra and Baranzini (1971, pp. 242–3)):

1. First, historically, the interest rate has been considerably lower than the average profit rate of the system, except for some periods characterized by recession or high inflation. In general a ratio of $2:3$ is more likely to reflect the realities of the world than a ratio of $1:1$. This observation implies one of two things: either the economy is not on an equilibrium growth path and there is no evident hope of ever achieving such a path; or it becomes necessary to incorporate into the model a different hypothesis which explicitly takes into account the observed difference between the rate of interest on normal life-cycle savings and the overall profit rate.

2. Secondly, one might argue that the act of saving and the act of investing are two distinct operations, as pointed out above, since they refer to two distinctive acts of appropriation: one is strictly connected with the wage-rate and only indirectly with the average profit rate of the economy; the latter, on the contrary, is more directly connected with capital and its profit rate. One might also say that saving is essentially a passive act, while investment is more active. Not surprisingly a higher remuneration is normally attached to the active act of investing.

3. Thirdly, a different way of looking at the same phenomenon is to postulate that there is a risk factor associated with the act of investing. This risk should be reflected in the differential between rate of interest on riskless savings and overall profit rate. We shall consider in the final part of this work the implications of the introduction of a risk asset in the model.

4. Finally, it may be said that investment, to be profitable, must be

larger than a certain minimum. The workers, taken individually, are not able to exploit the profit opportunities of large investment. Their saving, accordingly, is likely to carry a smaller reward. This of course does not mean that we would have to introduce the argument of increasing returns to scale on savings. We simply maintain that the interest rate is not necessarily identical to the profit rate. It should, however, be stressed that in this context by interest rate we mean *the rate at which the workers place their savings* in the hands of the capitalists (or in the hands of the state in a socialist society).

The distribution of capital in the case of a differentiated interest rate for the two classes. At this point it is important to define the distribution of wealth between the two classes in order to assess their relative weight in the economy, the distribution of income, and the weighted average of the overall rate of profit. Assuming that r_c^* is equal to ϕr_w^*, where ϕ is possibly higher than unity (but it could be smaller than one), and solving with respect to B^w/K, the workers' share of the total inter-generational capital stock we get:

$$B^w/K = \frac{\phi Y/K - r_c^*}{r_c^*(\phi - 1)},$$
(5.51)

where r_c^* is the optimal interest rate relative to the capitalist class. Relation (5.51) may be rewritten as:

$$B^w/K = \frac{\phi Y/K - g - (1 + b)\dfrac{2 + \delta}{1 + \delta}}{(\phi - 1)\left(g + (1 + b)\dfrac{2 + \delta}{1 + \delta}\right)}.$$
(5.51')

In Figure 5.2 we have represented graphically the value of B^w/K and B^c/K respectively, i.e. the value of the share of the inter-generational stock of the two classes respectively. If we retain the assumption that $\phi = r_c^*/r_w^* > 0$, i.e. that the rate of interest of the capitalist class is higher than that of the workers, we observe that both classes can hold a positive share of the inter-generational capital stock as long as the inverse of the capital/output ratio is greater than $r_c^* = (P/K)_c^*$; since this condition is probably always satisfied (as a matter of fact no rate of profit ought to be higher than Y/K) we may conclude that the model which allows for a differentiated interest rate also allows for the existence of two types of inter-generational assets in the system: one belonging to the capitalists and the other to the workers.

If, on the contrary, we retain the assumption that the rate of return of the capitalists is lower than that of the workers ($r_c^* < r_w^*$), a fairly

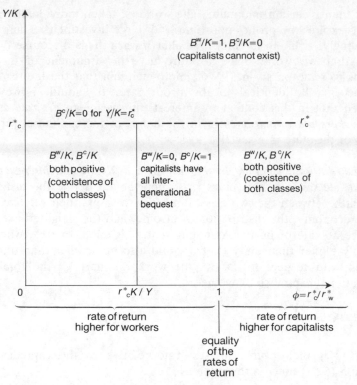

Where: Y/K is the inverse of the capital/output ratio;
$r_c^* = g + (1 + b) \frac{2+\delta}{1+\delta}$, the optimal equilibrium interest rate of the capitalists;
$r_w^* = [Y/K - B^w/K(g + (1 + b) \frac{2+\delta}{1+\delta})] . (1 - B^w/K)^{-1}$, idem for the workers;
B^w/K is the share of the inter-generational bequest of the workers;
B^c/K is the share of the inter-generational bequest of the capitalists (in the total capital stock);
b is the bequest discount rate (equal for both classes).

Fig. 5.2 The value of the two classes' inter-generational bequest in equilibrium and as a function of $\phi r_c^*/r_w^*$ and of the capital/output ratio in the case of a differentiated interest rate

unrealistic proposition, then two possible solutions are possible, always assuming that Y/K is greater than r_c^*.

First when ϕ is less that unity but greater than the value r_c^*/Y, which means that the rate of interest of the workers' class is *just* higher than that of capitalists, then the latter hold the totality of the inter-generational capital stock, leaving to the workers the possibility of accumulating life-cycle savings only.

Second, if ϕ is less than unity and less than the value r_c^*K/Y, which means that the rate of return on workers' savings is *much* higher than the rate of return on capitalists' savings, both classes can hold a positive share of the inter-generational capital stock; and in this case the overall rate of profit $P/K = r$ will be a weighted average of the two distinct rates of returns on savings.

Before considering the partial derivatives of the inter-generational bequests we might emphasize that if we retain the more realistic assumption that $\phi = r_c^*/r_w^*$ is more than unity, i.e. that the rate of return on capitalists' assets is higher than that of the workers, both classes can hold a positive share of the inter-generational capital stock, as well as of life-cycle savings. This analytical result (as can be seen in Figure 5.2) confirms the validity of the assumption of a differentiated interest rate in two- or multi-class growth models of income distribution. The literature dealing with this specific field, which first appeared in the late 1960s, has considered many aspects of this problem but, as far as we know, has never incorporated explicitly the problem of the size of the inter-generational bequest as opposed to life-cycle savings. Of course in this case the overall rate of interest of the system, in equilibrium, will be equal to:

$$r^{**} = (r_w^* K^w/K + r_c^* K^c/K), \tag{5.52}$$

where K^w/K and K^c/K stand for the share of the total capital stock of the two classes respectively. Each capital stock is, as pointed out in the initial sections of this chapter, made up by inter-generational capital stock plus life-cycle savings. Both capital stocks are functions of all parameters of the model, including the rate of growth of population and the capital/output ratio. They would be analytically defined through the equilibrium B^w/K ratio given in relation (5.51').

In order to assess the relevance of the B^w/K ratio we may write (where we assume, for the sake of simplicity, that ϕ is greater than unity, which means that the optimal rate of return of the capitalists is higher than that of the workers):

$$\partial B^w/K/\partial \phi = (r_c^* - Y/K)/r_c^* (\phi - 1)^2 > 0 \tag{5.53a}$$

$$\partial B^w/K/\partial g = -\frac{\phi Y/K}{r_c^{*2}(\phi - 1)} < 0 \tag{5.53b}$$

$$\partial B^w/K/\partial Y/K = \phi(\phi - 1)^{-1}/r_c^* > 0 \tag{5.53c}$$

$$\partial B^w/K/\partial b = \frac{2 + \delta}{1 + \delta} \frac{r_c^* - \phi Y/K}{r_c^{*2}(\phi - 1)^2} < 0 \tag{5.53d}$$

$$\partial B^w/K/\partial \delta = \frac{1 + b}{(1 + \delta)^2} \frac{\phi Y/K}{r_c^*(\phi - 1)} > 0. \tag{5.53e}$$

These results are interesting and confirm the general properties of the model encountered so far. The least straightforward interpretation relates to (5.53*a*), which shows that an increase in the differential between the two rates of return (here represented by ϕ), meaning a relative weakening of the workers' class in economic terms, leads to a higher B^w/K ratio, i.e. to a higher intensity of the workers' inter-generational assets. Paradoxically though it appears, it may be explained by the fact that the workers' relative strength, weakened by a lower rate of return on their capital (both life-cycle and inter-generational), may be maintained only through a stronger position here represented by the share of their inter-generational bequest. This result is typical of steady-state models, where equilibrium positions have to be maintained in the long-run. Outside a steady-state situation an increase in the differential between the two rates of return would of course weaken the overall economic position of the workers' class, leading most probably to a lower B^w/K share.

Relation (5.53*b*) shows that an increase in the rate of growth of population has a negative effect on the share of long-term capital owned by the workers, due to the fact that their rate of return is negatively correlated with g (see relation 5.40). On the other hand the capitalists' rate of return (relation 5.41) is positively correlated with g. From this point of view a faster rate of population growth exercises a positive effect on the capitalists' economic power, while it tends to reduce that of the workers (who may well respond by increasing their investment in human capital, i.e. education). The same impact may be observed in the case of an increase in the capital/output ratio, i.e. of capital intensity in general in the economy. This is clearly visible in relation (5.51′) and, of course, in (5.53*c*). Hence an economy that is rapidly becoming more capital-intensive is bound to reduce the long-term capital stock of the workers; this is in line with the result obtained above: a fast rate of growth means more profits for the entrepreneurs and hence a relative weakening of the position of the workers' class. This result is clearly in contrast with what would be seen in a neoclassical model, where the relative scarcity of one factor (in this case labour) increases the economic strength of the class that owns it.

The last two results concern the discount rates for consumption and for bequests. A general increase in b, the bequest discount rate, which means less willingness to leave assets to the next generation, will depress the share of inter-generational or long-term capital of the workers' class in the total capital stock. This does not necessarily mean that the capitalists will make up for the workers' loss: it means that there will be a switch from inter-generational capital to life-cycle savings. Finally, we come to relation (5.53*e*), which shows that an increase in the consumption discount rate of both classes tends to reduce the inter-generational bequest of the workers (and possibly that of the capitalists as well) by increasing life-cycle savings.

5.9.4 The case of a differentiated rate of interest with a differentiated bequest discount rate

In order to fit the two classes into the same balanced growth path, both with a positive share of the long-term capital stock (or inter-generational bequest), one may postulate the existence of both a differentiated interest rate *and* a differentiated rate of discount for the bequest, i.e. willingness to endow one's children. In this case we should retain the inequalities $b_c \neq b_w$ and $r_c^* \neq r_w^*$. From relations (5.40) and (5.41), setting, for the sake of simplicity, the condition $\phi = r_c^*/r_w^* > 1$ (which means that the rate of interest on capitalists' assets is higher than that of the workers' — quite a realistic assumption indeed) we get:

$$(B^w/K)^* = \frac{\phi Y/K - r_c^*}{(\phi - 1)g + \dfrac{2 + \delta}{1 + \delta}(\phi - 1 + b_w - b_c)}$$

$$= \frac{\phi Y/K - g - (1 + b_c)\dfrac{2 + \delta}{1 + \delta}}{(\phi - 1)g + \dfrac{2 + \delta}{1 + \delta}(\phi - 1 + b_w - b_c)} \tag{5.54}$$

which depends on all parameters of the model (including both bequest discount rates b_w and b_c) and on $\phi = r_c^*/r_w^*$, the ratio between the two interest rates, which may well be determined by the relative economic strength of the two classes in the process of determination of the rates of return on accumulated assets.

Once again we focus on the properties of the workers' share of long-term capital in the total capital stock by writing:

$$\partial(B^w/K)^*/\partial r_c^* = -D^{-1} < 0. \tag{5.55a}$$

$$\partial(B^w/K)^*/\partial(Y/K) = \phi D \; (= Dr_c^*/r_w^*) > 0 \tag{5.55b}$$

$$\partial(B^w/K)^*/\partial g = D^{-2}\left(\frac{2 + \delta}{1 + \delta}(\phi b_c - b_w) - (\phi - 1)\phi Y/K\right) < 0$$

$$\text{for } b_c \ll b_w \tag{5.55c}$$

$$\partial(B^w/K)^*/\partial b_w = -\frac{2 + \delta}{1 + \delta}D^{-2}\left(\phi Y/K - g - (1 + b_c)\frac{2 + \delta}{1 + \delta}\right) < 0$$

$$\tag{5.55d}$$

$$\partial(B^w/K)^*/\partial b_c = \frac{2 + \delta}{1 + \delta}D^{-2}\left(\phi(g + Y/K) - \frac{2 + \delta}{1 + \delta}(\phi + b_w)\right)$$

$$(> 0), \hspace{3cm} (5.55e)$$

where $D = (\phi - 1)g + (2 + \delta)(\phi - 1 + b_w - b_c)/(1 + \delta)$.

The interpretation of the above results is straightforward and supports our intuition. First (5.55a) shows that, other things being equal, an increase in the rate of return earned by the capitalist class has a negative effect on the share of the workers' inter-generational bequest in the total capital stock: this is surely due to the positive effect that such a change has on the capitalists' capital stock. The fact that an increase in the rate of return on capital of a given class is bound to weaken the relative economic strength of the other classes should not come as a surprise. The same result is obtained through the derivative with respect to $\phi = r_c^*/r_w^*$, which we do not report here since it appears analytically complicated.

Relation (5.55b) shows that the share of the workers' bequest in the total capital stock is positively associated with the value Y/K, and hence negatively with the capital/output ratio, K/Y. This can be more easily observed in relation (5.40), which shows that a higher capital/output ratio exerts a negative effect on the equilibrium rate of return on workers' financial assets. On the other hand, relations (5.13) and (5.41) show that the optimal rate of return for the capitalist class is independent of technology. After all, a higher capital/output ratio, even in the Kaldor–Pasinetti model (where $P/Y = P/K \cdot K/Y = g/s_c \cdot K/Y$) has the effect of shifting income from labour to capital, or from wages to profits; and since the latter accrue mainly to 'pure' capitalists and only partially to workers the result is thus explained. Again in this case the relative strength of the capitalists is enhanced by an increase in the P/Y ratio, which reflects itself negatively on the share of the inter-generational bequest of the workers.

Relation (5.55c), which can be compared to (5.53b), proves that an increase in the rate of growth of the system negatively affects the inter-generational capital share of the workers. As we have already pointed out, a faster rate of population growth will force the capitalists to accumulate at a faster rate in order to endow all their children with the same amount as they inherited themselves, so forcing down, in equilibrium, the share of the workers' inter-generational capital stock. The same result applies for relation (5.55d): a higher bequest discount rate of the workers' class, meaning less willingness to endow one's children, depresses the equilibrium inter-generational capital stock of the same class. Obviously the opposite result is obtained if we consider

(5.55c), which shows that an increase in the bequest discount rate of the capitalist class has a positive effect on the inter-generational capital stock of the other class.

It should be remembered that these results apply to the special case in which the rate of return of the capitalist class is higher than that of the other class (the workers) *and*, at the same time, the capitalists exhibit a stronger propensity to leave inter-generational assets to their children. This is one of the three conditions which ensures equilibrium growth to the system; and this confirms once again the fact that in the life-cycle model considered strong elements of class differentiation must be incorporated. (Such elements may be put into relation with elements of 'market imperfections' within the theory of the firm.) More than this: in certain cases such imperfections or elements of differentiation must be fairly strong as the only way to ensure that the system stays in equilibrium.

One additional remark may be added. In order to ensure equilibrium growth of the system (with both classes holding inter-generational assets) one may further postulate for the two classes (*a*) a different consumption discount rate, and/or (*b*) a different rate of population growth. It is obvious that these two cases deserve additional attention; but in order to generalize the model we have excluded the analysis of these alternatives. As King (1985, p. 285) points out, 'For some households, although probably a minority, bequests are likely to represent one of the main motives for accumulation of wealth'; for this reason we have chosen to concentrate on the analysis of different attitudes towards bequests by the two socio-economic classes.

5.10 CONCLUSION

This chapter had several aims. The first was to build a simple model which would reconcile the micro-economic decisions of individuals with a macro-economic framework allowing for the study of the mechanisms which define the process of capital accumulation, income distribution, and profit determination. As stated, the model set up is quite simple, since it includes the simplest version of the life-cycle model; it does however provide a number of insights into the laws which regulate the relationships among economic variables.

The second aim of this chapter was to provide a general framework within which the relevance and the historical dimensions of the inter-generational capital stock or bequest could be studied. In other words the distinction between life-cycle savings and inter-generational bequests, founded on a simple bequest utility function and on a few other assumptions, allows the relative strength of both kinds of capital or accumulated assets to be determined.

The third objective of the analysis was to check the importance or strength of the socio-economic classes or groups of individuals, namely consumers or families on one side, and capitalists or firms on the other. More precisely it was important to enquire into the forces that are at the basis of the distribution of (*a*) total life-cycle savings and (*b*) total inter-generational bequests among the socio-economic groups in a model which allows both classes to hold such assets. To do this we considered a steady-state long-term growth path where the relative strength among the classes is supposed to remain unchanged: in other words we tested the conditions under which 'social peace' among classes is preserved. This gave interesting answers regarding the conditions which must be satisfied if the system is (*a*) to reach a situation of equilibrium and (*b*) to maintain this equilibrium. The requirements concerning the equilibrium conditions are relevant, since, among other things, they tell us how a given class may maintain its relative economic strength and reveal the elements that lead to a (perpetual, or in any case long-term) formation of different classes.

The fourth aim of the analysis was to define the analytical value of the most important variables of the model, in particular that of the equilibrium interest and profit rate. The equilibrium value of the rate of profit played a central role in the controversy on income distribution and capital theory that took place in the 1960s and early 1970s. The models put forward by post-Keynesian authors like Kaldor, Robinson, and Pasinetti had the specific aim of showing that the distribution may be determined independently of the marginal productivity of production factors, but on the basis of behavioural and other technological and institutional factors. In particular this school of thought proved that in a situation of steady-state growth the profit rate is determined uniquely by the exogenously determined rate of growth of the system and the thrift of the entrepreneurial class. At the same time the distribution of income between wages and profits is shown to be determined by the rate of growth of the system, the thrift of the entrepreneurs, and the capital/ output ratio of the system, the latter corresponding to the technological state of the economy. The results obtained in this chapter are interesting since, possibly for the first time, the micro-economic pure exchange model (or utility-maximization model) is encompassed by the post-Keynesian framework in order to define a more flexible model of income and wealth distribution. The analysis has two main conclusions.

1. In a model where the transmission of inter-generational financial assets is a prerogative of the entrepreneurial class, the equilibrium rate

of interest turns out to be a function of the behavioural parameters of the capitalists, but not of those of other classes nor of technology. The fact that the equilibrium rate of interest is independent of the technological factors (i.e. of the capital/output ratio) is particularly relevant, and seems to confirm the validity of the Cambridge equation.

2. When both classes are allowed to pass on inter-generational assets (excluding education) to their children, then in order to have a steady-state path, the capitalists must have a much stronger will to bequeath capital to their children than the other classes. It is only in such a situation that all classes will hold a positive share of the total capital stock. Can this analytical result be reconciled with economic reality and common sense? To a certain extent the answer may be positive, since (*a*) the workers' class, by definition, derives a high proportion of its income from human capital stock, so that the class may be inclined to discount its inter-generational bequest at a rate lower than average (on this point see Flemming, 1979); and (*b*) it is not unrealistic to posit a situation where, in general, low-income families give higher priority to life-cycle consumption and, consequently, a lower one to the inter-generational capital stock. On the other hand those classes that derive a high proportion of their income from inter-generational wealth (and the remaining part from life-cycle savings) in a long-term perspective are bound to give weight to the accumulation of such wealth, by discounting it at a rate higher than average. Notwithstanding this different approach to the inter-generational bequest, as we have shown in this chapter, there exists a real possibility of a balanced growth of the system, where the classes maintain a constant relative economic strength and a constant share of the capital stock. Obviously the system may well leave such a path: this would happen if the capitalists were to show a too low propensity to pass on bequests to their children, so diminishing their strength; similarly a much stronger desire to transmit inter-generational wealth by the workers would eventually achieve the same result.

In this chapter we also considered the possibility and implications of a double capital market, i.e. of remuneration of savings according to ownership. The issue will be further considered in the following chapters. As a matter of fact this hypothesis has often been considered in the literature which has been prompted by the Kaldor–Pasinetti and Meade–Samuelson and Modigliani models. Since these models consider two distinct classes of economic agents, i.e. workers–consumers and capitalists–entrepreneurs, it is appropriate to enquire into the implications of different rates of return on capital according to whether it is connected with the act of saving ('the negative act of refraining from spending the whole of his current income on consumption' according to Keynes) or with the act of investment ('the positive act of starting or maintaining some process of production' always according to Keynes). The overall rate of return on capital would of course be a weighted average of the two distinct rates, and its determination would be connected with the theoretical framework of analysis chosen, so as to leave unaltered the whole structure of the system.

The introduction of this hypothesis has led to interesting new results and in the present framework it appears to play a crucial role since it allows the existence of a steady-state growth path in the case where classes hold and transmit inter-generational assets without having to postulate a different attitude towards future generations (i.e. a different bequest discount rate). In other words this version of the capital market ensures the conditions for the coexistence of all classes, each with a positive share of inter-generational and life-cycle assets. In this way what appears to be a simple hypothesis becomes an optimality condition ensuring coexistence of the socio-economic classes.

The latter point is of particular importance since the inter-generational capital stock represents the backbone of all industrial systems, and the issue of the coexistence of the classes, at least over fairly long periods of time, often characterized by economic prosperity and sustained growth, must be relevant. Yet it appears to be impossible, within such a framework, to have at the same time a situation where all classes can transmit financial or material wealth and where there also exists a single capital market and the same common bequest discount rate (meaning that all classes attach the same relevance to the inter-generational capital stock). One condition must give way in order to have a balanced growth path with a multi-class system.

Clearly in a world dominated by perfect competition, equal opportunities for all, and no (or little) class distinction the existence of a steady growth path would be threatened. The results obtained show that a given degree of market imperfection or class differentiation must be taken into account in order to allow for status quo among the classes. In this case the degree of market imperfection refers to a double capital market (with different rates of return on capital), while the concept of class distinction refers to the different values attached to the inter-generational transmission of wealth. We may conclude that once a different economic role for the various classes is accepted, the economic system may reproduce itself with a continuity of 'social contract' only where the classes retain their relative economic strength and *only* if one allows for an extra degree of class differentiation. In other words a given degree of market imperfection is necessary if one requires the long-term survival of all classes existing in the system. Otherwise one class or the other is bound to disappear in an economic sense, while the other is bound to gain economic strength and to take over.

The introduction of socio-economic classes into the model of income and wealth distribution, both in the short and long run, not only reflects the different roles of economic agents in a capitalistic economic system, but allows us to determine that distribution independently of the concept of marginal productivity of the productive factors.

A number of our conclusions are confirmed, at least to a certain extent and in a slightly different context, by Wolff's (1988, pp. 261–80) analysis of the 'life-cycle savings and the individual distribution of wealth by class'. Wolff in fact develops a similar life-cycle model for the workers' class, but supposes that capitalists save a fixed proportion of their income. In particular he focuses on the significance of modifications in steady-state wealth inequality of the system resulting from changes in the following six parameters: (*a*) changes in productivity growth; (*b*) changes in the capitalists' propensity to save; (*c*) changes in the life-span and retirement age; (*d*) changes in the relative size of the capitalist class; (*e*) changes in the covariance of earnings with age; and (*f*) changes in the social security system. As the author points out, some of these factors may have played an important role in the historical decline in wealth inequality. Wolff concludes that:

Two principal theoretical results emerge from the model developed in this paper. First, the specification of a life cycle savings model for workers in a two-class model is found to be consistent with the Pasinetti results regarding the rate of interest and productivity growth in steady-state equilibrium. Second, in steady-state equilibrium, wealth inequality among individuals is found to remain constant over time (Wolff, 1988, p. 276).

Such conclusions reinforce the validity of our approach, especially because Wolff stresses that he has not proved that there is always a two-class solution. 'In particular, it is possible that under certain conditions (parameter values) the workers' savings propensity is so high that they accumulate wealth faster than the capitalists. In this case, the only equilibrium which results is a one-class worker economy' (Wolff, 1988, p. 277). One may note the similarity of these results with ours, although we have explicitly considered a life-cycle model for the capitalists as well.

Finally, the results that we have summarized in Table 5.2 may be compared with the following long-term properties of Wolff's model:

Various factors were adduced which might help to explain the observed reduction in personal wealth inequality over the last 50 years or so. Of these, the increased life expectancy and reduction in work life and hence increase in the number of years of retirement seems the strongest force leading to increased wealth inequality. Second, a slowdown in productivity growth and a decline in the profit (or real interest) rate may have led to greater wealth equality. Third, an increasing size of the capitalist class may have contributed to a decline in personal wealth inequality. Fourth, a decline in the rate of return to age or experience on wages may have led to reduced wealth inequality. Fifth, the increase of the social security tax rate from zero % in 1934 to 7% or so today has probably led to increasing wealth inequality (Wolff, 1988, p. 278).

In a certain sense Wolff's inequality in personal wealth distribution may, in our model, be partially replaced by the distinction between workers' and capitalists' inter-generational capital stock, while a number of his other conclusions coincide with those indicated in the various sections of this chapter.

In Chapter 6 we shall consider a number of issues raised here (for instance the length of the retirement period, the relevance of the social security system, i.e. pension rates, and the role of technological progress) in a more comprehensive continuous life-cycle model. On the significance of the long-term trends in the concentration of personal and class wealth and income we shall return in the final chapter.

6

The Accumulation of Capital in a Two-Class Life-Cycle Model in Continuous Time

6.1 INTRODUCTION

In the preceding chapter we considered a two-class life-cycle model in which we explicity derived the value of the equilibrium variables of the model, namely the optimal interest rate and rate of profit by which both a steady growth and individuals' utility maximization are achieved. In order to obtain explicit analytical solutions we considered a very simple two-period model based on some restrictive assumptions which we proceed now to relax in order to observe the effects of the various parameters on a few relevant variables (like initial consumption-, saving-, and accumulation-rates) in a more generalized life-cycle model of income and wealth distribution. Additionally this analysis, with particular reference to the saving- and consumption-rates, will allow us to compare the results obtained in a deterministic life-cycle model with those valid for a corresponding stochastic model (see Chapter 7) in order to observe the effects of uncertainty in a life-cycle model under optimality.

In this part of the volume we shall prove how life-cycle consumption- and saving-theories can close the traditional two-class post-Keynesian macro-model and help to determine the variables of the model. More precisely we shall show that:

1. In a life-cycle model 'history', as described by the bequest function k_o (the bequest that each capitalist inherits at the beginning of his life), is just as important as the other behavioural and technological parameters in the determination of the equilibrium variables of the model if we do not introduce a bequest utility function as in the previous chapter.

2. In a life-cycle model, under general conditions, when each capitalist bequeaths the same capital stock k_o to each of his children as he himself has inherited, the saving supply function $s_c = g/r$ is always valid; however there is a fundamental difference from Pasinetti's equation $r = g/s_c$; more precisely in the latter relation s_c is exogenously given, while in the former it is a function of all parameters of the model.

3. In a life-cycle model where the bequest of the capitalists is exogenously given and there exists no bequest utility function the rate of

interest which keeps the system in equilibrium is a function of all parameters of the model, including the behavioural parameters of the workers' class.

4. The hypothesis of perfect altruism (where individuals plan to leave the same bequest to their children as they have inherited themselves) relative to the workers' class leads, under general conditions, to a result following which the workers might never start accumulating wealth and leave a positive bequest. Note that this hypothesis is different from that considered in Chapter 5 where the workers were given an initial positive bequest and a bequest utility function.

5. The special case in which the rate of interest equals the natural rate of growth raises some interesting questions in a dynamic context, due to the fact that in this case the capitalists cannot consume a positive share of their income. This point does not however arise if we assume a higher than average rate of return for the capitalist class.

These are the questions we seek to answer in this chapter. As we have already pointed out we do not introduce here a bequest utility function and we treat the initial inter-generational capital stock as an exogenous variable. This means that we shift the attention of our analysis away from the role of the long-term capital stock of the system in order to concentrate on the behaviour of other variables, in particular the consumption and saving rates. Moreover, instead of considering both classes as an aggregate, we introduce at the micro-level the life-cycle hypothesis where each individual makes his plans in order to maximize, throughout his expected life-span, the value of the flow of the discounted utilities from consumption. The individual consumption- and saving-plans thus obtained are then aggregated in order to arrive at the total consumption- and saving-function of each class.

Plan of the Chapter. In Sect. 6.2 the basic assumptions of the model are specified, by postulating a perfect capital market, i.e. with a rate of return on capital equal for all classes. In Sect. 6.3 we consider the complete model: first both micro- and macro-models, then the aggregate macro-model. In Sect. 6.4 we analyse the consequences of the removal of the assumption of 'perfect selfishness' which states that every worker bequeaths no assets to his children. In the following section we shall discuss the Golden Rule path and its implications in a life-cycle model.

6.2   THE BASIC ASSUMPTIONS OF THE MODEL

A. *Demographic and biological assumptions*

1. Individuals are fully trained adults at $t = 0$ when they start earning (or being active if they are pure rentiers) and when, at the same time, they set up an independent household.

2. Each individual (worker or rentier) works, or is active, for R years and then retires.
3. Each individual dies at age T, so enjoying T − R years of retirement.
4. At the age of R years each individual has e^{gR} children, so that the number of births is rising at the constant rate g (where e^{gR} is not necessarily a whole number).
5. Labour input is measured in efficiency units so as to allow for Harrod-neutral (labour-augmenting) technical progress. The rate of growth is exogenously given and is constant; it will be denoted by $n = g + m$ (the natural rate of growth), where g is the rate of growth of population and m is the rate of labour-augmenting technical progress. Since we shall be confining our analysis to steady-state growth paths (*a*) the rate of growth of total output, total capital, consumption and savings, will be equal to n and (*b*) the rate of growth of output, capital, etc. per head and of the wage-rate will be equal to m, the rate of technical progress.

B. *Capital accumulation*

As in most two-class growth models we make the assumption that the classes are inter-generationally stable, i.e. of a rigid segmentation between capitalists and workers. (Bevan, 1974, Sect. 7, considers a model in which this assumption is partially relaxed. We shall consider this aspect at the end of this chapter and in the next chapter incorporating uncertainty.) We shall make the following assumptions:

1. The *workers*, when they are born, inherit no financial capital and, in the same way, when they retire at T − R they leave no bequest to their children (more precisely they leave neither assets nor debts). They will nevertheless, during some part of their lives (usually the first part) accumulate some financial assets in order to arrange their consumption streams in an optimal way.

2. The *capitalists*, on the other hand, when they set up an independent household inherit a certain amount of assets (k_o) from which they will derive all their income; they are by definition non-wage-earners. When they reach age R they bequeath a certain amount of assets per child (who is just setting up a new household). Since, as stated above, we are confining our analysis to steady-state growth paths only, each capitalist born at time t = 0 will bequeath, when he retires, an amount of assets equal to $k_o e^{(g+m)R} = k_o e^{nR}$ so that each child will inherit $k_o e^{mR}$, where m is the rate of technical progress.

C. *Income*

As stated earlier, the capitalists derive all their income from the financial capital they own. The workers have two types of income: the first one from their work, i.e. a wage-rate w(t) supposed to be known and growing at rate m (we suppose that all workers face the same wage-rate and pension-rate); the second income is derived from their accumulated assets (which they own possibly indirectly). The rate of interest r that they earn on these accumulated savings equals the average rate of profit P/K of the system; additionally we assume that there is a perfect capital market so that each individual may borrow or lend at the same interest rate (r). Finally we suppose that during the retirement period every worker receives a pension equal to pw(t), corresponding to a fixed proportion of the wage-rate he would earn if he was still working ($0 \leq p \leq 1$). For the sake of convenience we assume that pensions are postponed wage-incomes so that the labour share includes the wage-rates paid to workers and the pensions paid to the pensioners.

D. *Utility function*

The utility function for consumption considered here will be, as in the preceding chapter, $U(c_t) = \frac{1}{a}(c_t)^a$, which yields iso-elastic marginal utility. (Since uncertainty is not introduced here, a has nothing to do with risk-aversion; it simply represents something about time-preference; we shall, moreover, consider the same utility function for both classes.) While most of our results are valid for values of a lower than unity, we shall at times assume that it is non-negative.

6.3   THE MODEL

As we are considering a two-class model we shall start by defining both micro-models and then each class as a whole. The plan of the analysis is more or less the same for each class. First of all we shall define the consumption- and saving-plans of a single individual. This will enable us to determine the initial consumption and initial saving (which might also be a dissaving if an individual starts by borrowing) and define the capital accumulation, or disaccumulation, during his life-cycle. When the entire micro-model is completed, we define the entire model for both classes, and finally the whole macro-model, which we shall consider against a (post-Keynesian) background where the capital/output ratio is given and the level of full-employment investment is also exogenously given.

6.3.1 *The two micro-models*

For both individuals (capitalist and worker) the criterion of choice is such as to select that plan of consumption which maximizes the value of the discounted utilities:

$$U = \int_0^T e^{-\delta t} U(c(t)) dt = \int_0^T e^{-\delta t} \cdot \frac{1}{a} (c(t))^a dt, \qquad (6.1)$$

where δ is the pure time-preference (constant and non-negative), $c(t)$ is consumption at time t, T is the date of death.

Optimal consumption plan. Since one unit of consumption at time t is interchangeable with e^{rk} units of consumption at time $t + k$ we may write:

$$U'(c(0)) = e^{-\delta t} U'(c(t)) e^{rt}$$

i.e.

$$c(t) = c(0) e^{g^* t}, \text{ where } g^* = \frac{r - \delta}{1 - a}. \qquad (6.2)$$

Since the worker leaves no assets at time T, while the capitalist bequeaths $B(R) = k_0 e^{(g+m)R} = k_0 e^{nR}$ at time R to his children,[1] we may write the following budget equations for the capitalist and the worker respectively:[2]

$$\int_0^T c_c(t) e^{-rt} dt - k_0(1 - e^{(n-r)R}) = 0,[3] \qquad (6.3a)$$

$$\int_0^R (w_o e^{mt} - c_w(t)) e^{-rt} dt + \int_R^T (p w_o e^{mt} - c_w(t)) e^{-rt} dt = 0, \quad (6.3b)$$

which combined with (6.2) yields the two consumption rates:[4]

$$c_c(t) = c_c(0) e^{g^* t} = k_0(r - g^*) \frac{1 - e^{R(n-r)}}{1 - e^{T(g^* - r)}} e^{g^* t}, \qquad (6.4)$$

where, to recall, $g^* = (r - \delta)/(1 - a)$, and

$$c_w(t) = c_w(0) e^{g^* t} = w_o A \frac{r - g^*}{r - m} e^{g^* t}, \qquad (6.5)$$

---

[1] In order to make this procedure feasible, in the long run, r must be greater than n, the overall rate of growth. We shall explore the case $n \geqslant r$ later. Note that for $m = 0$ (i.e. for a zero rate of technical progress) the capitalist will leave the same bequest k_0 to each of his children.

[2] As usual the subscripts c and w refer to capitalists and workers respectively for any variable (or parameter) to which they are attached.

[3] When an individual is born, at $t = 0$, he has the following expectations: he knows that he will retire at time R and die at time T; if he is a worker he knows that his labour income will in the interval $(0, R)$ be equal to $w(0)e^{mt}$, where $w(0)$ is his income at $t = 0$, and during his retirement (R, T) equal to $pw(0)e^{mt}$ $(0 \leqslant p \leqslant 1)$; if he is a capitalist he knows that he will bequeath $k_0 e^{nR}$ at time $t = R$ to his children (where k_0 is the capital stock that he has inherited at $t = 0$); moreover everybody knows that the rate of interest r earned on the accumulated savings and capital will remain constant. For the sake of simplicity we have assumed that if an individual starts off borrowing he will pay an interest rate equal to r.

[4] Note that $r \neq m$ must be valid (a very reasonable assumption).

where

$$A = \frac{1 - e^{R(m-r)} + p(e^{R(m-r)} - e^{T(m-r)})}{1 - e^{T(g^*-r)}}.$$

Since we have excluded the case $n \geq r$ we note immediately that the initial consumption rate is always positive, at least for positive values of the parameters. To analyse the properties of $c_{c,w}(0)$ we differentiate them partially with respect to the individual parameters:[5]

$$\partial c_{c,w}(0)/\partial \delta > 0, \tag{6.6a}$$

$$\partial c_{c,w}(0)/\partial R > 0, \tag{6.6b}$$

$$\partial c_w(0)/\partial p > 0, \tag{6.6c}$$

$$\partial c_c(0)/\partial m, g, n < 0 \tag{6.6d}$$

The other derivatives are more complicated and ambiguous (especially for $c_w(0)$). For the sake of simplicity, and without much loss of generality, we derive them by setting $p = 0$ in (6.7a), (6.7c), and (6.7e), $a = 0$ (i.e. a log u-function) in (6.7d) and (6.7e) and $\delta = 0$ in (6.7c). We obtain the following results:

$$\partial c_{c,w}(0)/\partial T|_{p=0} < 0, \tag{6.7a}$$

$$\partial c_w(0)/\partial m|_{p=0} > 0, \tag{6.7b}$$

$$\partial c_{c,w}(0)/\partial a|_{\substack{\delta=0 \\ p=0}} < 0, \text{ when } 1 > \left(1 - T\frac{ar}{1-a}\right)e^{Tar/1-a}, \tag{6.7c}$$

$$\partial c_c(0)/\partial r|_{a=0} > 0, \tag{6.7d}$$

$$\partial c_w(0)/\partial r|_{\substack{a=0 \\ p=0}} < 0. \tag{6.7e}$$

The results obtained may be interpreted in the following way. Relation (6.6a) shows that an increase in the pure time-preference has a positive effect on both initial consumptions: as a matter of fact an increase in δ has the effect of discouraging saving and hence stimulating initial consumption. The same result is obtained in relation (6.6b): as R (the date of retirement) is postponed, total disposable income is increased so that initial consumption is positively affected; not surprisingly the opposite result applies with respect to T, the date of death: this is shown in relation (6.7a), where, for the sake of simplicity but without much loss of generality, we have assumed that no pension is paid to retired workers. Relation (6.6c) tells us that as p, the pension/

---

[5] We do not give here the analytical results since they are lengthy without being particularly instructive.

wage ratio, is increased, the worker will start with a higher consumption rate (since he will need less saving for his retirement period).

Relations (6.6d) and (6.7b) show that an increase in $n(=g+m)$ has an opposite effect on the two initial consumption rates $c_w(0)$ and $c_c(0)$. More precisely as m increases the disposable income of the worker is also increased so that initial consumption $c_w(0)$ is raised. On the contrary an increase in n, the overall rate of growth of the system, has a negative impact on $c_c(0)$: this is easy to explain since an increase in n has the immediate effect of reducing the total disposable income of the capitalists who in equilibrium are bound to leave a bequest equal to $k_o e^{nR}$ (hence an increase in n clearly reduces the life-cycle disposable income). It is worth noting that this result has been reached by keeping r constant; and by now we do know that an increase in the rate of growth of the economy normally has a positive effect on the rate of profit (see, for instance, the case of the Kaldor–Pasinetti theorem $P/K = n/s_c$).

Relation (6.7c) states that as long as $[(1 - T)\ ar/1 - a] \exp(ar/1 - a)$ is smaller than unity, which is likely to happen in the real world, an increase in a, the elasticity of the u-function, has a negative effect on both initial consumptions. (For realistic values of the parameters as $a = -2$, $r = 0.05$, and $T = 50$ (years) we can indeed rewrite the above inequality as: $0.507 < 1$.)

An increase in the interest rate r has a positive effect on $c_c(0)$, while it has a negative effect on $c_w(0)$. When r is increased, a rational worker will tend to increase initial saving to enjoy a larger income later: for this reason he will reduce initial consumption. (Note that relation (6.7e) has been derived by assuming w_o as a constant, and hence independent of r.) The opposite applies for the capitalist: when r is increased his income (being a direct function of the rate of interest) is also increased, so stimulating initial consumption. Note that this increase in disposable income offsets the other effect that an increase in r has upon a rational individual, who tends to increase initial savings in order to enjoy more income later. We turn now to the capital accumulation process.

Capital accumulation. We shall start by defining the capital stock k_w^a owned by a worker during his working life $(0 \leqslant t \leqslant R)$:[6]

$$k_w^a(t) = \int_0^t (w_o e^{mv} - c_w(v)) e^{r(t-v)}\, dv$$

$$= \frac{w_o}{r - m}\, [e^{rt} - e^{mt} + A(e^{g^*t} - e^{rt})]. \tag{6.8}$$

---

[6] The superscripts a and p stand for 'working age' and 'retirement age' respectively.

Then we write the capital stock k_w^p owned by a worker during his retirement period ($R < t \leqslant T$):

$$k_w^p(t) = k_w(R)e^{r(t-R)} + \int_R^t (pw_o e^{mv} - c_w(v))e^{r(t-v)}dv$$

$$= w_o \frac{e^{rt}}{r-m} [p(e^{T(m-r)} - e^{t(m-r)}) + A(e^{t(g^*-r)} - e^{T(g^*-r)})].$$

$$(6.9)$$

Denoting by $k_c^a(t)$ the capital stock owned by a capitalist who is active ($0 \leqslant t \leqslant R$):[7]

$$k_c^a(t) = k_o e^{nt} + \int_0^t ((r-n)k_o e^{nt} - c_c(v))e^{r(t-v)}dv$$

$$= k_o e^{rt}(1 - B(1 - e^{(g^*-r)t})),$$

$$(6.10)$$

where

$$B = (1 - e^{R(n-r)})/(1 - e^{T(g^*-r)}), \text{ independent of time.}$$

Note that $k_c^a(t)$ includes the endowment to the following generation. We define now $k_c^p(t)$, the financial capital stock of a retired capitalist:

$$k_c^p(t) = (k_c^a(R) - k_o e^{Rn})e^{r(t-R)} - \int_R^t c_c(v)e^{r(t-v)}dv$$

$$= k_o e^{rt}[e^{(g^*-r)t} - e^{(g^*-r)T}].$$

$$(6.11)$$

In Appendix 6.1 we shall graphically represent the above consumption and accumulation rates for both individuals.

Continuity in the standard of living. From relations (6.4) and (6.5) we deduce that at time R (when the parent retires and, at the same time, his children start a new household) the ratio z of the son's to the parent's standard of living is:

$$z_{c,w} = e^{(m-g^*)R},$$

$$(6.12)$$

which is valid for both classes. Clearly if $g^* = (r - \delta)/(1 - a) > m$ the parent, during his retirement, will enjoy a better standard of living than his children and vice versa. We shall reconsider this question when we relax the basic assumption of perfect selfishness for the workers' class (following which they cannot hold inter-generational assets; cf. Sect. 6.4 below).

Having analysed the behaviour of a single individual, we are now in a position to spell out the aggregate model for both classes.

---

[7] Note that at time $t = R$ the capitalist owns two capitals: the first one that he leaves to his children and the second one which will finance his consumption during the retirement age.

6.3.2 *The two macro-models*

For analysing the aggregate sub-models we shall first assume that the number of working people belonging to cohort 0 (i.e. born at $t = 0$) is equal to N_w, while the number of active capitalists is N_c.

Now at time t only the people setting up an independent household in the interval $(t - T, t)$ are still alive (retired or working); their number will be equal to $N_w e^{gt}(1 - e^{-gT})/g = N_w(t)$ and $N_c e^{gT}(1 - e^{-gT})/g = N_c(t)$ respectively, since population is growing at rate g.

Moreover let w_o be the wage-rate at time $t = 0$; the wage-rate at time t will hence be $w(t) = w_o e^{mt}$. On the other hand we have assumed that every capitalist inherits the same capital stock $k_o e^{mt}$ when he sets up a new household at time t. Everybody faces the same wage-rate (if worker), bequest (if capitalist), interest rate, and u-function.

We shall start by defining, for each class, the aggregate consumption and then the aggregate capital stock, from which we shall derive the equilibrium aggregate saving.

Aggregate consumptions. Denoting by $C_c(t)$ and $C_w(t)$ the consumption of the capitalist and worker classes respectively, we may write:

$$C_c(t) = \int_0^R N_c e^{g(t-v)} e^{m(t-v)} c_c(v) dv + \int_R^T \phi N_c e^{g(t-v)} e^{m(t-v)} c_c(v) dv$$

$$= N_c k_o e^{nt} B \frac{r - g^*}{n - g^*} [1 + (\phi - 1)e^{R(g^*-n)} - \phi e^{T(g^*-n)}], \quad (6.13)$$

and

$$C_w(t) = \int_0^R N_w e^{g(t-v)} e^{m(t-v)} c_w(v) dv + \int_R^T \phi N_w e^{g(t-v)} e^{m(t-v)} c_w(v) dv$$

$$= N_w w_0 e^{nt} \frac{A}{n - g^*} \frac{r - g^*}{r - m}$$

$$\times [1 + (\phi - 1)e^{R(g^*-n)} - \phi e^{T(g^*-n)}]. \quad (6.14)$$

Differentiating $C_{c,w}(t)$ with respect to time we obtain at once $nC_{c,w}(t)$.[8,9]

Aggregate capital stocks. We may now write the sum of the assets owned, at time t, by the capitalist class $(K_c(t))$ and by the workers' class $(K_w(t))$.

---

[8] Note that, at time t, the number of retired workers and capitalists is equal to $\phi N_w(t)$ and $\phi N_c(t)$ respectively, where $\phi = (T - R)/[R + e^{gR}(T - R)]$.

[9] Note that for $r > n$ in equilibrium $C_w(t)$ is greater than the aggregate wage-income (and pension) of the class. This is due to the fact that for r greater than n the total capital stock of the class is always positive, yielding a positive profit income. Always for $r > n$, $C_c(t) > 0$: as a matter of fact, in equilibrium, the capitalist class can survive only when the rate of interest is greater than the natural rate of growth.

$$K_c(t) = \int_{t-R}^{t} N_c e^{gv} e^{mv}(k_c^a(t-v)) dv$$

$$+ \int_{t-T+R}^{t} \phi N_c e^{gv} e^{mv}(k_c^p(t-v)) dv$$

$$= N_c K_o \frac{e^{nt}}{r-n} B \frac{r-g^*}{n-g^*} [1 + (\phi - 1)e^{R(g^*-n)} - \phi e^{T(g^*-n)}],$$

(6.15)

and

$$K_w(t) = \int_{t-R}^{t} N_w e^{gv} e^{mv}(k_w^a(t-v)) dv$$

$$+ \int_{t-T+R}^{t} \phi N_w e^{gv} e^{mv}(k_w^p(t-v)) dv$$

$$= N_w w_o \frac{e^{nt}}{r-n} \left[\frac{e^{-g} - 1}{g} + \phi \frac{p}{g} (e^{-g}) - e^{-gR} \right)$$

$$+ A(r - g^*) \frac{1 + (\phi - 1)e^{R(g^*-n)} - \phi e^{T(g^*-n)}}{(r - m)(n - g^*)} \right].$$

(6.16)

Whether workers will be property-owners or not will depend on whether $K_w(t) > 0$ or not. In the latter case the workers will be net debtors as a class, and there will be two types of assets in the economy: the capital goods and the bonds issued by the workers' class when it is a net debtor. In this way the capitalist class will hold capital goods and bonds issued by the workers and there will be an inter-class trading where young human-capital-owners borrow from the capitalists and pay their debts in the second part of their lives.

Aggregate savings. We may now define the aggregate savings $S_c(t)$ and $S_w(t)$ of the two classes:

$$S_c(t) = rK_c(t) - \int_{0}^{R} N_c e^{g(t-v)} e^{m(t-v)} c_c(v) dv$$

$$- \int_{R}^{T} \phi N_c e^{g(t-v)} e^{m(t-v)} c_c(v) dv$$

$$= rK_c(t) - N_c k_o e^{nt} B \frac{r - g^*}{n - g^*}$$

$$\times [1 + (\phi - 1)e^{R(g^*-n)} - \phi e^{T(g^*-n)}];$$

(6.17)

$$S_w(t) = rK_w(t) + \int_0^R N_w e^{g(t-v)} e^{m(t-v)} s_w^a(v) dv$$

$$+ \int_R^T \phi N_w e^{g(t-v)} e^{m(t-v)} s_w^P(v) dv$$

$$= rK_w(t) - N_w w_o e^{nt} \left[\frac{e^{-gR} - 1}{g} + \phi \frac{p}{g} (e^{-gT} - e^{-gR}) \right.$$

$$\left. + A(r - g^*) \frac{1 + (\phi - 1)e^{R(g^*-n)} - \phi e^{T(g^*-n)}}{(r - m)(n - g^*)} \right]. \tag{6.18}$$

The above relations prove that as long as each capitalist leaves $k_o e^{mt}$ to each of his children (i.e. what he himself has inherited *plus* an 'allowance' for technical progress) the saving of the class is equal to n times the capital stock. This applies to the workers as well, for whom we have set $k_o = 0$; while they earn a wage-rate. Note that when there is no technical progress ($m = 0$) for this to be valid the capitalists must leave an amount equal to k_o only to each of their children.

6.3.3 *The aggregate life-cycle model*

The analysis of the determination of the equilibrium of the aggregate model may be first carried out in the following general terms, without any loss of generality, since we shall recall the more general and detailed results obtained in the preceding paragraphs.

We shall start by rewriting the two basic micro-models in order to facilitate the macro-approach; moreover, for the sake of simplicity, but again without much loss of generality, we shall omit the Harrod-neutral technical progress. Let us start by considering the 'pure' capitalist class.

'Pure' capitalists. Following our basic assumptions, a man of age t consumes $c_c(t)$ and has a total capital stock of $k_c(t)$.[10] Except at t = R (when he retires) $k_c(t)$ is differentiable and we may write:

$$c_c(t) = rk_c(t) - \dot{k}_c(t). \tag{6.19}$$

We know also that $k_c(0) = k_o$ and that $k_c(R-) - k_c(R+) = e^{nR}k_o$; integrating (6.19) from 0 to T we obtain:[11]

$$\int_0^T e^{-nt} c_c(t) dt = r \int_0^T e^{-nt} k_c(t) dt - \int_0^R e^{-nt} \dot{k}_c(t) dt - \int_R^T e^{-nt} \dot{k}_c(t) dt,$$

---

[10] For $0 < t < R$, $k_c(t)$ includes the inter-generational bequest $k_o e^{nt}$.

[11] Where there is no risk of confusion or forgetfulness we drop the suffix t from the aggregate variables C, S, and K, and from r and w as well.

i.e.

$$C_c = rK_c - e^{-nR}k_c(R-) + k_c(0) - e^{-nT}k_c(T)$$
$$+ e^{-nR}k_c(R+) - nK_c$$
$$= (r - n)K_c, \qquad (6.20)$$

where C_c and K_c are the aggregates for a balanced group of $\int_0^T e^{-nt}dt = (1 - e^{-nT})/n$ capitalists (and where the number of capitalists born at time t has been set equal to unity). The same relationship obtained in (6.20) may be deduced, in the preceding paragraph, from relations (6.13) and (6.15).

Workers' class. The same kind of argument may be applied to the workers' class. As we have seen in the preceding paragraphs, a worker of age t consumes $c_w(t)$; and $k_w(t)$, his life-cycle capital stock, is differentiable (except at $t = 0, R$) so that we may write (assuming here that the pension rate is equal to zero):

$$c_w(t) = w(t) + rk_w(t) - \dot{k}_w(t), \qquad (6.21)$$

where $k_w(0) = 0$ and $w(t)$ is the per capita wage-rate at time t. After the necessary manipulations we obtain the following result:

$$C_w = (r - n)K_w + w(1 - e^{-nR})/n, \qquad (6.22)$$

for a balanced population of $(1 - e^{-nT})/n$ workers, of whom $(1 - e^{-nR})/n$ are active. Again, we have set the number of workers born at time t equal to unity. Relation (6.22) may be compared with relation (6.14) which gives us the aggregate consumption of the workers' class in the preceding section.

Aggregating the model. Suppose now that there are θ capitalists born for every worker (where $\theta = N_c/N_w$ in the micro-model considered in the previous paragraphs). Hence, always in equilibrium, by multiplying (6.20) by θ and adding it to (6.21), we may write:

$$C = \theta C_c + C_w = (r - n)K + wL, \qquad (6.23)$$

where $L = (1 - e^{-nR})/n$ is the number of active workers.

A word about the two aggregate consumptions C_c and C_w may be useful at this point. From life-cycle theory we know that the consumption of the two classes may be written as:

$$C_c = C_c(k_o, r; \text{parameters of the capitalist class})$$

and

$$(6.24a)$$

$$C_w = C_w (w, r; \text{parameters of the workers' class}),$$

which in the case of our life-cycle model (relations (6.13) and (6.14)) may be written as:

$$C_c = C_c(k_o, r; n, R, T, N_c, \delta, u\text{-function, technology})$$

and

$$C_w = C_w(w, r; n, R, T, N_w, \delta, u\text{-function, technology}),$$

(6.24*b*)

where $r = P/K$, the profit or interest rate.

The above relations show that the aggregate consumption of the model depends on the two variables (w, r) and on all parameters of the model. The parameters of a standard life-cycle model (like that analysed in this chapter) may be divided into behavioural, demographic, and bequest parameters. By behavioural parameters we mean the u-function (here iso-elastic), the pure time-preference (δ); while the demographic parameters are the rate of growth of population ($g = n$ if we do not consider technical progress), the dates of retirement and death (R and T, which are known), the number of capitalists and workers born at $t = 0$ (N_c and N_w) and the number of capitalists born for every worker ($\theta = N_c/N_w$). The bequest parameter is the capital stock inherited by the capitalists at the beginning of their lives (k_o), which is possibly the more appealing parameter in a two-class life-cycle model since in this specific case (a) it applies to the capitalist class only and (b) it determines the weight of the capitalists' inter-generational assets in the total capital stock, so determining the relative share of the capital of both classes in the system. We shall reconsider this aspect of the bequest function below.

It may be worth noting that there exists a fundamental difference between the present model and that of the previous chapter, where we derived explicitly the equilibrium value of the rate of interest and where we were able to define the equilibrium share of the inter-generational bequest explicitly. In the present model we consider k_o as exogenously given, and it does not depend on the form of the utility function. This allows us to concentrate on the determination of the equilibrium rate of interest in a more general life-cycle model.

The other parameters, g (in the case of a positive technical progress) and the technology of the system (as expressed by the capital/output ratio) may be called the 'technological parameters' and will help to determine the variables of the system, in particular the equilibrium rate of interest and the wage-rate. From (6.24*a*, *b*) we may rewrite (6.23) as follows. (Remember that in order to ensure, in long-run equilibrium, the existence of the capitalist class, r must be greater than n.)

$$\theta C_c(r; k_o; \text{other parameters}) + C_w(w, r; \text{parameters})$$

$$= [(r - n) k + w]L,$$

(6.25)

where L is the labour force. As pointed out above (6.25) determines the endogenous variables r^*, w^*, and k^*, which are all related by technology, in equilibrium. An even simpler way of putting all this is to use the basic relationship for an economy in balanced growth, since $C + I = W + P$:

$$c + nk = w + rk, \tag{6.26a}$$

i.e.

$$c = (r - n)k + w, \tag{6.26b}$$

which is just (6.25). In other words in our life-cycle model $c = \theta c_c + c_w$ is just a deterministic function of the variables w and r; and this closes the model when the bequest k_o is given (as well as the other parameters of the model). Therefore history, as described by the inter-generational bequest k_o, is just as important in this model without a bequest utility function, as the intertemporal preferences and the other parameters in determining the equilibrium variables of the model. Note that in the previous chapter the inter-generational capital stock was associated with a bequest utility function (similar to the consumption utility function—or final consumption); so endogenizing the inter-generational capital stock from which we have derived directly the equilibrium variables of the model.

We can now consider the aggregate variables of the model described in this chapter. For the sake of convenience and without loss of generality we shall compute $p = 0$, meaning that during the retirement period the workers receive no pension allowance. In this case, from relations (6.15) and (6.16) we obtain $K(t)$, the total capital stock, in equilibrium, of the entire economy:

$$K(t) = K_c(t) + K_w(t) = \frac{e^{nt}}{r - n} \left[N_w w_c \left(\frac{e^{-gR} - 1}{g} \right. \right.$$

$$\left. \left. + AD \frac{r - g^*}{(r - m)(n - g^*)} \right) + N_c k_o BD \frac{r - g^*}{n - g^*} \right] \tag{6.27}$$

where

$$D = (1 + (\phi - 1)e^{R(g^* - n)} - \phi e^{T(g^* - n)}),$$

and A and B have been defined in relations (6.5) and (6.10) respectively. From (6.17) and (6.18) we can now write the aggregate savings $S(t)$ which turn out to be equal to:

$$S(t) = S_c(t) + S_w(t) = nK(t), \tag{6.28}$$

where the value of $K(t)$ corresponds, in equilibrium, to that given in relation (6.29) above. Finally from (6.13) and (6.14) we obtain total consumption $C(t)$:

$$C(t) = C_c(t) + C_w(t) = e^{nt}D\,\frac{r - g^*}{n - g^*}\left(A\,\frac{N_w w_0}{r - m} + BN_c k_0\right). \quad (6.29)$$

Therefore, in equilibrium, we may write:

$$\dot{K}(t)/K(t) = \dot{S}(t)/S(t) = \dot{C}(t)/C(t) = n. \quad (6.30)$$

The equilibrium interest rate r^*. A formal proof of the existence of a unique or multiple positive equilibrium interest rate r^* which solves our model is not given here, as it would be too difficult to carry out in this context. The outline of a possible treatment is however easily sketched.

In a post-Keynesian framework, as pointed out, for instance, by Pasinetti (1974a, p. 135) the capital/output ratio is not necessarily a monotonically decreasing function of the rate of interest as is the case of the neoclassical or marginalist model; its trend may be similar (with $\bar{g}$ constant) to the one reported in Figure 6.1. (Note that in this figure, on the vertical axis, the capital/output ratio of Pasinetti is replaced by $I/K \cdot K/Y$, where $I/K = \bar{g}$, assumed to be constant; the supply side of savings is equal to S/Y.) On the other hand the supply of capital here represented by the S/Y (S referring to both life-cycle and inter-generational stock) is, or at least in general should be, an increasing function of the rate of interest. As a matter of fact in the case in which the rate of interest is low the life-cycle savings of the system are small (see Chapter 5 on this point) so lowering the overall capital per capita; on the other hand as the rate of interest increases individuals will find it

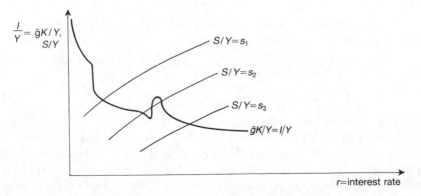

Fig. 6.1 The supply and demand of savings (S/Y and I/Y) as a function of the rate of interest

more convenient to accumulate life-cycle savings and, indirectly, inter-generational wealth as well.

Then, under these conditions, the equilibrium rate of interest of the system would normally be unique (and of positive value); but we may well have a multiple solution (cf. $S/Y = s_2$ in Figure 6.1). The case of a multiple equilibrium is rather simple to interpret: the system may, for different (as many as three) values of the K/Y ratio, i.e. of the technology, have an equilibrium for a unique value of the S/Y ratio, i.e. propensity to save of the system. This outcome contrasts with the solution put forward by Britto (1969) who, by considering a similar life-cycle model of capital accumulation concludes that there is a unique equilibrium value of the rate of interest.

The point is that in this model the equilibrium rate of interest may not be unique; but in any case it will be determined by the forces which define the strength of capital accumulation for all classes, and hence the whole system. In other words this means that the rate of interest is a function of *all parameters of the model*, including the behavioural parameters of the workers' class. The fact that the rate of interest is not independent of the behavioural parameters of the workers and of other parameters (like the capital/output ratio) is in contrast with the traditional Kaldor–Pasinetti theorem. But within this context the dividing line between the two classes is blurred since the rate of interest is the outcome of optimal conditions for which *both* classes will accumulate at a constant rate.

Since insights into the quantitative importance of our analysis and into the properties of the equilibrium rate of interest which solves the system for several economically significant values of the parameters could be provided by considering a given technology (K/Y^*).

6.3.4 The propensity to save of the capitalist class

The results obtained above show that within a life-cycle context the Kaldor–Pasinetti Equation $(P/K = n/s_c)$ has become a tautology, in that, whatever is the rate of interest, the capitalists as a group adjust their savings so that by relation (6.20):

$$\bar{s}_c = (rK_c - C_c)/rK_c = n/r. \tag{6.31}$$

This is seen to be the supply-function of saving, but it is no help at all in determining equilibrium. More precisely in all non-life-cycle two-class growth models as Kaldor's, Pasinetti's and Meade–Samuelson and Modigliani's the propensity to save of the two classes is exogenously given and hence constant for any value of the variables (and other parameters). In a life-cycle model, however, the saving behaviour of the capitalists (and of the workers as well) is a function of all parameters of the model, including technology. Therefore we might rewrite the above relation (6.31) as:

$$\bar{s}_c = \bar{s}_c \text{ (all parameters of the model).} \tag{6.32}$$

Hence in a life-cycle model Kaldor and Pasinetti's and Meade–Samuelson and Modigliani's elegant solutions ($P/K = n/s_c$ and $P/K = P/Y \cdot n/s_w$) no longer apply since, in this case, the rate of interest is determined, *inter alia*, by the behavioural parameters of both classes.

Secondly it may be stressed that (6.32) holds even if r is not the equilibrium interest rate and the economy is not on the balanced growth path; $\bar{s}_c$ will adapt itself to a change in r. Two cases may be considered here:

1. When from relation (6.12) $z_{c,w} = 1$, i.e. when at time R the children have the same standard of living of their retired parents, we get $s_c^{**} = n/(\delta + m(1 - a))$. In this case of 'perfect altruism' the aggregate propensity to save of the capitalist class is a function of the parameters a, n, m, and δ alone. Note that in the case of a zero technical progress $s_c^{**} = n/\delta$, which means that in order to have the same standard of living through generations, the propensity to save of the entrepreneurial class must be equal to the rate of growth of population divided by the consumption discount rate.

2. The second case arises when $r = n$, i.e. when the rate of interest is equal to the rate of growth of population. In this case the propensity to save of the entrepreneurs should be equal to unity in order to ensure a steady growth of their capital stock.

6.4 THE EXTENSION OF INTER-GENERATIONAL TRANSFERS TO BOTH CLASSES

We shall now remove the assumption following which the workers cannot bequeath financial assets to their children.[12] This approach is different from that considered in Chapter 5, where we introduced a workers' bequest utility function. This is due to the assumption, made here, that every worker does not inherit financial assets; none the less we allow them to leave a certain amount of assets, at $t = R$, to their children in order to maximize the flow of the discounted consumption-utilities of themselves and of their children. It must be stressed that in

---

[12] We implicitly assume the institutional principle following which no negative bequest may be made. We have considered this question in Sect. 4.5.3. For negative inheritances to be considered we should introduce the concept of perfect altruism of Meade (1966*b*; 1968 ch. 13). For the case of a negative bequest it turns out that, instead of parents endowing their heirs, children have to support their parents.

this particular case the decision-maker has some degree of concern for his children's (but not grandchildren's) welfare, but not for his parents' welfare, from whom he receives no bequest.[13]

The consequences of this assumption are the following: (*a*) there will be a continuity of consumption throughout the generations; and (*b*) the second generation will enjoy, in the case of a positive bequest, a higher standard of living. Our subject will hence try to maximize:[14]

$$U = \sum_{i=0}^{1} \left[e^{igR} \int_{iR}^{iR+T} e^{-\delta t} U(c_w(t)) dt \right],$$ (6.33)

since in the interval $(T, 2T)$ the dynasty will have e^{gR} households. This enables us to write the initial expenditure of the dynasty:[15]

$$c_w(0) = w_o \frac{\Sigma_{i=0}^{1} [e^{igR} \int_{iR}^{(1+i)R} e^{(m-r)t} dt] + p \Sigma_{i=0}^{1} [e^{igR} \int_{iR}^{iR+T} e^{(m-r)t} dt]}{\Sigma_{i=0}^{1} [e^{igR} \int_{iR}^{iR+T} e^{(g^*-r)t} dt]}$$

$$= w_o G \frac{r - g^*}{r - m}.$$ (6.34)

It is now easy to write the capital stock that our worker will have at $t = R$, i.e. just before retiring:[16]

$$k_w(R) = \frac{w_o}{r - m} [e^{rR} - e^{mR} + G(e^{g^*R} - e^{rR})],$$ (6.35)

from which we may deduce the discounted value (at $t = R$) of the consumption during his retirement $(R_w(R))$:

$$R_w(R) = \frac{w_o}{r - m} e^{rR} [G(e^{(g^*-r)T} - e^{(g^*-r)R}) + p(e^{(m-r)R} - e^{(m-r)T})],$$ (6.36)

so that we obtain $B(R)$, the amount of assets bequeathed to the second generation:

$$B(R) = w_o \frac{e^{rR}}{r - m} [1 - e^{(m-r)R} + G(e^{(g^*-r)T} - 1)$$

$$+ p(e^{(m-r)R} - e^{(m-r)T})].$$ (6.37)

[13] We assume that the decision-maker (or the founder of the dynasty) leaves his bequest at age $t = R$, i.e. when he retires and his children start a new household. The problem would not change, essentially, assuming that he leaves his bequest at any point of the interval (R, T) since we are assuming a perfect capital market.

[14] The subjective rate of consumption discount is supposed to remain constant throughout the generations.

[15] The procedure adopted in finding $c_w(0)$ is basically the same considered in Sect. 6.3.1.

[16] Recalling that, from (6.2) $c(t) = c(0)e^{g^*t}$, i.e.

$$c_w(t) = w_o e^{g^*t} \cdot G \cdot \frac{r - g^*}{r - m}, \text{ for } 0 \leq t \leq 2T.$$ (6.34′)

Since every individual has e^{gR} children, each of them will inherit an amount of assets equal to $b(R) = B(R)/e^{gR}$. As r is supposed to be greater than both g and m (the rate of growth of population and the rate of technical progress respectively) the sign of the bequest will depend on the sign of the expression between the square brackets of (6.37). If this expression is positive then the bequest will also be positive; if negative it will mean a zero bequest, since we have excluded the possibility of a negative bequest. Assuming, for example, the values of the parameters $g = m = 0.02$, $1 - a = 3$, $r = 0.06$, $\delta = 0.03$, $R = 40$ (years), and $T = 50$ (years), and, for the sake of simplicity, $p = 0$ (which means that there is no pension scheme), we obtain $G = 0.971$ and $c_w(0) = 1.21w_o$; this means that the worker would start by borrowing instead of saving. The same values give us the following value for the *total bequest* at $t = R$: $B(R) = -25.03$.

Hence, in this case, it turns out that the workers would not start by accumulating wealth. In other words the concept of 'altruism' for the workers' class would lead to the conclusion that no positive bequest is built up. (The same conclusion applies if we consider an infinite-time horizon, instead of a two-generation horizon as in this example. We do not reproduce here the analytical results since they would need too much space.) This result cannot compare with that derived in Sect. 5.9 above, since there we consider equilibrium values of the rate of interest with an initial positive bequest and a bequest utility function.

6.5 THE GOLDEN RULE PATH: SOME IMPLICATIONS

In this section we briefly discuss the Golden Rule Path using the theorem that consumption per capita is maximized, among states of balanced growth, when the profit rate r is equal to the overall rate of growth $n = g + m$. As we have already pointed out in Sect. 6.3.2 we know that, in equilibrium, the capitalists can enjoy a positive consumption only if r is greater than n. (It should be stressed that this is a tautological proposition about saving behaviour, not a golden rule theorem concerning technology.) Considering long periods of historical time, from an empirical point of view this is probably a reasonable assumption.

However it might happen that at some time the rate of profit equals the natural rate of growth. (Actually it may be lower; in general we shall confine ourselves to the case $r^* = n$.) In this case some basic hypothesis of our two-class model should be changed in order to let the capitalists consume a positive quantity of their income, given that in the steady-state they must let their assets grow at a rate $n = m + g$ and then transfer them to their children. More precisely the capitalists may react in one (or more) of the following ways:

1. They might decide to have fewer children. In this model the rate of growth of population of both classes has been considered as a para-meter. However there appears, now and then, in the economic literature trials to consider it as an endogenous variable. More precisely in most of these cases the rate of growth of population is considered as a function of the capital/labour ratio. It is then clear that if the capitalists (as well as the workers) make their decisions on the basis of life-cycle plans, then in this case the rate of growth of population would depend on the interest rate and on the wage rate.

2. They might decide to leave fewer assets to their children than the equilibrium value $k_o e^{nR}$, where k_o is the capital stock that they have inherited.

3. They might decide to work and earn a wage rate in order to supplement their property income.

When the latter applies the basic distinction between the two classes is directly affected and the difference between the two classes would consist in the fact that one class inherits and bequeaths assets, while the other does not. In any event the model would still be characterized by the presence of two socio-economic classes, where the 'bequest motive' is bound to draw a dividing line. When 1 and 2 apply it turns out that, in the very long run, the system ends up with only one class, i.e. the workers who are mixed income-earners.

6.6   CONCLUSION

In this chapter we have shown that one of the most important features of life-cycle models is that the saving rates of the socio-economic classes and the patterns of accumulation of capital are no longer simply a function of an exogenously given propensity to save, but in general are a function of all parameters (technical, behavioural, and demographic) of the model.

In this model the consequence of a change in the pure time-preference on the aggregate capital stock of each class, and hence of the whole system, is unambiguous. A lower (higher) rate of pure time-preference of both capitalists and workers will lead, other things being equal, to a system with a higher (lower) supply of savings.[17]

[17] This is not necessarily the case when the saving propensities are constant and exogenously given and there is a once-for-all change in the saving behaviour of one group. This is due to the fact that in the fixed-propensities-to-save model a change in the asset distribution between capitalists and workers would, under general conditions, exactly offset the corresponding change in the saving propensities. On this point see Britto (1968).

On the other hand it may be stressed that in the Kaldor–Pasinetti and Meade–Samuelson and Modigliani models it is not always true that a change in the saving propensity of just one class will modify the rate of return on capital, since each of the two roots $P/K = n/s_c$ and $P/K = nP/Y \cdot 1/s_w$ do not depend on both s_c and s_w, the fixed saving propensities of the two classes. The point is that in a life-cycle model which does not incorporate a bequest utility function (as it is the case of the preceding chapter) the equilibrium interest rate depends on all parameters of the model. The supply of savings has however to fulfil the requirements for steady-state growth dictated by the macro-economic framework as pointed out in the Introduction.

The discussion of the golden rule path of this specific case has also provided additional insight into the possible behaviour of the 'pure' profit-earners; in this case the role of the inter-generational bequest is bound to play a dividing line between the socio-economic classes.

Appendix 6.1

IN this Appendix we represent the consumption- and accumulation-plans of a rational worker and capitalist. Let us start considering the worker first, in the two cases of a positive and negative initial saving. Figure A6.1 shows the income- and consumption-plan of the human-capital-owner in both cases of an initial positive and negative saving. Figure A6.2 shows the capital accumulation (or disaccumulation) also for both cases. From the figures it is easy to deduce that (except for the very first years in the case of initial negative saving) the capital of a worker is always positive; it reaches its maximum at $t = R$ (just before the retirement) and approaches zero for $t \to T$.

The consumption- and accumulation-plans of the capitalist may be graphically represented as shown in Figures A6.3 and A6.4. Figure A6.3 shows (on log-scale) the optimal consumption path of the capitalist; Figure A6.4 shows his optimal accumulation of capital, starting from k_0 and leaving $k_0 e^{nR}$ to his children.

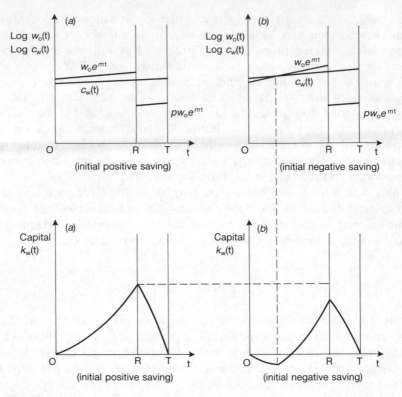

Figs. A6.1 and A6.2 Consumption- and Accumulation-Plans of the Worker

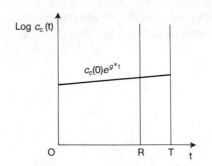

Fig. A6.3 Consumption-plan of the capitalist

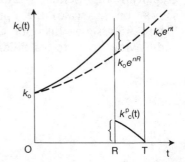

Fig. A6.4 Accumulation-plan of the capitalist

7
The Dynamic of Capital Accumulation in a Stochastic World

7.1 INTRODUCTION

The topic of this short chapter is only partially connected with the main argument of this volume, since it does not deal with the issue of profit determination and income distribution in a macro-economic framework. It is however connected with the issue of the dynamic of capital accumulation at the micro-level in a stochastic world. More precisely we shall be concerned with:

1. the dynamics of capital accumulation in a stochastic world where individuals or families have the choice between consumption and saving over a given time-horizon;
2. the choice of individuals or families with respect to the kind of financial investment chosen, i.e. risky or safe assets;
3. the conditions under which uncertainty, via the portfolio choice, may give rise to class differences, thus reinforcing the hypothesis of a society characterized by the presence of different socio-economic classes as in the case of the classical, post-Keynesian (as well as neoclassical) models of growth and income distribution analysed in the earlier chapters.

This chapter has a double purpose. First, that of expanding the analysis of the micro-foundations of the economic behaviour of individuals or families, with particular regard to their influence on long-term saving and consumption. Secondly—and this may seem more interesting in the context of our study—that of bringing closer the 'real' and 'monetary' research lines of the post-Keynesian research programme, which as we have pointed out, has concentrated on different topics; the former with particular reference to growth, income distribution, and capital accumulation, the latter with emphasis on the integration of money and uncertainty into the Keynesian framework.

We are well aware that this is only a first step in this direction, and that more effort will have to be made to formulate an exhaustive macro-economic framework which includes all elements of the two separate research lines.

After recalling the seminal contributions in the field of optimal portfolio choice, we shall spell out the basic assumptions of the stochastic model and consider the implications of the solutions obtained for the long-term consumption- and saving-path of the economic system and for the long-term rates of capital accumulation. It will then be interesting to consider the conditions under which a permanent class division may be generated, according to the different behaviour of individuals in the face of uncertainty. This may well, as stated earlier, reinforce the hypothesis of different socio-economic classes, even when taking into account a certain deal of inter-class mobility as postulated by Vaughan (1979).

The seminal papers by Tobin (1958) and Markowitz (1959) on efficient portfolios, i.e. those for which the expected value of return is maximized for each level of risk, have generated a substantial literature on the relationship between rate of return, risk for securities, and optimal investment behaviour. On this basis the selection of optimal portfolios may be reduced to the allocation of income between current consumption and savings, and to the allocation of accumulated savings between an efficient risky asset and a risk-free asset. We have taken up this issue because, although the fundamental and basic results have already been reached by Merton (1969, 1971) and Flemming (1974), the implications for long-term accumulation of capital and class distinction have not yet been fully considered, possibly because of a different focus of analysis.

Most models which consider the issue of optimal portfolios introduce the concept of risk-aversion (or risk-love) that individuals have *vis-à-vis* investment in risky assets; this concept is usually incorporated in the utility function. For instance Pratt (1964) states that if the amount invested in risky assets increases with wealth, the investor has decreasing absolute risk-aversion (and vice versa). On the other hand if the proportion of wealth invested in risky assets increases with wealth, the investor has decreasing relative risk-aversion (and vice versa). Later Tobin (1958) showed that in order to obtain utility indifference-curves yielding unique solutions to the choice between safe and risky assets, it was sufficient to use a monotonically increasing and strictly concave wealth utility-function.

The uncertainty structure (relative to the rate of return on the risky assets) that we introduce in this chapter is the so-called Markowitz–Merton–Flemming continuous-time optimal-portfolio approach where investment opportunities are stationary and consumption preferences are isoelastic. This assumption, as Flemming (1974, p. 137) has pointed out 'enormously simplifies the arguments—and the results'.

Merton (1969, 1971) considers a continuous-time consumption-portfolio problem for an individual whose income is generated by capital gains on investment in assets with prices assumed to satisfy the geometrian Brownian motion hypothesis and where the stationariness of the problem leads to (*a*) a policy of consuming at a rate proportional to wealth, and (*b*) an optimality of a constant portfolio composition.

In this way Merton's analysis (which has the merit of considering a finite time-horizon) yields explicit solutions for optimal consumption and portfolio composition.

Flemming's analysis (1974, p. 137) was motivated by the desire to 'present Merton's continuous time portfolio analysis in a form more accessible to those who, like the author, are intimidated by the terminology of stochastic processes and integrals'. By assuming an infinite time-horizon Flemming arrives at the same results as those obtained by Merton.

Our analysis will be based on the models of both Merton and Flemming; however we shall focus our attention on the consumption and mean accumulation rates of the rational agent. Moreover we shall consider in detail the influence of the variance and of the risk-aversion on all variables, deriving some results which have passed unnoticed in the previous literature.

The plan of the chapter is as follows. In Sect. 7.2 we study the various effects of interest uncertainty in a life-cycle model with portfolio choice. The basic assumptions of the model are specified in Sect. 7.2.1, while in the following Sect. 7.2.2 we define the optimal portfolio selection and its properties with particular reference to the variance of the interest rate and to the Arrow–Pratt relative risk-aversion measure. In Sect. 7.2.3 we study the value of the optimal consumption rate associated with the portfolio selection, while in the following paragraph we define the rate of growth of the mean wealth. In Sect. 7.3 we set out some numerical and graphical results, while an analysis of the long-term properties of the model will be given in Sect. 7.4. An appraisal of the relative risk-aversion measure will be provided in a final section.

7.2 THE MODEL OF OPTIMAL CONSUMPTION AND PORTFOLIO CHOICE

7.2.1 *The basic assumptions of the model*

In this section we provide a simple theoretical framework in which we explore the consequences of the introduction of interest uncertainty on the portfolio-, consumption-, and saving-plans of a rational agent.

For this purpose we shall assume the existence in the economy of two assets (or capital markets) in which the decision-making unit will be able to invest that part of financial assets which are not consumed; one asset will have a risky return, while the other will have a certain return.

Moreover we shall, as commonly postulated in the literature, disregard labour income (which, by the way, could be without much difficulty introduced into the model, but without much advantage).

In addition we will make the following assumptions:

1. *Time-horizon*. If uncertainty about the interest rate is introduced into a life-cycle model where individuals make their plans with a finite horizon, from an analytical point of view the problem is not easy to solve. Therefore, for the sake of simplicity, an infinite time-horizon is assumed; this is equivalent to considering an entire dynasty of rational consumers. The results do not however diverge from those obtained in a finite-horizon context (see Merton, 1969, 1971).

2. *Transaction costs*. They are not usually considered in this context; this simplifying assumption has the advantage of not complicating the mathematics any further.

3. *Utility function*. We shall use an additively separable utility function yielding constant relative risk-aversion of the form $U(c_t) = 1/a(c_t)^a$, where c_t is the consumption rate at time t. In this case the Arrow–Pratt relative risk-aversion measure is $R_R = 1 - a$. While most of the results of our analysis are valid for the more general case $a < 1$, we shall confine our analysis to the case $a < 0$, without much loss of generality.

It is assumed that the risky capital market has a serially independent random return $R(\theta)$ with positive mean $r\theta$ and finite variance $v\theta$ proportional to the period of holding θ (note that higher moments disappear in the limit since they are less than proportional to time θ, as described in the random-walk hypothesis considered for instance by Cootner; Wiener processes and Brownian motions conform to these requirements).

We can hence define for both capital markets:

$E(R(t)) = r(t)$, the rate of return on the risky capital stock with

$$\text{var}\, R(t) = v(t) > 0, \tag{7.1}$$

$E(i(t)) = i$, the rate of return on the safe capital stock, with

$$\text{var}\, i(t) = 0 \tag{7.2}$$

(also defined as the riskless rate of interest).

Note that the two assets could be, for instance, consols and money, or treasury bills and shares, or bonds and deposit accounts. Additionally throughout the analysis it is assumed that short sales are not allowed; this assumption is often introduced for the sake of mathematical simplicity.

We assume now that:

$z(t)$ is the constant proportion invested in risky assets, where

$$0 \leqslant z(t) \leqslant 1, \tag{7.3}$$

and

$1 - z(t)$ the constant proportion invested in safe assets, where

$$0 \leqslant 1 - z(t) \leqslant 1. \tag{7.4}$$

Hence a rational agent who, at time t_o, inherits a financial capital stock B_o, from which he will derive all his income, will make his plans in order to maximize, in continuous time, the flow of the discounted utilities from consumption. And since utility is, by definition, isoelastic and the investment opportunities themselves are stationary, the stationariness of the whole problem ensures the optimality of the policy of consuming at a rate proportional to total wealth (i.e. $c_t = cB_t$). Therefore the basic problem is:

$$\phi(B_t) = \underset{c,z}{\text{Max}} \int_0^\infty e^{-\delta t} U(c\widetilde{B}_t) dt, \tag{7.5}$$

where c is the constant proportion of capital consumed; z is the proportion of capital invested in risky assets (constant through time); δ is the subjective discount rate; B_t is the total financial capital stock at time t. Since the stochastic process of R has mean and variance proportional to time (as explained above), from the definition of the utility function we may rewrite relation (7.5) as follows:[1]

$$\phi(B_t) = \underset{c,z}{\text{Max}} \frac{1}{a} c^a B_o^a \int_0^\infty e^{(a[(1-z)i+zr-(1-a)z^2 \cdot v/2-c]-\delta)t} dt. \tag{7.6}$$

---

[1] This may be obtained considering the following discrete-time budget differential equation which is the generalization of the continuous-time budget equation under uncertainty (on this point see also Flemming, 1974, pp. 143–4):

$$dB = (1 - z)Bidt + zBdR - cBdt, \tag{a}$$

so that

$$d\left(\frac{1}{a} B^a\right) = B^a\left(\left[(1 - z)i - (1 - a)z^2 \cdot \frac{v}{2} - c\right]dt + zdR\right). \tag{b}$$

Hence:

$$\frac{d}{dt} E\left(\frac{1}{a} B^a\right) = E(B^a)\left[(1 - z)i + zr - (1 - a)z^2 \cdot \frac{v}{2} - c\right], \tag{c}$$

which yields:

$$E\left(\frac{1}{a} B^a\right) = \frac{1}{a} B_o^a e^{a[(1-z)i+zr-(1-a)z^2 \cdot v/2-c]t}, \tag{d}$$

Integrating (7.6) we obtain:[2]

$$\phi(B_t) = \underset{c,z}{\text{Max}} - \frac{1}{a} c^a B_o^a (a[[(1 - z)i + zr$$

$$- (1 - a)z^2 \cdot \frac{v}{2} - c] - \delta)^{-1}. \qquad (7.7)$$

7.2.2 The implications of the optimal portfolio selection

We have now to maximize relation (7.7) with respect to consumption, c, and the proportion of risky assets, z, held; this may be done by maximizing it with respect to z first. By setting:[3]

$$\frac{\partial \phi(B_t)}{\partial z} = r - i - zv(1 - a) = 0 \qquad (7.8)$$

and solving it with respect to z we obtain:[4]

$$z^* = \frac{r - i}{v(1 - a)} \quad (\text{where } 0 \leqslant z^* \leqslant 1). \qquad (7.9)$$

Relation (7.9) gives us the value of the optimal proportion of risky assets that our individual will hold in his portfolio. We note immediately that z^*, in this context, is independent of time, of the initial bequest B_o, and of the subjective discount rate δ.

This result is not original in the economic literature and was first formulated by Merton in his seminal paper of 1969, with the merit of considering a finite horizon with a positive final bequest. Then, a few years later, it was confirmed by Flemming (1974) who derived the same result by working in the context of an infinite time-horizon: we have followed here his analysis, of which we try below to analyse some implications with more attention.

Before deriving the consumption rate, c^*, it may be worth considering

and therefore

$$c^a \int_0^\infty e^{-\delta t} E\left(\frac{1}{a} B^a\right) dt = \frac{1}{a} c^a B_o^a \int_0^\infty e^{a[(1-z)i+zr-(1-a)z^2 \cdot v/2-c]-\delta)} dt. \qquad (e)$$

[2] Provided that:

$$\left(a\left[(1 - z)i + zr - (1 - a)z^2 \cdot \frac{v}{2} - c\right] - \delta\right) < 0 \qquad (7.7')$$

otherwise

$$\phi(B_t) = \underset{c,z}{\text{Max}} (- \infty); \qquad (7.7'')$$

we shall reconsider this condition in relation (7.17) below.

[3] The second-order condition is also satisfied, as $(1 - a)$ is always positive.

[4] An asterisk denotes optimal values.

the properties of z^*. In order to do this we differentiate it with respect to the individual parameters:

$$\partial z^*/\partial v = - \frac{r - i}{v^2(1 - a)} = -z^*/v < 0,$$ (7.10)

$$\partial z^*/\partial(1 - a) = - \frac{r - i}{v(1 - a)^2} = -z^*/(1 - a) < 0,$$ (7.11)

$$\partial z^*/\partial a = \frac{r - i}{v(1 - a)^2} = z^*/(1 - a) > 0,$$ (7.12)

$$\partial z^*/\partial r = \frac{1}{v(1 - a)} = z^*/(r - i) > 0,$$ (7.13)

$$\partial z^*/\partial i = \frac{-1}{v(1 - a)} = -z^*/(r - i) < 0.$$ (7.14)

These results may be interpreted in the following way. First we note that as v, the variance, increases, the proportion of risky assets decreases. This result is not surprising and confirms that risk and uncertainty discourage investment in risky assets. Secondly, from relation (7.10) we observe that an increase in relative risk-aversion leads to a decrease in the value of z^*. The results obtained in relations (7.13) and (7.14) are not surprising either: an increase in the mean rate of return of the risky capital increases z^*; while an increase in the rate of return of the safe capital tends to lower z^*.

Hence we observe that the proportion of risky assets held under optimality is an increasing function of their rate of return, while it diminishes with their riskiness.

7.2.3 The optimal consumption rate under uncertainty

Having examined the implications of the optimal portfolio selection we now turn our attention to the consumption rate, c^*. Differentiating relation (7.7) partially with respect to c we find the following first-order condition for a maximum:[5,6]

$$c^* = (1 - a)^{-1}\left(\delta - a\left[(1 - z^*) i + z^*r - (1 - a)z^{*2}\cdot\frac{v}{2}\right]\right),$$ (7.15)

i.e. since $z^* = (r - i)/v(1 - a)$,

$$c^* = (1 - a)^{-1}\left(\delta - ai - \frac{a(r - i)^2}{2v(1 - a)}\right).$$ (7.16)

---

[5] The second-order condition is also satisfied.

[6] This result was first given by Flemming (1974, p. 144, n. 13). He did not however focus on the implications of this relationship (nor on the rate of growth of the mean wealth) since he was more interested in the optimum portfolio choice problem, while we are more interested in the optimal accumulation rate.

We see that as long as a is negative c^* is always positive and never reaches zero (this is not the case when there exists a risky capital market only). Moreover we note that when the relative risk-aversion is equal to one (which implies $a = 0$), c^* equals the value of the pure time-preference; while as the risk-aversion tends to infinity c^* tends to i from above or below, depending on the value of the expression $2v(\delta - i) + (r - i)$ which we shall consider below.

We have thus obtained the consumption rate. We note that, like z^*, it is independent of time and of the size of the initial bequest. If we substitute this result in relation (7.7) above we obtain:

$$(1 - a)^{-1}\left(ai - \delta + \frac{a(r - i)^2}{v(1 - a)}\right) < 0 \qquad (7.17)$$

which, at least for negative values of a, is always true. Therefore we may conclude that the inequality expressed in (7.7′) is always satisfied, so that the validity (and uniqueness) of (7.15) is assured. We can now write the following relations:[7]

$$\partial c^*/\partial i = \frac{a}{1 - a}\left(\frac{r - i}{v(1 - a)} - 1\right) = \frac{a}{1 - a}(z^* - 1) \geq 0; \qquad (7.18)$$

$$\partial c^*/\partial r = -\frac{a}{1 - a}\frac{r - i}{v(1 - a)} = -\frac{a}{1 - a}z^* > 0; \qquad (7.19)$$

$$\partial c^*/\partial v = \frac{a(r - i)^2}{2v^2(1 - a)^2} = a(z^*)^2/2 < 0; \qquad (7.20)$$

$$\partial c^*/\partial \delta = 1/(1 - a) > 0; \qquad (7.21)$$

$$\partial c^*/\partial a = (1 - a)^{-2}\left[\delta - i - (1 + a)\frac{(r - i)^2}{2v(1 - a)}\right]. \qquad (7.22)$$

These results may be interpreted in the following way. An increase in both (mean) interest rates and in the subjective interest rate has a positive effect on consumption. The former is common to most stochastic and non-stochastic models; the latter confirms that an increase in pure impatience stimulates initial consumption. On the other hand we note that an increase in the variance of the risky asset has a negative effect on c^*. Broadly speaking these findings suggest that in this context, uncertainty (i.e. a positive variance) discourages consumption under optimality.

Relation (7.22) is more ambiguous and has no definite sign. To measure the influence of the elasticity of the utility function a on the consumption rate, we solve the right-hand side of relation (7.22) with

---

[7] Where we assume, as pointed out at the beginning, $a < 0$.

respect to a (which we continue to assume negative):[8]

$$\partial c^*/\partial a < 0 \text{ for } 2v(\delta - i) + (r - i)^2 < 0, \tag{7.23a}$$

$$\partial c^*/\partial a < 0 \text{ for } \frac{2v(\delta - i) - (r - i)^2}{2v(\delta - i) + (r - i)^2} < a < 0 \quad \left.\begin{array}{l} \\ \\ \text{for} \\ \\ 2v(\delta - i) + (r - i)^2 > 0. \end{array}\right.$$

$$\partial c^*/\partial a \geqslant 0 \text{ for } \frac{2v(\delta - i) - (r - i)^2}{2v(\delta - i) + (r - i)^2} > a \qquad \tag{7.23b}$$

The first conclusion to be drawn is that the above results are more complicated than those obtained in the corresponding stochastic model with a single risky capital market,[9] since they are associated with the value z^*, a function of the parameters r, i, v, and a.

We note that where $2v(\delta - i) + (r - i)^2 < 0$ an increase[10] in the relative risk-aversion measure has a positive effect on optimal consumption; this is specified in relation (7.23a). On the other hand when $2v(\delta - i) + (r - i)^2 > 0$ the consumption rate has a maximum for the value $a = a^+$ given in relation (7.23c). For lower values of a the derivative of c^* (with respect to a) is negative, while the opposite applies for higher values of a.

Then the intuitive deduction following which an increase in the relative risk-aversion should have a definite effect on consumption is, at least partially, removed. For as we see that it may happen that c^*,[11] as $1 - a = R_R(B)$ increases, is first stimulated, then attains a maximum before starting to decline. In Sect. 7.3, to gain some insight into the quantitative importance of the above results we shall give the value of c^* for several combinations of the parameters.

7.2.4 The optimal path of accumulation of capital with portfolio selection

In a stochastic model of economic growth the variables are clearly random variables whose probability varies with time. Since in this model

---

[8] We obtain $c^*(\text{max})$ for

$$a = a^+ = \frac{2v(\delta - i) - (r - i)^2}{2v(\delta - i) + (r - i)^2}, \tag{7.23c}$$

in relation with (7.23b).

[9] Cf. Baranzini (1977). In the case of a single risky capital market as the risk-aversion increases, optimal consumption is first increased, attains a maximum (for average values of the risk-aversion), and then decreases slowly reaching zero for high values of the risk-aversion.

[10] Note that for econometrically reasonable values of the parameters (7.23a) usually applies. Let $\delta = 0.03$, $i = 0.05$, $r = 0.06$, and $v = 0.005$; then we get $2v(\delta - i) + (r - i)^2 = -0.0001$ and therefore (7.23a) applies.

[11] In the particular case where $2v(\delta - i) + (r - i)^2 > 0$.

mean and variance are proportional to time and since the variance of the rate of return of the risky capital is positive, it only makes sense to discuss the expected (or average, or mean) value of future wealth of a rather large group of people (dynasty or class) since, as said, it is a function of a random variable.

Hence we write directly the rate of growth of the mean wealth as:[12]

$$g^* = (1 - z^*)i + z^*r - c^*, \tag{7.24}$$

i.e.

$$g^* = (1 - a)^{-1} \left[i - \delta + (2 - a) \frac{(r - i)^2}{2v(1 - a)} \right], \tag{7.25}$$

since $z^* = (r - i)/v(1 - a)$. Therefore the rate of growth of mean wealth is a function, *inter alia*, of the optimal portfolio. In this way the risk-aversion measure has a double effect on g^*: first on the consumption rate and secondly on z^*, so that the result obtained in relation (7.25) cannot be compared with the corresponding result obtained in the case of a single risky capital market.

We note that, again, g^* is independent of time and of B_o, the initial bequest. On the other hand it depends on all parameters of the model as follows:

$$\partial g^*/\partial i = (1 - a)^{-1} \left[1 - (2 - a) \frac{r - i}{v(1 - a)} \right], \tag{7.26}$$

$$\partial g^*/\partial r = (2 - a) \frac{r - i}{v(1 - a)^2} > 0, \tag{7.27}$$

$$\partial g^*/\partial v = -(2 - a) \frac{(r - i)^2}{2v^2(1 - a)^2} = -\frac{2 - a}{2} (z^*)^2 < 0, \tag{7.28}$$

$$\partial g^*/\partial \delta = -1/(1 - a) < 0, \tag{7.29}$$

$$\partial g^*/\partial a = (1 - a)^{-2} \left[i - \delta + (3 - a) \frac{(r - i)^2}{2v(1 - a)} \right] > 0, \tag{7.30}$$

as long as

$$2v(i - \delta) + (r - i)^2 > 0.^{13}$$

[12] Note that $0 \leqslant z^* \leqslant 1$. For empirical values of $z^* = (r - i)/v(1 - a)$ outside this range, we consider the upper (or lower) limit given and we retain relations (7.24) for g^* and (7.15) for c^*.

[13] Note that when $2v(i - \delta) + (r - i)^2 < 0$ (which is very unlikely to happen in the real world since the pure time-preference is usually lower than the interest rates in a life-cycle model) we would get $\partial g^*/\partial a > 0$ for:

$$\frac{2v(i - \delta) + 3(r - i)^2}{2v(i - \delta) + (r - i)^2} < a \text{ and } \partial g^*/\partial a < 0 \text{ for } a < \frac{2v(i - \delta) + 3(r - i)^2}{2v(i - \delta) + (r - i)^2}.$$

Three of the above results are unambiguous. Relation (7.27) shows that an increase in the mean risky rate of interest has a positive effect on g^*. On the other hand an increase in the variance and in the pure time-preference has a negative effect on g^*.[14]

We focus now on relation (7.28) which does not confirm the rather general proposition following which the variance has a positive effect on the rate of growth of the mean wealth. The outcome obtained here may be interpreted in the following way. As we have already pointed out, the value g^* is associated with z^*, the proportion of risky assets. But we see from relation (7.10) that the variance has a negative effect on z^*; more precisely $\partial z^*/\partial v = -z^*/v$, which is a very low value since v is very small. This behaviour of z^* at the end offsets the basic tendency of g^* to react positively to an increase in the variance (cf., for instance, Baranzini (1977)).[15]

Relations (7.26) and (7.30) are more ambiguous and need further investigation. Solving (7.26) with respect to v we have the signs:

$$\partial g^*/\partial i > 0 \quad \text{for} \quad v > (r - i)(2 - a)/(1 - a), \tag{7.31}$$

$$\partial g^*/\partial i \leq 0 \quad \text{for} \quad v \leq (r - i)(2 - a)/(1 - a). \tag{7.32}$$

Since the expression $(2 - a)/(1 - a)$ is always greater than unity, it is very unlikely that in the real world the variance of the rate of return r will be higher than $(r - i)(2 - a)/(1 - a)$, otherwise everybody would invest in the riskless asset. Therefore we may conclude that, in general, relation (7.32) applies: hence an increase in the rate of return of the riskless asset has a negative effect on the accumulation of capital. This result may be interpreted as follows: as i increases the proportion of risky assets held diminishes: this offsets the increase in the overall rate of return so that the rate of growth of capital tends to decrease.

Let us now consider relation (7.32). As already pointed out the partial derivative $\partial g^*/\partial a$ is positive as long as $2v(i - \delta) + (r - i)^2$ is positive: this is the case which is more likely to happen since in a life-cycle model δ, the pure time-preference should be lower than all mean interest rates. As a matter of fact in the case where the proportion of risky assets held is low, a pure time-preference higher than the riskless interest rate i would imply dissaving (or no accumulation of capital at all when dissaving is not permitted).

Hence in this model with portfolio choice the rate of growth of the mean wealth reacts positively to an increase in a, the elasticity of the

---

[14] Relations (7.27) and (7.28) are not surprising and their economic interpretation is straightforward.

[15] Note that these two effects (i.e. $\partial z^*/\partial v$ and $\partial g^*/\partial v$) play in opposite directions, and the average return on the portfolio is reduced by more than consumption per unit wealth.

utility function. In other terms g^* is a monotonic decreasing function of the risk-aversion measure $1 - a = R_R(B)$, at least under general conditions.

Therefore it is clear that in this context with portfolio choice more risk-aversion will lead to a lower mean accumulation; while in a model with risky assets only the opposite result applies (at least for high values of the risk-aversion). This difference may be related to the fact that g^*, the rate of accumulation of mean wealth with portfolio choice, is associated with z^* which is negatively correlated with the risk-aversion measure.

7.3   SOME COMPUTATIONAL RESULTS

To gain some insight into the quantitative importance of our findings the value of the optimal variables of the model, for several combinations of economically reasonable values of the parameters, is given in Tables 7.1

Table 7.1 Optimal portfolio (z^*), consumption (c^*), and mean accumulation (g^*) rates for different combinations of the risk-aversion measure when $\delta = 3\%$, $i = 5\%$, $r = 6\%$, and $v = 0.005$ (variables in percentages)

$1 - a = R_R(B)$	z^*	c^*	g^*	$i + z^*(r - i)$
1	100	3.00	3.00	6.00
2	100	4.25	1.75	6.00
3	67	4.56	1.11	5.67
4	50	4.69	0.81	5.50
5	40	4.76	0.64	5.40

with a the elasticity of the u-function $U(c_t) = \dfrac{1}{a}(c_t)^a$;

$\quad 1 - a = R_R(B)$ the Arrow–Pratt risk-aversion measure;
$\qquad \delta$ the subjective discount rate;
$\qquad i$ the rate of return on the risk-free assets;
$\qquad r$ the mean rate of return on the risky assets;
$\qquad v$ the variance of r;
$\qquad z^*$ the optimal proportion of risky assets held;
$\qquad c^*$ the optimal consumption rate;
$\qquad g^*$ the optimal rate of growth of the mean wealth.

Note: c^* and g^* are optimal values associated with z^*.

and 7.2 below. More precisely we focus our attention on the effects of the variance, v, and of the relative risk-aversion measure, $1 - a = R_R(B)$, on the optimal variables of the model. These effects will be easily deduced from Figures 7.1 and 7.2 that we give after the numerical tables.

In Table 7.1 we can observe the behaviour of the four optimal variables (portfolio, consumption, accumulation, and mean average return) as risk-aversion increases. We note that these parameters c^*, g^*, and z^* are very sensitive to changes in the low value range of the risk-aversion. Moreover, as $1 - a = R_R(B) \to \infty$, z^*, $g^* \to 0$ and $c^* \to i$ from below since there is no $c^*(\max)$.

In Table 7.2 we observe the behaviour of the variables as the variance of the risky rate of return changes; its effect is not definite: this may be observed on the rate of growth of mean wealth which first increases and then decreases as the risk-aversion increases, due to the fact that z^* cannot be higher than unity, a particularity that was not spotted in relation (7.20).

Figures 7.1 and 7.2 graphically illustrate these numerical results and give an easy representation of the behaviour of the variables c^*, g^*, and z^*, respectively optimal consumption, accumulation, and proportion of risky assets.

Table 7.2 Optimal consumption (c^*), and mean accumulation (g^*), rates for different combinations of the variance, $v(r)$,[1] when $\delta = 3\%$, $r = 6\%$, $i = 5\%$, and $(1 - a) = R_R(B) = 3$ (variables in percentages)[2]

$v(r)$	$(1 - a)^{+3}$	z^*	c^*	g^*	$c^*(1 - a)^+$	$g^*(1 - a)^+$
0.001	3.33	100	5.44	0.56	5.45	0.55
0.003	-4	100	4.70	1.30	-4	—
0.005	-4	67	4.56	1.11	-4	—
0.007	-4	48	4.49	0.99	-4	—
0.009	-4	37	4.46	0.91	-4	—
0.015	-4	22	4.41	0.81	-4	—

[1.] The list of symbols is given in Table 7.1 above.
[2.] All variables are associated with z^*, the optimal proportion of risky assets.
[3.] $a^+(c^*(\max))$, the value at which $c^*(\max)$ as shown in relation (7.23c).
[4.] $2v(\delta - i) + (r - i)^2 < 0$ and hence no $c^*(\max)$.

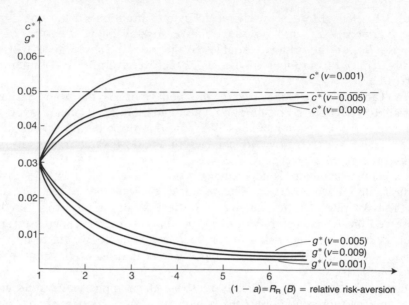

Notes: 1. The list of symbols is given in Table 7.1 above.
2. For very high values of the relative risk-aversion all c^* curves approach i asymptotically, while all g^* curves approach zero.

Fig. 7.1 The behaviour of optimal consumption (c^*) and optimal accumulation (g^*) as the risk-aversion $(1 - a) = R_R(B)$ and variance $v(r)$ change when $\delta = 3\%$, $i = 5\%$, and $r = 6\%$

7.4   THE LONG-TERM PROPERTIES OF THE MODEL

Armed with the results obtained in the previous sections we are now in a position to analyse the effects of interest uncertainty and risk-aversion on the distribution of financial wealth among classes of individuals sharing a common behaviour. More precisely we shall focus on a particular long-term property of the model and show that, under some fairly general and realistic conditions, as the generations pass the economy tends to converge towards a two-class society, where one class has a high ever-increasing capital per capita and the other a much lower one. For the sake of completeness we shall compare this outcome, obtained in the case of a mixed capital market, with that expounded in Baranzini (1977, pp. 418–21) in which only a risky capital market is assumed.

The main argument of this section is fairly straightforward and is based on the assumption that the relative risk-aversion $(1 - a = R_R(B))$ is a decreasing function of the financial wealth owned by a rational individual. (In other words a wealthy individual is supposed to be more

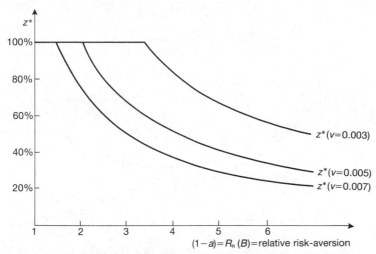

Note: The list of symbols is given in Table 7.1 above.

Fig. 7.2 The behaviour of the optimal proportion of risky assets (z^*) as the risk-aversion $(1 - a) = R_R(B)$ and the variance $v(r)$ change for $i = 5\%$ and $r = 6\%$

of a risk-taker than a less wealthy individual.) The dynamic element of the argument is represented by the presence in the economy of closed dynasties or families of wealth-owners which through the generations accumulate or disaccumulate the wealth of their initial founder.[16] Of course these dynasties also consume a part of this wealth (and its interest) following the optimal consumption plan expounded in Sect. 7.2 above.

Hence it is not unrealistic to assume that the dynasties of wealth-owners revise periodically (for instance with each new generation) their consumption- and savings-plans according to the size of the bequest that they have inherited. (Note that the concept of financial wealth could be easily extended to include human capital as well, in order to consider income from work and from capital.)

The dynamics of the process may be observed in Figure 7.3, in which we assume a constant rate of the growth of population g_e, and average values of the parameters (i.e. $\delta = 0.03$, $i = 0.05$, $r = 0.06$, and

---

[16] The relevance of the concept of family or dynasty in the process of wealth accumulation (or maintenance) is discussed by Phelps Brown (1988, pp. 394–464) in his chapter on 'The Formation and Distributions of Income and Wealth'. Social status and political influence are often elements which determine a coordinated long-term behaviour of successive generations.

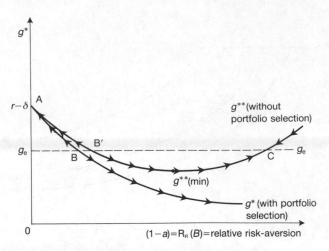

where: g^* is the rate of growth of mean wealth with portfolio selection;
        g^{**} is the rate of growth of mean wealth without portfolio selection;
        g_e is the constant rate of growth of population;
        $r - \delta$ is the value of g^* and g^{**} for $(1 - a) = R_R(B) = 1$.

Fig. 7.3 The dynamics of the accumulation process under uncertainty with and without portfolio choice and under the hypothesis of decreasing relative risk-aversion

$v = 0.005$). In the case of a double capital market the optimal rate of growth of the mean wealth is g^* and for all points to the left of B the dynasties are initially little risk-averse and hence, following the optimal plan described in the previous sections, will accumulate at a rather higher rate, certainly higher than the rate of the growth of population. As time passes these dynasties, by increasing their per capita wealth, will become less risk-averse so increasing their accumulation rate further and converging towards point A, where the maximum rate of growth of mean wealth will be reached for the value $r - \delta$ (greater than g_e).

The opposite will happen to those who start off under the g_e-line: they accumulate at a rate which is too low, so becoming increasingly more risk-averse. The point is that, in the very long-run, the fraction of capital stock per person (owned by the dynasties starting off below the g_e-line) becomes zero, which of course does not mean that they own no financial capital at all. So, in the very long run and under the assumption specified above, we would end up with a two-class society: one class with a large, ever-increasing financial bequest per capita and another class with an irrelevant bequest per capita.

Let us now consider the case of a unique and risky capital market, where by definition $z^* = 1$ for all levels of risk-aversion and which corresponds to the model expounded in Baranzini (1977). Here the mean rate of growth of wealth, g^{**}, as shown in Figure 7.3, is high for low values of risk-aversion; as risk-aversion increases g^{**} first decreases, attains a minimum (always positive) for average values of risk-aversion, and then tends to increase again for high values of risk-aversion. Hence in this model with a unique and risky capital market we would end up with a different two-class society from the one described above: here one class would have a relatively small (but positive) bequest per capita (those converging towards point C, who will be rather risk-averse), while the other class would end up with a much larger bequest per capita (those converging towards point A, who will be little risk-averse).

The point is that for both cases (i.e. with and without portfolio selection) uncertainty seems to be an element capable of generating class distinction in terms of wealth. It should however be stressed that these results are based on the following three assumptions:

1. The rate of growth of population must be *higher* than g^{**} (min) (see Figure 7.3) and *lower* than $r - \delta$ (where r is the mean rate of return on the risky asset and δ is the subjective discount rate), a very reasonable assumption indeed. If the first condition were not satisfied in the case of a unique and risky capital market we would end up with one class only (of very rich people). If the second condition were not satisfied we would end up with a one-class society characterized by a very low accumulation of capital.

2. The rate of growth of population is assumed constant and homogeneous for all dynasties, and the rate of growth of their wealth does not affect it at all.

3. Dynasties here are supposed to be inter-generationally stable; however, in the long run, the relaxation of this assumption should not have too great an effect on the results obtained.

It should be pointed out that in the long run a third class may be added to those generated by the uncertainty of the capital market. As a matter of fact one may well postulate that there exists a class or a group of people who do not inherit non-human wealth, and/or do not plan to leave any bequest to the next generation(s), and/or are not in a position to accumulate financial (or other non-human) means in excess of their life-cycle savings. The analysis in Chapters 5 and 6 has highlighted the conditions under which classes or dynasties cannot, in an equilibrium situation, hold inter-generational assets. On the other hand in the case of portfolio choice this bequestless class would be rejoined by dynasties starting off with a positive (average or small) inter-generational capital stock on the right-hand side of point B of Figure 7.3.

Thus, at the end of our journey, we rejoin the old classical, post-Keynesian, and neo-Ricardian proposition of a society characterized by the presence of different socio-economic classes (with different propensities to consume, to save, and to accumulate), but with a different perspective. As a matter of fact our results are the outcome of optimal behaviour, whereas in the above-quoted frameworks it is an assumption.

7.5   THE PROCESS OF WEALTH ACCUMULATION AND THE MEASURE OF RELATIVE RISK-AVERSION

A number of arguments put forward above have been expounded on the assumption that the level of relative risk-aversion $R_R(B)$ decreases with the amount of the wealth held by a dynasty. This assumption, which has been used in a large number of analyses, is in accordance with intuition and was in particular confirmed by the work of Cohn, Lewellen, Lease, and Schlarbaum (1975) who explicitly concluded that the Arrow–Pratt measure of attitude toward risk called relative (or proportional) risk-aversion declines as wealth increases across households. There is, in addition, a large collection of data showing that, in general, the proportion of risky assets[17] held is higher for large estates (see, for example, Flemming and Little (1974, p. 19)[18] and Phelps Brown (1988, p. 457)).[19]

In recent years at least two analyses have appeared which seem to challenge this commonly held view, the first by Friend and Blume (1975) and the second by Siegel and Hoban (1982). In the latter, for instance, it is argued that the study of Cohn, Lewellen, Lease, and Schlarbaum (which, as we said, concludes that households exhibit decreasing relative risk-aversion) 'is limited, however, in three respects: (1) their sample is from a highly selected population (customers of a large brokerage firm); (2) they measured wealth as total marketable

---

[17] Riskless assets are defined as financial assets which 'have certainty of nominal value' (Siegel and Hoban, 1982, p. 486): cash, deposit account balances, and savings bonds are typical riskless assets held by households. Marketable risky assets may be converted into cash at any time, but at an uncertain price and include stocks, bonds, mutual funds, and loans held.

[18] Flemming and Little (1974, p. 19) give the following figures for the most important risky asset: *Estimated Composition of Individuals' Wealth Holdings, Great Britain, 1971*

Wealth Range £000s	Shares (%)
under 10	2.3
10–15	6.5
15–20	12.1
20–50	23.4
50–100	43.8
100–200	51.9
200+	51.6

[19] 'In British personal wealth in 1976 . . . stocks and shares formed 12 per cent of all holdings, but 42 per cent of the biggest' (Phelps Brown, 1988, p. 457).

assets rather than as net worth; and (3) they did not adjust their risk-aversion measure for taxes' (Siegel and Hoban, 1982, p. 481). Such drawbacks were, according to Siegel and Hoban, avoided by the study of Friend and Blume (1975) who: (*a*) developed a theoretical model from which they were able to derive an estimate equation for the coefficient of the relative risk-aversion of households; (*b*) were able to use net worth as their wealth variable; and finally (*c*) incorporated non-marketable assets (i.e. human capital) into a global measure of wealth (the sum of net worth and non-marketable assets). The contribution of Siegel and Hoban (1982) is grafted on to the model of Friend and Blume mainly by eliminating the interaction of age and wealth effects. As the authors point out:

The division of total resources into net worth and nonmarketable wealth is age dependent. Retired people have no capitalized labour income, and presumably low nonmarketable wealth. A young person, in contrast, is likely to have high nonmarketable wealth and low marketable wealth. By restricting the analysis to a single cohort, households with males between the ages of 50 and 64 in 1971, the impact of age differences is reduced in this study. Furthermore, this age group probably have translated their risk preferences into observable patterns of wealth accumulation while younger cohorts have not (Siegel and Hoban, 1982, p. 482).

Starting from these considerations Siegel and Hoban develop their own model and conclude by stating that:

By restricting the data and procedures to conform to those used by the previous researchers, this research reaffirms their results. However, when these restrictions are removed different conclusions are reached. If wealth is defined narrowly, RRA [relative risk-aversion] is seen to increase for less wealthy households probably because their repayment of debt dominates their acquisition of risk assets. For higher wealth households, the opposite phenomenon is seen. When housing is included in net worth, increasing RRA is observed for both the lower wealth and higher groups. When the measure of wealth is expanded to include both net worth and nonmarketable assets, RRA again is seen to increase with wealth. Hence, increasing relative risk aversion, rather than the constant relative risk aversion used as an assumption in a number of theoretical models of decreasing relative risk aversion, would appear to have the most empirical support (Siegel and Hoban, 1982, p. 485).

We want however to argue that the results obtained by Siegel and Hoban do not necessarily invalidate the conclusions that we have drawn from the analysis above and concerning the long-term dynamics of the accumulation process under uncertainty and its role for the generation of different economic classes. This may be explained on the basis of the following considerations. First the above-quoted analyses do not consider the role of consumption of households (or dynasties): as illustrated by Table 7.2 and Figure 7.1 (where the rate of optimal consumption (c^*) and optimal accumulation (g^*) are expressed as a percentage of the total marketable wealth of the dynasty) the absolute level of consumption depends on the level of wealth. By postulating that consumption increases at a lower rate than accumulated wealth (and hence indirectly at a lower rate than global disposable income) it follows that relative risk-aversion must decrease as wealth increases through a higher rate of accumulation g^*. Otherwise one would have to postulate that consumption increases more than proportionally (and saving less than proportionally) as wealth and disposable income rise, as it would be in the case of increasing relative risk-aversion (with respect to wealth).

A second element which seems to suggest a decreasing relative risk-aversion concerns the inclusion of human capital in the above-quoted works of Friend and Blume (1975) and Siegel and Hoban (1982). As a matter of fact when one considers, as in the models of this chapter, the long-term inter-generational transmission of wealth (and the way in which it is accumulated) one should not include in the same terms human capital, which cannot be transferred to the next generation in the same way as financial or marketable wealth in general. (One could, of course, take into account the financial effort made by parents for their children's education, but this has not been taken into account here.) For this reason we should retain here the results of the analyses previous to those of Friend and Blume which indicate, in general, a decreasing relative risk-aversion.

The third reason for retaining the hypothesis of decreasing relative risk-aversion is that risk-aversion probably tends to increase over the life-cycle, as it has been observed that mature and retired people prefer to invest in safe assets so avoiding risks. Since middle-aged and retired persons, as the life-cycle theory explains, tend to own higher financial resources than younger ones, this element might be relevant in explaining why, within the same socio-economic group, relative risk-aversion increases with wealth. From the point of view of the long-term accumulation of capital and of its inter-generational transfer this element tends to disappear since younger generations are more numerous than older ones.

These three aspects of the inter-generational transfer of wealth make the hypothesis of decreasing risk-aversion more realistic; and in such a way the endogenous generation of different financial classes would be maintained. However, even in the case of increasing relative risk-aversion with wealth (as postulated by the four authors quoted above) such an endogenous explanation of different classes would remain.

This may be observed in Figure 7.4 in which we have reproduced the dynamics of the accumulation process under uncertainty with and without portfolio choice and under the hypothesis that relative risk-aversion

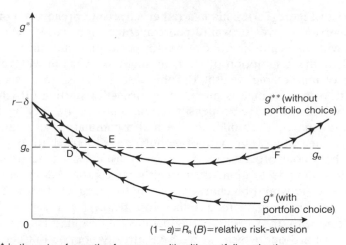

where: g^* is the rate of growth of mean wealth with portfolio selection;
g^{**} is the rate of growth of mean wealth without portfolio selection;
g_e is the constant rate of growth of population;
$r - \delta$ is the value of g^* and g^{**} for $(1 - a) = R_R(B) = 1$, i.e. for a unitary relative risk-aversion;

Fig. 7.4 The dynamics of the accumulation process under uncertainty with and without portfolio choice and under the hypothesis of increasing relative risk-aversion

increases as wealth grows; so that on the left-hand side of the graph we find poor dynasties and on the right-hand side wealthier ones. (Note also that all remaining hypotheses, already expounded in connection with Figure 7.3, are maintained here as well.) We note immediately that in the case in which individuals have to choose between consumption or investing in some form of risky assets, two distinct groups of wealth-owners are generated in the long run. The first one will be made up by small-wealth-owners (those on the left-hand side of point E) who, under the hypothesis of increasing risk-aversion, will progressively save a lesser amount and slowly converge towards point E characterized by a rather low wealth per capita, according to the mean rate of return of the risky assets and to its variance. Towards the same point E will converge all dynasties characterized initially by an average level of risk-aversion and whose mean wealth grows at a rate lower than g_e (the constant rate of growth of population); their wealth will progressively become less important until its mean rate of growth will reach, at the point E, the value g_e thanks to a lower level of risk-aversion in the investment process. In this way, and in the long run, if the three conditions discussed at the end of the previous paragraph hold, the dynasties belonging to the medium-wealth group will end up with the same wealth per capita held by the initially low-wealth dynasties considered before (point E of Figure 7.4). This is a rather surprising process of concentration/dispersion of wealth where poor, average, and fairly rich dynasties end up with the same amount of wealth per capita; and this outcome is ensured by the assumption of an increasing risk-aversion with respect to the size of marketable wealth. But this case gives rise to a second class of wealth-owners, which is made up by dynasties starting off (thanks to their lower than average propensity to consume) with a very high capital per capita (maybe the upper decile) and accumulating at a rate higher than g_e, the rate of growth of population supposed to be constant during the whole process. In this case dynasties will tend to increase, generation after generation, their wealth per capita. Adding up, in this case the society would be characterized by two distinct classes of wealth-owners: the first one with a rather low bequest per capita, and the second one with an ever-increasing bequest per capita. To this class we may add a third one which, as we have already pointed out above, may correspond to those dynasties not in a position (or not willing) to pass on financial or real wealth to their children.

We may now consider the case (illustrated again in Figure 7.4) with portfolio selection, for which analytical solutions for the mean accumulation rate have been set forth at the beginning of this section. Apparently in this case uncertainty is bound to generate one class only of capital-owners. On the one hand dynasties starting off with a low capital per capita (on the left-hand side of D) slowly converge towards D where the rate of growth of mean wealth is equal to the constant rate of growth of population, so that wealth per capita remains steady at a low but positive value, depending on the value of the parameters considered. On the other hand richer dynasties—and in this case quite risk-averse by hypothesis, due to an initial low propensity to invest in risky assets— register too low an accumulation of mean wealth and, in the long run, their offspring will be endowed with smaller and smaller estates. During this process of dispersion of wealth, these dynasties, by hypothesis, become increasingly less risk-averse and, consequently, accumulate at a faster rate so that they eventually converge towards the point D where their wealth per capita remains constant through time. In this way uncertainty tends to generate a unique class of (positive) wealth-owners; but to this class we may again and realistically add the bequestless class, made up of households which explicitly choose to save exclusively for life-cycle purposes and not for inter-generational transfer of wealth (and a class which cannot be easily introduced into the stochastic model expounded above).

Hence even in a model where—according to the findings of Siegel and Hoban (1982)—it is assumed that households exhibit increasing risk-aversion with respect to wealth-holding, uncertainty is bound to generate a multi-class society. This is obvious in the case of a unique (and risky) capital market, while it is less evident, but still true, in the case of a double capital market.

7.6 CONCLUSION

In this chapter we have studied the effects of interest uncertainty on the variables of a stochastic life-cycle model with portfolio selection (where individuals may invest their savings on safe or risky assets), by focusing our attention on the rate of growth of mean wealth and on the long-term implications of the model on the distribution of wealth among individuals or groups. (The model of uncertainty chosen is that of Markowitz–Merton–Flemming formulated in the late 1960s and early 1970s.) Among other things our analysis has shown that the variance of the risky rate of return has a negative effect on the optimum accumulation of wealth, while, at least for reasonable values of the parameters, risk-aversion has a negative effect on the rate of growth of mean wealth.

Looking at the above results from a historical point of view in order to throw some light on the different patterns of accumulation of capital, we have shown that (under the realistic assumption, for our model, of decreasing risk-aversion with the amount of wealth) in the case of a double capital market uncertainty may contribute to generating a two-class society. In fact, other things being equal, one class should end up with a very high capital stock per capita, while the other would register an accumulation rate which decreases continuously with time.

Uncertainty also tends to generate (or to perpetuate) a two-class society in a model considering only risky assets (and no safe investment); but while here one class ends up with quite a large amount of financial stock per capita, the other class with an initial average or high risk-aversion reaches a constant mean accumulation rate (equal to the rate of growth of population) so endowing their children with a fixed and limited amount of marketable wealth. Finally we have shown that even in the quite unlikely case of increasing risk-aversion with the amount of wealth, uncertainty is bound to generate or perpetuate a two- or multi-class society. On the relevance of these results, and on their capacity to throw light on the actual patterns of accumulation of wealth in industrial societies, we shall return in the final chapter. We might however recall that the main purpose of this chapter was not that of studying the patterns of income distribution in a macro-economic framework, but more simply that of enquiring into the possible generation or perpetuation of endogenous socio-economic classes by interest uncertainty within the Markowitz–Merton–Flemming model. In this specific case uncertainty tends to lead to less ambiguous results than in the case of a number of stochastic models, and the conclusions yield additional insights into the long-term process of wealth accumulation (or dispersion).

We may conclude by emphasizing that the process of wealth accumulation (including human capital in a more comprehensive model) may also be studied in this context by assigning to different groups a specific rate of growth of population or specific investment opportunities. But in this case the 'endogenous explanation' of different patterns of wealth accumulation would have a more restricted value.

8
Main Conclusions and Perspectives for Further Enquiry

8.1 AIM OF THE RESEARCH PROGRAMME AND METHODOLOGY CHOSEN

The aim of this last chapter is essentially threefold. First of all we want to give an assessment of the methodology used for seeking answers to the questions outlined in Chapter 1. Secondly, and this will be the main theme of this chapter, we want to draw together and assess the main conclusions of the research programme and to point out the implications of the results obtained by providing an economic and possibly historical interpretation. Thirdly and finally, we shall try to make some suggestions for an extension of the research programme, since we are well aware of the incompleteness of the answers that we have provided and of the necessity to explore alternative and more sophisticated grounds of study. We shall fuse these three objectives in the present and following three sections, since they are closely connected with one another.

First of all let us reconsider the methodology and the technique adopted in framing and solving our task, a way of proceeding which is often used in complex (but not necessarily difficult) issues. We first considered the compatibility between two different theoretical approaches (the life-cycle model which has been encapsulated into the post-Keynesian macro-model of distribution and accumulation); then we first set up a very simple two-period model (without technical progress, pension rate, and so on, and with just one member for each socio-economic class—distinguished here on the basis of the composition of their income) including most of the main issues in which we are interested, i.e. the patterns of income distribution, capital accumulation, and the mechanisms of class differentiation.

In this first framework, thanks to the relative simplicity of the model we are analysing, we derive a number of basic results (which generality is later confirmed in most cases) and try to capture some further implications of the problem. In this way the line of research becomes a thread much easier to evaluate and to follow in order to acquire additional insights. For instance we are able to write down explicitly the value of the equilibrium interest rate (on which, for obvious reasons, we focus part of our attention), and on the other equilibrium variables of the model whose properties are studied in detail. This approach, among other things, enables us to compare the results obtained with those formulated in the classical post-Keynesian as well as neoclassical models which do not include some sort of micro-foundations. On the other hand it is also possible to compare a number of the results obtained in the traditional life-cycle saving- and consumption-models, without class distinction, with those of our model which includes a socio-economic class division. In this way the relevance and significance of such class distinction may be appreciated.

It is worth pausing for a moment on the strategy followed in order to reach the results obtained, a strategy which may well be altered or even reversed in future research programmes. Individuals, during the first part of their life-cycle, may choose to allocate their income to consumption, life-cycle savings, or the next generation (the latter decision may be taken later on in the life-cycle). Additionally in the case of the 'pure' profits earners, there is a unique rate of interest (a) which they earn on their inter-generational and life-cycle savings, (b) which optimize their consumption and saving plans (on the basis of a given utility function), and (c) which ensures an equilibrium growth of their inter-generational capital stock, so making certain a steady-state growth of the system. Hence on the basis of such simultaneous constraints we are able to define the equilibrium and optimal distribution of income and to study the properties and the patterns of wealth accumulation. Note that this strategy implies that equilibrium and optimal positions are reached (at least for the entrepreneurs' class) and maintained in the long run—a condition that might seem rather restrictive, but which represents an exclusive and precious tool of analysis and which seems to be justified by the convergence analysis.

As pointed out earlier alternative strategies may be chosen. One may, for instance, postulate a certain relationship between the life-cycle and the inter-generational capital stock, perhaps associated with a given composition of income or a given socio-economic status. However, this approach would have the drawback of leading to an almost constant process of development and would not allow for differentiation among the classes other than the life-cycle savings/long-term capital stock ratio. Another strategy, quite common in neoclassical models, would consist in assuming constant factor shares instead of a fixed capital/output ratio and by considering the bequest as exogenously given and not determined via a bequest utility function. Other approaches would still be possible, and the rather large literature shows a variety of methods of analysis in this field. However, it seems to us that the two major constraints associated with the post-Keynesian framework (i.e. that of a constant capital/output ratio and of the presence of a class of 'pure' capitalists in the system) are amongst the least restrictive and have allowed us to expound in detail the mechanisms of long-term capital accumulation which would not necessarily have been observable with other kinds of methods of analysis.

Additionally, one should not overlook the fact that our analysis, both in a deterministic and stochastic framework, has confirmed the existence in the system of long-term mechanisms which maintain and in certain cases lead to the formation of different classes. In other terms the cycle of analysis seems to be complete, since the outcome, in general terms, has confirmed the validity of one of the most important hypotheses of most classical and Keynesian models of distribution, i.e. the presence of different socio-economic classes with different compositions of income and wealth and different propensities to allocate disposable income.

As it might be observed the methodology and the choice and relevance of the constraints and hypotheses, together with the specific goals of the analysis, all play an important role. On the other hand alternative goals would require a change of strategy as we shall see.

The initial rigidity of our strategy (see Chapter 5) was of course relaxed after the initial stage. In this perspective the next step consisted in lifting a crucial (as well as implicit) assumption of most classical and post-Keynesian models of distribution that the workers' or 'pure' consumers' class does not hold inter-generational assets, but only life-cycle savings, and analysing the implications of this relaxation. (One might note that the original models of distribution of Ricardo, Kaldor, and Robinson do not even allow the workers to accumulate life-cycle savings, while in those formulated by Pasinetti, Meade, Samuelson, and Modigliani both classes save and earn a rate of interest on their savings. The assignment of inter-generational capital to all classes of the model seems to represent a further generalization of the model.) The results obtained provide us with a more flexible and exhaustive picture of the historical reasons which determine the long-term economic strength of the socio-economic classes and of the conditions for which one class may come to modify its relative position.

Some of the insights derived within the two-period model are somewhat limited by its specific framework. However, it should be pointed out that some (if not most) problems are more easily dealt with, and comprehended, in a more general framework and that some difficulties associated with particular cases become easier to treat in a slightly more general context. Some of the limitations of our two-period model may for instance be inferred from the numerical examples that have been provided. It is worth performing such calculations to observe the basic behaviour of the variables, even if the absolute values are not always realistic in empirical terms.

These are the reasons why in a further step we consider a fully fledged continuous-time model where we introduce more realistic assumptions and parameters like technical progress, a pension rate during an extended retirement period, and so on, in order to refine the whole framework. In so doing we necessarily lose some of the simplicity of the previous model and, for instance, we cannot formulate an explicit expression for the equilibrium interest rate; but on the other hand we have the advantage of being able to define more realistically, and to study, most of the equilibrium variables with greater accuracy (like the consumption-, saving-, and accumulation-plans of the dynasties and classes). The first implication of this approach consists in an improvement of the qualitative value of some of the results obtained.

It is at this stage that we are in a position to test modifications of three original assumptions, i.e. the existence of different rates of return on the savings of the two classes (an interesting hypothesis in a two-class growth model, which has already drawn a good deal of attention in the literature) and the possibility of a different rate of bequest discount for the classes, meaning that the dynasties, according to their source of income, exhibit an unequal propensity to endow their children and grandchildren with a bequest. (We also consider the case of a different consumption utility function for the socio-economic classes, although this possibility seems less justifiable.) We may note that in these special cases the framework of the model remains basically the same; but the results obtained give us an elucidation of the implications associated with the introduction of market imperfections, and/or of different utility functions into an integrated consumers' model.

Finally, we introduce uncertainty into a simplified model of consumption and accumulation. This assumption needs a much simpler framework, due to the analytical difficulties associated with stochastic processes. However, the approach used must reflect the general methodology used in the preceding deterministic analysis. Of the various kinds of uncertainty we have retained the one relative to interest-uncertainty because it fits better into the framework of capital accumulation chosen, while the models developed by Merton and Flemming provide an excellent support for our study on the long-term consumption- and saving-plans of families. The results obtained throw additional light on the behaviour of consumers and, more importantly, on the process of capital accumulation. In particular they show that in the very long run the system may explain the evolution towards a two-class (or multi-class) society of financial-capital-owners.

In general the interpretation of the analytical results obtained has been fairly simple, even in the case of complicated analytical expressions. This is due to the fact that, in these cases, the strength of certain elements is much greater than that of others; additionally the chain of causality in the decisional process of individuals and in other processes had been identified with exactitude beforehand; in this way the interpretation of the analytical results has been easier. (First- and second-order derivatives help considerably in most cases.) In other cases the results obtained have been more ambiguous, but an analysis of the possible reasons for this has in most cases been provided. We would like, however, to emphasize once again that in this framework of analysis it is far more important to understand the chain of causality of the process of accumulation than simply to derive a number of analytical results.

8.2 PERSONAL AND FUNCTIONAL DISTRIBUTION OF INCOME AND WEALTH

8.2.1 An appraisal of the long-term hypotheses of our framework of analysis

Throughout this volume we have made a limited reference to the possible links between personal and functional (i.e. relative to factors of production or, in this case, to specific socio-economic classes) distribution of income and wealth. We have also provided little or no reference to the empirical evidence of historical accumulation and distribution of wealth (both life-cycle and inter-generational). This is to be connected with the main objective of our research programme, which is that of studying the laws of functional distribution of wealth in a growth context especially with respect to the long-term transmission of dynastic wealth and to a model based on micro-economic foundations.

This element must however be integrated with the mechanisms which, both in a deterministic and stochastic context, might contribute directly or indirectly to the maintenance and even to the generation of different socio-economic classes. (These two qualifications of the whole model are equally relevant.) In order to do this, not surprisingly we had to formulate a number of restrictive assumptions, not unusual in a long-term context. In this section we shall first consider the relevance of the particular assumptions made (and of their role in the general patterns of the whole process of growth) and then the links between personal and functional distribution of wealth with the aim of providing a much wider historical perspective for our research programme.

There is a precise reason for first considering the relevance of the most important assumptions formulated throughout most of the analysis, and in particular in Chapter 7, on the role of interest-uncertainty in the process of accumulation; in fact they do not only refer to the process of concentration or of dispersion of economic power (i.e. of income and both types of wealth) but they are at the very basis of all growth models considering multiple aspects of economic growth. In particular we shall refer to the role of a constant rate of growth of population, to the fact that such a rate of population growth must be neither too high nor too low, and to the inter-generational stability of dynasties.

The rate of growth of population. We have postulated that the rate of growth of population (both the growth rate of the working population and that of the wealth-owning population depending on the nature of the model) is equal for all socio-economic classes, and exogenously given, i.e. unaffected by economic changes. As pointed out by Meade a variation in the standard of living (thanks to a change in disposable income both from work and accumulated savings or inherited assets)

might affect the growth rate of population either through its effect upon mortality or through its effect upon fertility or through both influences. Suppose that a low standard of living led to malnutrition and that this caused (i) a higher incidence of disease and death and (ii) a lower biological fecundity among women. Then a fall in the standard of living would tend to raise death rates and lower birth rates and this in turn would tend to lower the rate of growth of population (Meade, 1968, p. 118).

But one may argue that, as has happened in certain cases in affluent societies, richer classes tend to have fewer children than average; in this case a progressive concentration of wealth should take place. (Note that the same process of concentration should take place in the case in which the whole, or the greatest part, of the estate is left to one of the children, normally the eldest son or daughter. On this point we shall return below.) In fact:

It is, however, not certain that a fall in the real income per head of a population will reduce the growth rate of that population and vice versa. It is conceivable that the opposite will be the case—namely that a rise in real income per head will reduce the growth of a population, and *vice versa*. It is in fact often maintained that a rise in the standard of living leads to a greater degree of birth control and to a smaller family pattern of life. In this case the demographic factor, instead of mitigating, could intensify the changes in the movements of labour's income. For suppose that a too rapid rate of growth of labour was causing the workers' income per head to fall. If then the fall in the workers' income caused the working population to grow more rapidly, the growth of labour relatively to other resources would be intensified. In fact in the real world we do often see a high fertility and consequently high rates of growth of population associated with poverty. But we must be careful not to conclude from this that poverty is necessarily the direct cause of high fertility and wealth the direct cause of low fertility (Meade, 1968, pp. 118–19).

We may note, to conclude these considerations on the role of the rate of population growth, that in a multi-class model the demographic constraint (as we have considered it) must be valid (*a*) for all socio-economic classes and (*b*) through the whole process considered—in our case in the very long run. For this reason it is obvious that demography may be considered as one of the central elements of the model. A differentiated rate of growth of population, as we shall point out again below, is bound to lead to a higher or lower concentration of wealth (and/or income), which in turn may lead to further changes in the demographic patterns.

The rate of growth of population must be neither too high nor too low. As may be observed in most models developed in Chapters 5 and 6, the rate of growth of population may be technically equal to zero; in particular the values of the equilibrium rate of profits derived in Chapter 5 is still positive even for $g = 0$, while this is not the case for the Kaldor–Pasinetti or Meade–Samuelson and Modigliani's solutions, where a non-positive rate of growth (of population and technical progress) implies a zero equilibrium rate of profits and hence no share for the national income. The analysis on the implications of interest uncertainty (see for instance Figure 7.3) has however proved that a low rate of growth of population could mean a higher concentration of personal wealth; and also in the case of a deterministic model a low value of the rate of growth of population (which may include technical progress) may imply an insufficient rate of profits. On the other hand a too high rate of growth of population may slow down the process of growth via a progressive dispersion of wealth per capita; this may be observed again in Figure 7.3, where a rate of growth of population higher than $r - \delta$ (where r is the mean rate of return on the risky asset and δ is the subjective discount rate) would prevent most dynasties from endowing their children with the same wealth as that inherited by their parents.

The point is that an average value of the rate of growth of population may, among other things, create or ensure the conditions for a steady-state system where the classes may accumulate positive wealth per capita and hold, possibly, a positive share of the inter-generational capital stock. Values for the same variable that are either too low or too high may not allow for the existence of such a steady-state path, and generate extreme situations like a rapid concentration or dispersion of wealth. Consequently an orderly or smooth development of the economic system may be difficult to achieve, and may prevent a given economy from completing all stages of the process of development.

The assumption of inter-generational stability of classes. Within our framework the concept of 'stability of classes' means that during the process of expansion dynasties belonging to one class do not mix with dynasties belonging to other classes; or that transfers are exactly compensated by counter-transfers. Classes are defined on the basis (*a*) of the composition of income: for the capitalists' class we have postulated an income predominantly from capital, mainly inter-generational; for the workers' class we have postulated an income from both work and capital (interest on savings); (*b*) of the capacity of transmitting inter-generational assets: capitalists in any case; workers in general not (and this reflects the formulation of most classical and early post-Keynesian models). Both classes are however allowed to transmit inter-generational wealth in a generalized model at the end of Chapter 5.

It is easy to see that in this case the stability of social classes has mainly to do with the way in which inter-generational wealth is transmitted. (We do not exclude that other elements like education, social contacts, and so on should be considered in the study of the patterns of transmission of economic power.) More precisely the way in which marriages take place in our society becomes relevant; this issue has been considered in great detail by Meade who has written that

In fact mating is somewhere between the completely random and the perfectly assortative. A bachelor at a given position in the bachelor's pecking order will not inevitably marry the spinster at the corresponding position in the spinster's pecking order; but the choice is not purely random; the nearer any given bachelor and any given spinster are at the same position in their two pecking orders the more likely they are to choose each other as mates. But as long as mating is not perfectly assortative there is some averaging and equalizing tendency at work. If Tom's and Mary's fortunes do not correspond, then the joint family's fortune will be an average of whichever is the greater fortune and whichever is the lesser fortune. This is an equalizing tendency; and if this were the whole of the story, inequalities would progressively disappear as the generations succeeded each other. For as long as differences of fortune persisted there would be a force at work taking two different fortunes, joining them together, and averaging them. This force is known as the regression towards the mean. . . . If this regression towards the mean were the whole of the story we would expect to find society continually moving towards a more and more equal distribution of endowments (Meade, 1974, p. 18).

But together with this factor of 'regression towards the mean' there exists another set of forces at work tending to reintroduce inequalities and hence to maintain a certain balance among the classes; in Meade's words:

But elements of random luck in genetic make-up, and in social and economic fortune cause a dispersion about the average; and the more marked are these elements, the greater will be the ultimate degree of inequality in society. Finally, the more marked are the positive feedbacks and the less marked the negative feedbacks .... of structured developments of endowments, the greater the ultimate degree of inequalities (Meade, 1974, p. 21).

In this way inequalities between the most and least able—as Meade himself points out—will be re-established: 'in their careers some will strike lucky in education, social contacts, investments, and jobs and will go uphill, while others will go downhill' (Meade, 1974, p. 21).

The degree of inter-generational stability of socio-economic classes (Meade's 'ultimate self-perpetuating degree of inequality' in the distribution of fortunes) is thus the outcome of the interaction of a number of forces. And in this perspective it is obvious that if the forces which account for the 'regression towards the mean' are equivalent to those which account for a greater dispersion, there might result a good degree of inter-generational mobility. It must however be pointed out that in order to ensure the stability of classes, such a complex process (*a*) must be supplemented by stability in the functional distribution of income, (*b*) must be considered in the long run, since different classes of people might have different ages, and hence different propensities to save and to endow their own children, and (*c*) must take place in association with a constant inter-generational/life-cycle wealth ratio.

The issue of inter-generational mobility of classes is of course much more complex than described here, but it is not the aim of this chapter to examine it exhaustively. We have confined ourselves to those elements which, in the context of an integrated model of income and wealth distribution, are directly connected with the issues raised.

8.2.2 *Personal and functional distribution of income and wealth: long-term trends*

At this point of our analysis we may set our results against the more general issue of the progressive concentration or dispersion of wealth. We have already pointed out in the Introduction that there exist a number of elements which are continuously at work in the determination of the progressive concentration or dispersion of wealth. Let us reassess such elements in the light of the results obtained in the preceding chapters, with particular attention to the way in which they may alter such results in the medium and long term. We shall start by considering the main elements of dispersion of wealth, which on the one hand may tend to level off life-cycle savings and on the other may reduce the relevance of inter-generational assets in total wealth. Such elements concern: (1) fiscal policies of redistribution; (2) falls in the value of holdings; (3) the drawing-down of savings; (4) transfers in the donor's lifetime; and (5) dispersion at death.

1. *Fiscal policies of redistribution*. This is an instrument of economic

policy whose role has become increasingly important in recent decades. In certain cases these policies[1] have been successful in stopping or slowing down the progressive concentration of wealth, while in other cases the forces acting in favour of such a concentration have been overwhelming. A large number of economists have considered in detail the relevance of all direct and indirect taxes on the process of wealth accumulation, and their conclusions have often been ambiguous. Nevertheless it seems clear that wealth taxes and estate duties have led to a lower concentration of wealth than one would otherwise have experienced, though we may argue that the substance of our results would remain valid even in the presence of the introduction of fiscal policies of redistribution.

In particular taxes on income from interest at a differential rate may come to modify (partially) the difference between the rate of return on capitalists' and workers' income from accumulated savings. On the other hand the inclusion in the bequest discount rate of an explicit tax on transfers should reinforce one of our main results, i.e. that in a steady-state situation, in order to maintain their relative economic power, 'pure' capitalists must exhibit a markedly higher propensity to leave assets to their children than average. (On this point see, for instance, Atkinson and Stiglitz, 1980, pp. 85–8, on 'Bequests and Wealth Transfer Taxation'.)

But we should also take into account the overall impact of taxes on savings, which represent the starting-point of the accumulation process. As Atkinson and Stiglitz point out:

When part of the motive for saving arises from uncertainty associated with future income or future needs, the effect of taxation on savings may be markedly different from that in the life-cycle model. Assume that a person expects to have a fairly high income next period; so that in the absence of uncertainty he would do no saving; but there is a small chance that he will be unemployed. He therefore sets aside a small amount of 'insurance' against this contingency. The interest income tax effectively increases the price of this insurance, and this may induce individuals to purchase less. On the other hand, assume that the person wishes to be sure that, after tax, he has a minimum level of consumption if he is unemployed. His precautionary saving is targeted at providing exactly that amount. Then, to maintain that minimum level of consumption, with an interest

---

[1] Atkinson and Stiglitz (1980, p. 63) indicate a variety of types of taxes on capital and return on capital: (*a*) taxes on interest income, either at the same rate as other income or at a differential rate (for instance the UK investment income surcharge); (*b*) taxes on (short-term or long-term) capital gains; (*c*) wealth taxes on the net value of assets owned (with special provisions that reduce the effective rate—like special treatment of housing, or life assurance and pensions, as well as certain tax-exempt bonds); and (*d*) special taxes, as those on houses, land, etc. (labelled as 'property taxes' in the US, 'rates' in the UK, and 'tassa sulla casa' in Italy).

income tax, the person must actually increase his savings. Thus, once again, we observe an ambiguity in the effect of taxation on savings, but now it depends on the individual's attitude towards the risks he faces (Atkinson and Stiglitz, 1980, p. 84).

For this reason it is clear that the implications of fiscal policies on the consumption- and saving-behaviour of individuals—especially in a stochastic context—deserve additional attention in the context of our research programme. As a matter of fact the fiscal component will be indicated below as a possible field of extension of the analysis of the present volume.[2]

2. *Falls in the value of holdings*. As pointed out by Phelps Brown this element occurs only occasionally:

Particular investments may collapse, a fall in farm prices may depress land values, or a depression may lower the valuation of all manner of assets. Since the proportion of assets held in the form of stocks and shares rises with the size of the holding, the wealth of the top 1 per cent of holders is particularly vulnerable to a fall in the stock market. The number of probated British estates of £100,000 and over, which had been rising steeply since the 1850s, hardly rose at all in 1875–9 and 1885–9, the two troughs of the great Victorian depression ... ; that the fall in another severe depression, that of 1930–4, was small may be explained by the rise in gilt-edged at that time (Phelps Brown, 1988, pp. 451–2).

Such phenomena, although of an occasional or sporadic nature might contribute to a drastic reduction in the inter-generational capital share of the 'pure' capitalists' class. This may lead to (*a*) an increase—however slight—in the inter-generational share of the other classes and/or (*b*) a fast increase in the 'pure' capitalists' propensity to bequeath (and this is more likely to happen). The latter result, which would be the outcome of an emergency situation, may paradoxically lead to a more stable long-term coexistence of the various classes of the system, since we have shown that in a deterministic model equilibrium growth is ensured only in the case in which the propensity to bequeath of the capitalists is markedly higher than that of the other class(es), and/or in the case in which there exists a minimum degree of market imperfection (which may be more likely to happen in a situation of

---

[2] On the normative aspect of taxes on wealth or on income from wealth we shall not enter. We shall confine ourselves to report a passage from Flemming and Little (1974) which raises a number of interesting points: 'Capitalism may well require reforms, which both prevent the accumulation of great personal wealth and disperse existing accumulations, if it is to survive. Some supporters of capitalism fear that a wealth tax would be particularly difficult for small but progressive businessmen. We do not think that this needs to be the case; indeed if we thought so we would not support so heavy a wealth tax as we do, since we believe that anything tending to lead to greater industrial concentration is undesirable, and inimical to capitalism' (Flemming and Little, 1974, pp. 1–2).

economic instability). Finally we note that phenomena like those described here may, in certain cases, have a rather neutral effect on the forces which account for distribution and accumulation of wealth; and in this event no particular problems arise. Such phenomena would be more relevant if 'neutrality' did not apply, or in the case in which there was more than one shock.

3. *The drawing-down of savings* to maintain a sustained level of consumption after retirement. This element of dispersion has been incorporated in our deterministic models; its relevance does determine the role of life-cycle savings. Phelps Brown (1988, p. 452) emphasizes that 'although it occurs in some cases, it is far from being a general practice' probably because nowadays pensioners tend to have a sufficient global disposable income for their needs. From a general point of view it may be argued that a better pension scheme and Medicare (which are important for old age) are bound not only to discourage overall savings (see for instance a number of works of Martin Feldstein) but basically to increase the share of the inter-generational wealth in total wealth.[3]

4. *Transfers in the donor's lifetime* are also an element of dispersion of wealth. It may however be noted that if transfers simply anticipate transmissions which would normally take place at death, then they are equivalent to a simple modification of the bequest discount rate, i.e. of the willingness to leave an estate to the next generation. Actually if practised by the richer classes (for instance for fiscal reasons) it would simply imply, other things being equal, that capitalists have a lower bequest discount rate than the other classes, a condition that we have found to be essential for the coexistence of all classes in equilibrium. However, as Phelps Brown has indicated, there is no reason to infer that transfers in the donor's lifetime 'play a substantial part in forming the British distribution; but we lack direct observations' (Phelps Brown, 1988, p. 452). If, on the other hand, transfers in the donor's lifetime are

---

[3] On this point Modigliani states that: 'The basic LCH (life-cycle hypothesis) implies that, with retirement, saving should become negative, and thus assets decline at a fairly constant rate, reaching zero at death. The empirical evidence seems to reveal a very different picture: dissaving in old age appears to be at best modest. . . . According to Mirer, the wealth/income ratio actually continues to rise in retirement. (Note, however, that his estimate is biased as a result of including education in his regression. . . . Most of other recent analysts have found that the wealth of a given cohort tends to decline after reaching its peak in the 60–65 age range . . ., though there are exceptions . . . To be sure, the results depend on the concept of saving and wealth used. If one makes proper allowance for participation in pension funds, then the dissaving (or the decline in wealth) of the old tends to be more apparent, and it becomes quite pronounced if one includes an estimate of Social Security benefits. But when the saving and wealth measures include only cash saving and marketable wealth, the dissaving and the decline appear weaker or even absent' (Modigliani, 1986, p. 306).

made to others than the natural heirs, or in different proportions among the heirs, then the outcome may be more complicated. First, endowments to non-heirs may imply concentration or dispersion of wealth according to the financial position of the beneficiary; secondly, transfers in unequal proportions to heirs imply in general a process of concentration of wealth; all this of course also depends on the number of children and heirs and on the amount transferred. We have already referred to the UK Royal Commission's findings (1977, para. 372) according to which in half of the estates with two or more children the bequests to the children were equal. With regard to the remaining half 'on average the most-favoured child received 74 per cent of the property bequeathed to two children, and about 51 per cent where there were three or four children'. But Phelps Brown goes further and adds that: 'The extent of inequality did not vary with size of the estate. Thus there was no dominance of primogeniture; and in the half of the cases where one child received more than an equal share, the others still had substantial portions. There were also significant bequests to grandchildren' (Phelps Brown, 1988, pp. 453–4).

If we consider the role of the bequest discount rate in the macro-economic model of Chapter 5 we note that an increase of this parameter (denoting a lower willingness of donors to leave assets to their children) would paradoxically lead to a lower proportion of inter-generational wealth in the total capital stock of the society, at least for econometrically reasonable values of the parameters. (Note that this result is likely to be obtained in all cases with one or both classes holding inter-generational wealth.)

Hence a modification of the patterns of transmission of wealth is likely to have more specific consequences for the value and relative strength of the aggregate variables of the system, including the long-term equilibrium rate of profits, the functional distribution of income and wealth among social groups, while such a modification will have a less clear influence on the personal distribution of income and wealth. This is due to the fact that it is not easy to identify the repercussions of such changes on the relationships among individuals or dynasties.

5. *Dispersion at death*, due to a large number of children, should also be considered here. This may easily be observed in the case of the accumulation of capital with interest-uncertainty: here the rate of growth of population will determine (*a*) the amount of wealth which is left to successive generations and, more importantly, (*b*) the relevance and even the existence of socio-economic classes. A link with the overall share of inter-generational wealth in the total capital stock may be, at this point, established. The results obtained in Chapter 5 show that such a share is, in general, negatively connected with the rate of growth of

population. In other words an increase in the rate of growth of population has a negative effect on the share of the inter-generational assets in the total capital stock (and a positive one on that of life-cycle savings). Hence a likely dispersion of inter-generational wealth at the personal level may be associated, *ceteris paribus*, with a lower share of total inter-generational wealth in the total capital stock. This result may be interpreted in various ways, but the more plausible may be that individuals who cannot rely on a large revenue from accumulated savings will be forced, other things being equal, to accumulate more life-cycle savings in order to enjoy a consistent level of consumption during their own lifetime.

One last element of dispersion of wealth concerns alternative ways of transmitting inter-generational economic power to a large family in the form, for instance, of education or social contacts in both an equal or unequal manner among the children or heirs.

To conclude this part on the chief factors that account for the progressive dispersion of personal wealth we may stress that: (*a*) only a number of such factors may alter the relative economic strength of social groups and classes; (*b*) their effect is not always clear on the functional distribution of income; and (*c*) it is not easy to work out with exactitude the implications of such factors on the aggregate values of the economic system. The implications of such modifications may however be much easier to observe in a model assigning a certain degree of rigidity of behaviour to socio-economic classes and assuming a fixed technology.

Let us now consider some of the forces which account for the progressive *concentration of personal wealth*, and their implications for its functional distribution. Among these forces we shall distinguish: (1) the unequal distribution of personal income; (2) the different propensities to save; (3) a different portfolio composition and hence a differentiated rate of growth of the mean wealth; (4) an unequal distribution of bequests and/or concentration at death due to a small number of children; and finally (5) the life-cycle accumulation of savings. Let us consider in detail these elements.

1. *The unequal distribution of personal income*, whose implications may be considered both at the micro- (i.e. personal) and macro- (i.e. functional) level. At the macro-level the models of growth developed in the literature to which the present volume refers consider different groups, with different propensities to save, to consume, and to endow their children with wealth. In this way relevant modifications in the distribution of personal income may be incorporated in class behaviour as we have endeavoured to show in this volume. However, strong modifications in such personal distribution, especially across the classes,

may significantly alter the value of the equilibrium solutions and lead, especially along the traverse, to results different from those obtained. It is also not clear in which circumstances (*a*) the traverse (i.e. the transition from one steady-state to another) will modify the relative position of wealth-owning dynasties or classes, or (*b*) the traverse will lead to a final steady-state situation with all classes present in the system.

2. *The different propensities to save*. This is an important element of the process of concentration of wealth. It has however been demonstrated that the propensity to save is not merely a function of the amount of disposable income and/or wealth; there are a number of other variables which come into play, as age, number of children, composition of income, and so on. In this sense the introduction of such differences within a life-cycle multi-class model as those developed in Chapters 5 and 6 seems to present a number of advantages. The propensity to save of individuals or dynasties is directly connected with the consumption discount rate, δ, as well as the bequest discount rate, b. In Table 5.2 we have indicated the relevance of these two parameters with respect to the process of distribution of life-cycle and inter-generational wealth. (We may recall that in the case of a unique equilibrium rate of interest, where non-capitalists do not transfer wealth from one generation to the next, an increase in the bequest discount rate has a positive effect on such a rate of interest, while the opposite result applies with respect to the consumption discount rate.) In general an increase in the bequest discount rate, b, indicating a lower willingness to leave assets to the next generation, has (not surprisingly) a negative effect on the inter-generational capital stock of the system. Less clear is the outcome in the case of an increase in the consumption discount rate. One would expect that an increase in δ, meaning a lower willingness to accumulate life-cycle savings, ought to lead to a higher proportion of inter-generational wealth in the total capital stock. The results that we have obtained indicate that although this may well be the general case, it is possible that in specific circumstances the opposite outcome applies. Again we may note that change in the propensity to save at whatever possible level (of a single individual or dynasty, of a single class or of all classes) exerts its influence on the distribution of income and wealth in general, and on the composition of the life-cycle and inter-generational capital stock.

3. *A different portfolio composition* and hence a different rate of growth of the mean wealth. This element may be considered at two different levels. In a deterministic context one may simply postulate a differentiated mean rate of return (due to factors already quoted, as the size of investment, different information, direct investment as against

passive savings, and so on). Always in the absence of risk we have been able to demonstrate that a differentiated rate of return on wealth may be a 'device' through which all classes in the system may be able to transfer wealth to the next generation; we have also been able to measure the implications of a smaller or larger difference between the mean rates of return. In general such variations have an influence over the value of all equilibrium variables of the model, and their implications for the equilibrium distribution of wealth among the classes is indicated in detail in Figure 5.2.

The portfolio composition has been explicitly considered in a stochastic context, first by enquiring into the sort of reasons which may lead to a different portfolio holding and then by analytically describing its effects on the mean rate of accumulation and consumption of households or dynasties. We have also studied the role of relative risk-aversion in the determination of the optimal portfolio holding. Again the effect of other changes in the parameters on the general composition of the portfolio has been outlined. In this way it is also easy to establish a direct link between personal and class distribution of income and wealth by taking into account the demographic composition of population and the characteristics of socio-economic classes.

4. *An unequal distribution of bequests* and/or a *concentration at death* due to a small number of children. The main elements at work in this case were considered above, when the forces accounting for the dispersion of wealth were analysed. In this case obviously the process of concentration concerns the systematic transmission of the largest (or whole) share of the estate to an only child. But we have seen above that unequal distribution of wealth does not often occur and, more importantly, that where it occurs there is no dominance of primogeniture. Obviously the number of children of dynasties or classes will also determine the speed of such a process of concentration; in particular if a class were to have fewer children than the other classes there would be an overall progressive concentration of wealth.

Of course relevant modifications in the distribution of wealth at the personal level may well be incorporated in macro-level analyses, for instance, with the introduction of a new class, characterized by a specific composition of income, wealth endowment, or bequest discount rate.

5. *The life-cycle accumulation of savings* which according to authors like Modigliani remains one of the most important elements of wealth concentration. We have seen that the patterns of life-cycle accumulation of wealth (see for instance Sect. 5.5 above) depend on all the main variables and parameters of the model, and in particular on the value of the consumption discount rate and bequest discount rate. Their impact at the personal and more aggregated level has been studied in detail.

At the end of this list of factors of concentration of wealth reference should be made to the conclusions drawn in connection with the factors involved in the dispersion of wealth. It should be recalled, however, that the assumption of specific socio-economic classes implies a minimum level of rigidity in the model, which is not to be found at the individual level. In other words a specific change in the behaviour of a given class may not always be fully compatible with steady-state growth, while it does not suffer any limitation at the individual or dynastic level.

8.2.3 Historical trends and analytical modelling

Let us reconsider one of the main conclusions reached within the deterministic framework. If we allow, in a simplified two-period life-cycle model, all socio-economic classes to accumulate both life-cycle and inter-generational assets, then the existence and continuity of such classes in equilibrium will be guaranteed provided that the propensity to bequeath of the 'pure' capitalists is markedly higher than that of the other classes. The theoretical implications of this result (as well as of a number of other results) are clear; and such results also describe the kind of conditions that must hold in a situation of long-term steady-state growth, both with respect to the nature and determination of the equilibrium variables and to the relative economic importance of the socio-economic classes.

It may be worth reassessing the significance of these conclusions in the light of recent trends in personal and functional wealth distribution.[4] As a matter of fact two historical phenomena concerning the distribution of wealth have occurred in developed countries since about 1920. The first one is a relative blurring of property ownership in the shape of widely dispersed ownership of homes, cars, durables, liquidities, and even social security wealth (and sometimes even stocks and shares). This diffusion (or dispersion), in the middle class, of these basically 'consumption assets' (that may be 'involuntarily' transmitted) is precisely what seems to justify the life-cycle theory component of wealth, the proportion of savings to income, and the apparent absence of class division in this model. But Modigliani himself accepts another non-irrelevant form of wealth 'earmarked for transmission' and concentrated among the wealthiest classes.[5] This is exactly the basis for a return (or

---

[4] I am grateful to a referee for pointing out this interpretation.

[5] In his Nobel Lecture Modigliani reports that the proportion of wealth held for bequests 'rises with wealth, reaching 1/3 for the top class. Similar, though somewhat less extreme, results are reported in the Brookings study . . . Thus the bequest motive seems to be limited to the highest economic classes. This hypothesis is supported by the findings of Menchik and David that for (and only for) the top 20 per cent, bequests rise proportionately faster than total resources, something which presumably cannot be explained by the precautionary motive. Furthermore, it is consistent, incidentally, with the observation that

the conservation) of a class division, which is not too far from the basic assumptions of Chapter 5, or at least of those of the more generalized models. In this case the capitalists could be defined as owning a minimum amount of non-life-cycle wealth making up the largest share of their property. In addition to the workers, a third class could also be distinguished, grouping the poor who have no hope of embarking in any life-cycle accumulation; or in a more sophisticated model (as the one developed in Sect. 5.9) with no bequest motive.

The second phenomenon concerns the increasing relevance of the process of accumulation and transmission of human capital, which for a number of authors appears to dwarf financial wealth accumulation. Some scholars consider that this Beckerian line of thought appears to constitute a serious challenge to the life-cycle hypothesis and, to a certain extent, to be an element of dispersion of wealth and hence a denial of class differentiation. The point, however, is that as long as there exists an inter-generational financial bequest, connected with a different way of discounting for different income-earners, our model of wealth and income distribution maintains its validity. Furthermore the process of accumulation and transmission of human capital may be, at least partially, assimilated to the process of accumulation and transmission of material wealth. Indeed, as Meade (1968, 1974) has repeatedly pointed out, investment in human capital is, in general, high on the list of priorities among the wealthiest classes. Secondly, there are other ways in which the younger generation may be endowed, i.e. through social contacts, which again may be better provided by classes with high incomes. Finally, if education is provided on a free or quasi-free basis by the state, then it will not directly enter the bequest function; its effect is that of providing better opportunities for the worse off (and hence it is an element of wealth dispersion).

Summing up we may stress that as long as (*a*) the development of our societies is characterized by the existence of an inter-generational capital stock; (*b*) the distribution of the latter is unequal among dynasties or classes; and/or (*c*) there is a different propensity to endow the next generation (both with material or human wealth), most of the analysis of the second part of this volume will be useful in providing additional

---

the decline in wealth with age tends to be more pronounced and systematic in terms of the median than of the mean. But, then the top fifth of the income distribution can be expected to account for substantially more than 1/5 of all bequests' (Modigliani, 1986, p. 310). Certainly this contrasts with Marshall's statement 'That men labour and save chiefly for the sake of their families and not for themselves, is shown by the fact that they seldom spend, after they have retired from work, more than the income that comes in from their savings, preferring to leave their stored up wealth intact for their families' (Marshall, 1890, iv, vii, p. 6; quoted in Phelps Brown, 1988, p. 449).

insights into the long-term process of wealth accumulation and distribution.

8.2.4 Positive and negative aspects of trends in wealth distribution

We come finally to the topic of the way in which it is possible to interfere with the forces that prevail in the continuous process of growth and distribution of wealth. In particular one may ask what is the role of uncontrollable elements and that of more controllable ones like the direct intervention of the state. The question is particularly relevant because there is a general agreement that a dynamic economy requires continuous adjustments in its distribution of economic potential and power. This issue has been taken up in a number of works; Meade, for instance, has pointed out that:

Many people and not only Marxists have maintained that we must rely more on structural changes in society's institutions which will basically readjust what I have called the structural endowments of good or bad fortune. But if Professor Jenks[6] is correct, we should on the contrary rely less on factors of educational, social, and economic reform which will equalize people's structural fortunes in life and should rely more on a continuing direct day-to-day redistribution of the unequal incomes and properties which the chances of luck will continually be re-establishing in society. Such measures—for example, progressive taxation of incomes and property, negative income taxes, social dividends and other social benefits, minimum wage rates, free education and medicine—would be needed simply because of their immediate direct effect on the standards of the lucky and the unlucky within any one generation (Meade, 1974, p. 28).

Beyond the issue of the relevance of the forces which act in favour of or against a higher concentration of wealth, there remains the question of the functional distribution of income and wealth and of the ratio between life-cycle and inter-generational wealth or capital. It may well be that a large number of modifications of the micro-foundations quoted above may take place without necessarily altering their functional distribution. (For instance the constancy—in certain cases over long periods of time—of the overall capital/output ratio may be a typical case.) In this way most of the results and conclusions of our analysis would remain valid, and the conditions for steady-state growth would remain unchanged. This is also due to the fact that the results obtained are in general unambiguous, and even relevant modifications in the value of most parameters will not substantially modify such results

---

[6] In his book entitled *Inequality* Jenks and his Harvard colleagues show that the factors which are usually associated with 'luck' are much more important in the determination of inequalities among households or dynasties than biological, demographic, social, and economic factors. (See, on this point, Meade, 1974, p. 28.)

(whose interpretation is normally straightforward). For instance in the case of a deterministic two-period life-cycle model most solutions are globally stable, and not simply locally, and convergence is ensured in most cases. The same considerations apply in the case of uncertainty, and the analysis of the results obtained (see derivatives and numerical computations provided) indicates that there exists a large band of applicability where the validity of the most important long-term conclusions is guaranteed.

These arguments, however, should not prevent us from outlining possible and more specific extensions of the research programme, with the aim of reinforcing the results obtained. This is what we shall seek to do in the final pages of this chapter after first looking again at a number of aspects connected with the generation or existence of socio-economic classes in a model of accumulation.

8.3   AGAIN ON THE EXISTENCE OF SOCIO-ECONOMIC CLASSES

A common thread of the various models developed in this volume concerns the link between the composition of income, the attitude towards the next generation, and the development, existence, and survival of different socio-economic groups or dynasties in the long-run equilibrium. Let us reassess this issue on the basis of the results that we have reached.

The results obtained in Chapters 5–8 seem to confirm at least two things: first there exist in the economic system (as we have sketched it) various mechanisms which in the long run may give birth to or maintain different socio-economic groups or classes; secondly, in the long run these groups or classes may coexist in equilibrium only if they assume a sharp profile and distinguish themselves in a clear manner. Let us consider in detail these two points.

A. *The birth of different socio-economic classes.*   The justification for the presence and the interaction of economic classes in classical, post-Keynesian, and neo-Ricardian models of growth and distribution, as we have pointed out in the first chapter, is connected with property rights (and hence the composition of their income) and/or the propensities to save and to consume. In general the existence of classes is exogenously imposed and linked to precise hypotheses. In our model however the existence of classes appears to be (*a*) the result of behavioural conditions (i.e. of the optimal allocation of consumption, savings, and bequests over the life-cycle) and (*b*) linked to mechanisms or qualifications that are present in our modern economic system.

In particular the presence of uncertainty may help to give rise to different classes of financial-wealth-owners, on the basis of the initial risk-aversion of individuals or dynasties. On the assumption that at the beginning of the process risk-aversion is not equal for all dynasties of the system (an assumption which we have discussed at length), the presence of a double capital market—safe and risky—tends to generate in the long run a class with a high capital stock per capita and another with an ever-decreasing rate of wealth accumulation.

But even outside a stochastic context our life-cycle model may help to generate two distinct classes of wealth-owners; indeed we have seen that in a two-period model in long-run equilibrium the classes of the system may hold a positive fraction of the inter-generational capital stock only if there exists a double capital market where one class (namely the workers with mixed income from work and from capital) earn a lower rate of return on accumulated savings than the other class(es). We may mention that the same argument applies in the case of different rates of bequest discount for the two classes; but this has nothing to do with institutions or market qualifications.

Of course the generation (or the concurrence to the generation) of distinct socio-economic classes, characterized by different capital endowments, and/or different compositions of income, and/or different propensities to consume, save and leave inter-generational assets, reinforces the legitimacy of those theories which take account of different groups.

B. *The difference between socio-economic classes.* Classes do not only exist (and in certain cases may be born) in our inter-generational model, but under given and fairly realistic conditions may continue to exist only if there are strong differentiating elements among them. Again, classes may, in the long-run equilibrium, hold a positive share of the system's inter-generational or long-term capital stock only if the capitalists have a much stronger desire to leave a bequest to their children than the other classes, and/or if the rate of return on their savings is much higher than the average. Otherwise the two classes would coexist only if one of them (the workers) gave up holding inter-generational assets, which seems to be an even stronger discrimination and a mile away from the 'equal opportunity' motto of certain frameworks of analysis. In this sense the coexistence of classes in optimal conditions and in a long-run growth path seems to be compatible only with strong elements of market imperfection or class differentiation relative to the consumption and/or bequest discount rate. This conclusion, which is the outcome of the optimal behaviour of the classes is surely more compatible within a post-Keynesian framework than within a neoclassical one.

8.4   ALTERNATIVE FRAMEWORKS OF ANALYSIS

At this point some possible extensions may be formulated. It is obvious that inheritance of financial capital and property in general accounts for only one aspect of the inter-generational continuity of dynastic income and economic strength. As pointed out in Part I, other elements may be taken into account, like genetic inheritance and the influence of the family on education, occupational choice, and personal relations. As Lydall points out: 'In one way or another, despite individual deviations, the biological family tends to perpetuate its own characteristics and hence the level of "permanent" family income' (Lydall, 1979, p. 290). This conclusion seems to provide support for the hypothesis of zero or very low inter-class mobility. One should also mention that the theory of investment in human capital is usually developed on the assumption of perfect foresight. In this case the above conclusions would not be directly affected, or only to a limited extent. Obviously investment in human capital is subject to a certain amount of risk, but so far few attempts have been made to incorporate this kind of uncertainty into a model similar to that expounded in this volume. Flemming (1971, pp. 18–19), for instance, has introduced into his model a 'human capital, or an entailed estate or, more prosaically, some assets for which the zero-trading-cost assumption is particularly implausible'. The results obtained are interesting, but the main objection to them is that human capital may be produced, but cannot be bought or sold on the market in the same way as financial wealth. A framework that overcomes these difficulties, at least partially, is that of Levhari and Weiss (1974).

Four main subjects for further research may therefore be suggested. First, the basic assumption that the capitalists are non-wage-earners could be, at least to some extent, relaxed. The borderline between the classes could be, as pointed out earlier, denoted by the size of their respective financial capital stock or by the rate of return earned on their bequest and life-cycle savings. A further step could consist in the relaxation of the assumption of inter-generational stability of the classes; in this case we would have non-hereditary castes and the analysis could include a random process towards the mean similar to that considered in Bevan (1974, 1979).

Secondly, wage-uncertainty could be introduced into a modified two- or multi-class model with interest-uncertainty. The purpose of this model would be that of providing a simple framework in which the various effects of wage- and interest-uncertainty could be analysed, bearing in mind that human capital can be produced during the first part of the life-cycle, but cannot be bought or sold at a later stage. It would be interesting to work out whether wage-uncertainty could represent an element of long-term class differentiation, as in the case of interest-uncertainty.

Thirdly, one might take up the thesis put forward by Desai and Shah (1983), who contrast the implications of the nuclear family arrangement with a joint family one (where generations do overlap for quite a while) and at the same time allow for important factors dealt with in earlier studies, such as uncertainty concerning length of life, optimizing behaviour, and bequest motives. Desai and Shah note that:

The overwhelming bulk of both theoretical and empirical research in this area has been concerned with nuclear families. Here, the amount transferred across generations has been shown to depend on the distribution of length of life, the degree of capital market imperfection, optimizing behaviour and bequest motives. But there are many societies at present times (and the majority of societies in the past) where non-nuclear or joint family arrangement is found. While most models allow only for property to pass from parents to children, from father to sons or to the eldest son, historical accounts or inheritance/bequest patterns present a bewildering variety of rules in different family arrangements (Desai and Shah, 1983, p. 193).

Through their enquiry the authors discover interesting differences in the arrangements about bequest/inheritance patterns, in the possibility of dynastic capital accumulation, and, not surprisingly, in the choice of a bequest transfer system. Such a research programme would surely prove fruitful in the framework of our analysis and possibly lead to new insights.

A fourth element concerns the role of the public sector in general and of taxation in particular as they affect income and wealth (including duties on inter-generational bequests). Indirect taxes may also be taken into account. It is clear that the modification of average and marginal tax rates may alter, among other things (a) the distribution of disposable income between current consumption and savings, (b) the ratio between life-cycle savings and inter-generational capital stock, and (c) the distribution of income and wealth (both life-cycle and inter-generational) among classes. These issues do have important implications for economic policies in general and on the patterns of development of an economic system, especially concerning point (b) above. On the ethical implications of economic policies see, for instance, Lydall (1979, pp. 291–6), who raises very important and interesting issues.

8.5 EPILOGUE

Before bringing this chapter to a close it may be worthwhile to sketch the path along which our research programme has led us. Along classical and Keynesian lines we started our analysis by considering a growth model where the borderline between the classes is seen in rigid terms. With the help of a life-cycle model we set up a number of models with the aim of defining the equilibrium variables, of studying their properties, and of focusing on different patterns of wealth accumulation. But our programme went further. We were able to illustrate the conditions under which (*a*) classes exist and may own a positive share of the total wealth in equilibrium and (*b*) one or the other class cannot, in long-term equilibrium, own a positive share of the inter-generational stock of wealth. Outside the equilibrium conditions we were able to point out the reasons why there might be a tendency to class differentiation in the society. So we have come full circle, and division of households into different groups is no longer to be connected with the classical hypothesis, but is the outcome of the rational and optimal behaviour of the very same households. These results appear particularly relevant since in the traditional two- or multi-class model little effort is made to explain the composition of total wealth (life-cycle or inter-generational), the reasons for perpetual class differentiation, and the role of the various kinds of market imperfections.

REFERENCES

ABEL, A. B. (1985) 'Precautionary Saving and Accidental Bequests', *American Economic Review*, pp. 777–91.
—— (1987) 'Operative Gift and Bequest Motives', *American Economic Review*, pp. 1037–47.
ADAMS, J. D. (1980) 'Personal Wealth Transfers', *Quarterly Journal of Economics*, pp. 159–79.
ADELMAN, I., and TAFT MORRIS, C. (1971) 'An Anatomy of Patterns of Income Distribution in Developing Countries', mimeo (Northwestern University, Evanston).
AHMAD, S. (1986) 'A Pasinetti Theory of Relative Profit Share for the Anti-Pasinetti Case', *Journal of Post-Keynesian Economics*, pp. 149–58.
ALLEN, R. G. D. (1967) *Macro-Economic Theory: A Mathematical Treatment* (Macmillan, London).
ANDO, A., and MODIGLIANI, F. (1963) 'The Life-Cycle Hypothesis of Saving: Aggregate Implications and Tests', *American Economic Review*, pp. 55–84.
APPELBAUM, E., and HARRIS, R. (1978) 'Imperfect Capital Markets and Life-Cycle Savings', *Canadian Journal of Economics*, pp. 319–24.
ARESTIS, P., and SKOURAS, T. (eds.) (1985) *Post Keynesian Economic Theory* (Wheatsheaf Books, Brighton; M. E. Sharpe, Inc., Armonk, New York).
ARROW, K. J. (1965) *Aspects of the Theory of Risk-Bearing*, Yrjo Jahnsson Lectures (Suomalaisen Kirjallisuuden Kirjapaino Oy, Helsinki).
—— (1967) 'Samuelson Collected', *Journal of Political Economy*, pp. 730–7
—— (1974) 'Limited Knowledge and Economic Analysis', *American Economic Review*, pp. 1–10.
ASIMAKOPULOS, A. (1980-1) 'Themes in a Post-Keynesian Theory of Income Distribution', *Journal of Post Keynesian Economics*, pp. 158–69.
ATKINSON, A. B. (1969) 'The Timescale of Economic Models: How Long is the Long Run?', *Review of Economic Studies*, pp. 137–52.
—— (1971) 'The Distribution of Wealth and the Individual Life Cycle', *Oxford Economic Papers*, pp. 239–54.
—— (1974) 'A Model of the Distribution of Wealth', mimeo (University of Essex and MIT).
—— (1975) *The Economics of Inequality* (Oxford University Press, Oxford).
—— (ed.) (1976) *The Personal Distribution of Incomes* (Allen & Unwin, London).
—— and HARRISON, A. J. (1978) *Distribution of Personal Wealth in Britain* (Cambridge University Press, Cambridge).
—— and STIGLITZ, J. E. (1980) *Lectures on Public Economics*, 8 (McGraw-Hill, London and New York).
ATSUMI, H. (1960) 'Mr Kaldor's Theory of Income Distribution', *Review of Economic Studies*, pp. 109–18.

BACKHOUSE, R. (1985) *A History of Modern Economic Analysis* (Blackwell, Oxford and New York).

BALESTRA, P., and BARANZINI, M. (1971) 'Some Optimal Aspects in a Two Class Growth Model with a Differentiated Interest Rate', *Kyklos*, pp. 240–56.

BALOGH, T. (1982) *The Irrelevance of Conventional Economics* (Weidenfeld & Nicolson, London).

BARANZINI, M. (1975*a*) 'A Two-Class Monetary Growth Model', *Revue Suisse d'Économie Politique et de Statistique (Schweizerische Zeitschrift für Volkswirtschaft und Statistik)*, pp. 177–89.

—— (1975*b*) 'The Pasinetti and the Anti-Pasinetti Theorems: A Reconciliation', *Oxford Economic Papers*, pp. 470–3.

—— (1976) 'On the Distribution of Income in Two-Class Growth Models', unpublished D.Phil. thesis, University of Oxford.

—— (1977) 'The Effects of Interest Uncertainty in a Life-Cycle Model', *Revue Suisse d'Économie Politique et de Statistique*, pp. 407–23.

—— (1978) 'Long-Run Accumulation of Capital and Distribution of Wealth in a Stochastic World', *Zeitschrift für die gesamte Staatswissenschaft*, pp. 503–11.

—— (1981) 'Taux d'intérêt, distribution du revenu, théorie des cycles vitaux et choix du portefeuille', *Kyklos*, pp. 593–610.

—— (1982*a*) 'Income Distribution in the Pasinetti Model: Comment on Woodfield and McDonald', *Australian Economic Papers*, pp. 200–6.

—— (1982*b*) 'Can the Life-Cycle Theory Help in Explaining Income Distribution and Capital Accumulation?', in M. Baranzini (ed.), *Advances in Economic Theory* (Blackwell, Oxford; St Martins Press, New York), pp. 243–61.

—— (1982*c*) 'Theorie der Einkommensverteilung, Profitrate, Kapitalbildung und "Life-Cycle" Theorie', *Jahrbücher für Nationalökonomie und Statistik*, pp. 329–35.

—— (1987) 'Distribution Theories: Keynesian', in *The New Palgrave Dictionary*, i (Macmillan, London), pp. 876–8.

—— (1988) 'Un quarto di secolo di dibattito', in Targetti (1988).

—— (1990) 'Reply to Miyazaki and Samuelson', *Oxford Economic Papers* (forthcoming).

—— and SCAZZIERI, R. (1986) 'Knowledge in Economics: A Framework', in Baranzini and Scazzieri (eds.), *Foundations of Economics; Structures of Inquiry and Economic Theory* (Blackwell, Oxford and New York), pp. 1–87.

—— —— (1987) 'Profit and Rent in a Three-Class Model of Capital Accumulation', mimeo (University of Oxford and University of Milan).

—— —— (eds.) (1990*a*) *The Economic Theory of Structure and Change* (Cambridge University Press, Cambridge).

—— —— (1990*b*) 'Economic Structure: Analytical Perspectives', in Baranzini and Scazzieri (1990*a*), pp. 227–333.

BECKER, G. S. (1964) *Human Capital* (Columbia University Press, New York).

—— (1967) *Human Capital and the Personal Distribution of Income*, W. S. Woytinsky Lecture No. 1 (University of Michigan, Ann Arbor).

—— and TOMES, N. (1979) 'A Theory of the Distribution of Income and of Intergenerational Mobility', *Journal of Political Economy*, pp. 1153–89.

BERGSON, A. (1938) 'A Reformulation of Certain Aspects of Welfare Economics', *Quarterly Journal of Economics*, pp. 310–34.

BEVAN, D. L. (1974) 'Savings, Inheritance and Economic Growth in the Presence of Earning Inequality', mimeo (St John's College, Oxford).

—— (1979) 'Inheritance and the Distribution of Wealth', *Economica*, pp. 381–402.

—— and STIGLITZ, J. E. (1978) 'The Wealth Distribution and Inheritance', Paper presented at the American Economic Association Meetings, Chicago.

BIDARD, C., and FRANKE, R. (1986a) 'On the Existence of Long-term Equilibria in the Two-Class Pasinetti–Morishima Model', mimeo (University of Paris X and University of Bremen).

—— —— (1986b) 'Les équilibres à long terme dans un modèle général à deux classes', mimeo (University of Paris X and University of Bremen).

BLATTNER, N. (1976) 'Corporate Finance and Income Distribution in a Growing Economy', *Zeitschrift für Wirtschafts- und Sozialwissenschaften*, pp. 223–38.

BLAUG, M. (1974) *The Cambridge Revolution* (Hobart Paperback, Institute of Economic Affairs, London).

BLINDER, A. S. (1973) 'A Model of Inherited Wealth', *Quarterly Journal of Economics,* pp. 608–26.

—— (1974) *Toward an Economic Theory of Income Distribution* (MIT Press, Cambridge, Mass.).

—— (1976) 'Inequality and Mobility in the Distribution of Wealth', *Kyklos*, pp. 607–38.

BLISS, C. J. (1975) *Capital Theory and the Distribution of Income* (North-Holland, Amsterdam and Oxford).

—— (1983) 'Two Views of Macroeconomics', *Oxford Economic Papers*, pp. 1–12.

—— (1986) 'Progress and Anti-Progress in Economic Science', in Baranzini and Scazzieri (1986), pp. 363–76.

BOMBACH, G. (1981) 'Ein Modell und sein Echo', *Kyklos*, pp. 517–39.

BORRELLY, R. (1975) *Les disparités sectorielles des taux de profit* (Presses Universitaires, Grenoble).

BORTIS, H. (1976) 'On the Determination of the Level of Employment in a Growing Economy', *Revue Suisse d'Économie Politique et de Statistique*, pp. 67–93.

—— (1978) 'Die "Renaissance" klassischer Ideen in der theoretischen Volkswirtschaftslehre', in P. Caroni, B. Dafflon, and G. Enderle (eds.), *Nur Oekonomie ist keine Oekonomie* (Paul Haupt, Berne and Stuttgart), pp. 49–78.

—— (1982) 'Dr. Wood on Profits and Growth: A Note', in Baranzini (1982b), pp. 262–70.

—— (1984) 'Employment in a Capitalist Economy', *Journal of Post-Keynesian Economics*, pp. 590–604.

—— (1988) *An Essay on Post-Keynesian Economics*, mimeo (University of Fribourg, Switzerland); forthcoming (Blackwell, Oxford and New York).

—— (1990a) 'Structure and Change within the Circular Theory of Production', in Baranzini and Scazzieri (1990a), pp. 64–92.

—— (1990*b*) 'Some Thoughts on the Role of the Labour Theory of Value in Pasinetti's Natural System', mimeo (University of Fribourg, Switzerland).

BREMS, H. (1979) 'Alternative Theories of Pricing, Distribution, Saving and Investment', *American Economic Review*, pp. 161–5.

BRITTAIN, J. A. (1973) 'Research on the Transmission of Material Wealth', *American Economic Review*, Papers and Proceedings, pp. 335–45.

—— (1977) *The Inheritance of Economic Status* (Brookings Institution, Washington, DC).

—— (1978) *Inheritance and the Inequality of Material Wealth* (Brookings Institution, Washington, DC).

BRITTO, R. (1968) 'A Study in Equilibrium Dynamics in Two Types of Growing Economies', *Economic Journal*, pp. 624–40.

—— (1969) 'The Life-Cycle Savings in a Two-Class Growth Model', Paper presented at the December 1969 meetings of the Econometric Society, New York.

—— (1972) 'On Differential Savings Propensities in Two-Class Growth Models', *Review of Economic Studies*, pp. 491–4.

—— (1973) 'Some Recent Developments in the Theory of Economic Growth: An Interpretation', *Journal of Economic Literature*, pp. 1343–66.

BRONFENBRENNER, M. (1971) *Income Distribution Theory* (Macmillan, London).

BURMEISTER, E., and TAUBMANN, T. (1969) 'Labour and Non-Labour Income Saving Propensities', *Canadian Journal of Economics*, pp. 78–89.

CAMPA, G. (1975) 'Indeterminatezza del saggio di profitto nel paradosso di Pasinetti', *Giornale degli Economisti e Annali di Economia*, pp. 16–55.

CASAROSA, C. (1970) Appendice IV: 'Macroeconomia', in A. Pesenti, *Manuale di Economia Politica*, 2 vols. (Editori Riuniti, Rome), pp. 377–510.

—— (1982) 'The New View of the Ricardian Theory of Distribution and Economic Growth', in Baranzini (1982*b*), pp. 227–39.

CASS, P., and YAARI, M. E. (1967) 'Individual Saving, Aggregate Capital Accumulation, and Efficient Growth', in K. Shell (ed.), *Essays on the Theory of Optimal Economic Growth* (MIT Press, Cambridge, Mass.), pp. 233–68.

CHAMPERNOWNE, D. A. (1958) 'Capital Accumulation and the Maintenance of Full Employment', *Economic Journal*, pp. 211–44.

—— (1969) *Uncertainty and Estimation in Economics,* iii (Oliver & Boyd, Edinburgh).

—— (1971) 'The Stability of Kaldor's 1957 Model', *Review of Economic Studies*, pp. 47–62.

CHANG, P. P. (1964) 'Rate of Profit and Income Distribution in Relation to the Rate of Economic Growth: A Comment', *Review of Economic Studies*, pp. 103–6.

CHANG, W. W. (1969) 'The Theory of Saving and the Stability of Growth Equilibrium', *Quarterly Journal of Economics*, pp. 491–503.

CHETTY, V. K., PRADHAN, B. K., and SARMA, A. (1987) 'Money, Debt and Taxes: Some Implications for Growth and Distribution', mimeo (Indian Institute, New Delhi).

CHIANG, A. C. (1972) 'Income Distribution and the Profit Rate in Two-Class

Models of Dynamic Equilibrium', *Rivista Internazionale di Scienze Economiche e Commerciali*, pp. 271–84.

—— (1973) 'A Simple Generalization of the Kaldor–Pasinetti Theory of Profit Rate and Income Distribution', *Economica*, pp. 311–13.

CHIODI, G., and VELUPILLAI, K. (1983) 'A Note on Lindahl's Theory of Distribution', *Kyklos*, pp. 103–11.

CODDINGTON, A. (1976) 'Keynesian Economics: The Search for First Principles', *Journal of Economic Literature*, pp. 1258–73.

COHN, R. A., LEWELLEN, W. G., LEASE, R. C., SCHLARBAUM, G. G. (1975) 'Individual Investor Risk Aversion and Investment Portfolio Composition', *Journal of Finance*, pp. 605–20.

COLLARD, D. (1978) *Altruism and Economy* (Blackwell, Oxford and New York).

CONLISK, J., and RAMANATHAN, R. (1970) 'Expedient Choice of Transforms in Phase-Diagramming', *Review of Economic Studies*, pp. 441–5.

COOTNER, P. H. (ed.) (1964) *The Random Character of Stock Market-Prices* (Cambridge, Mass).

COUTTS, K. J. W., GODLEY, W. A. H., and NORDHAUS, W. D. (1978) *Industrial Pricing in the United Kingdom* (Cambridge University Press, Cambridge).

CRAVEN, J. (1979) *The Distribution of the Product* (Allen & Unwin, London).

CROTTY, J. R. (1980) 'Post-Keynesian Economic Theory: An Overview and Evaluation', *American Economic Review*, Papers and Proceedings, pp. 20–5.

DALZIEL, P. C. (1989) 'Cambridge (UK) versus Cambridge (Mass.): A Keynesian Solution of "Pasinetti's Paradox"', *Journal of Post-Keynesian Economics,* pp. 648–53.

—— (1989) 'A Generalization and Simplification of the Cambridge Theorem with Budget Deficits', mimeo (University of Canterbury, NZ).

DARITY, W. A. (1981) 'The Simple Analytics of Neo-Ricardian Growth and Distribution', *American Economic Review*, pp. 978–93.

DAS, S. P. (1988) 'Economic Inequality, Capital Accumulation and Business Cycles', mimeo (Dept. of Economics, Indiana University, Bloomington).

DAVIDSON, P. (1968) 'The Demand and Supply of Securities and Economic Growth and its Implications for the Kaldor–Pasinetti versus Samuelson–Modigliani Controversy', *American Economic Review*, Papers and Proceedings, pp. 252–69.

—— (1978) *Money and the Real World*, 2nd edn. (Macmillan, London).

DAVIES, J. B. (1982) 'Uncertain Lifetime, Consumption, and Dissaving in Retirement', *Journal of Political Economy*, pp. 561–77.

—— and KUHN, P. (1988) 'Redistribution, Inheritance, and Inequality: An Analysis of Transitions', in Kessler and Masson (1988), pp. 123–43.

DEANE, P. (1978) *The Evolution of Economic Ideas* (Cambridge University Press, Cambridge).

DELLI GATTI, D. (1987) 'Il pensiero di Keynes (1923–1936) e l'interpretazione dei post-Keynesiani "soggettivisti"', unpublished Ph.D. thesis, Catholic University of Milan.

DEL VECCHIO, G. (1956) *Capitale e interesse*, 1st edn. 1915, under the title

Lineamenti generali della teoria dell'interesse (Edizioni Scientifiche Einaudi, Turin).

DENICOLÒ, V., and MATTEUZZI, M. (1989) 'Public Debt and the Pasinetti Paradox', mimeo (University of Bologna and University of Udine).

DERNBURG, T. F., and DERNBURG, J. D. (1969) *Macroeconomic Analysis. An Introduction to Comparative Statics and Dynamics* (Addison–Wesley, Reading, Mass.).

DESAI, M. (1986) 'Men and Things', *Economica*, pp. 1–10.

—— and SHAH, A. (1983) 'Bequest and Inheritance in Nuclear Families and Joint Families', *Economica*, pp. 193–302.

DIAMOND, D. A. (1965) 'National Debt in a Neoclassical Growth Model', *American Economic Review*, pp. 1126–50.

—— (1970) 'Incidence of an Interest Income Tax', *Journal of Economic Theory*, pp. 211–24.

—— and HAUSMAN, J. A. (1983) 'Individual Retirement and Savings Behavior', mimeo (Dept. of Economics, MIT, Boston, Mass.).

DIXIT, A. (1976) *The Theory of Economic Growth* (Oxford University Press, Oxford).

—— (1977) 'The Accumulation of Capital Theory', *Oxford Economic Papers*, pp. 1–29.

DOBB, M. (1973) *Theories of Value and Distribution since Adam Smith* (Cambridge University Press, Cambridge).

DOMAR, E. D. (1946) 'Capital Expansion, Rate of Growth and Employment', *Econometrica*, pp. 137–47.

DOMENGHINO, C.-M. (1982) *Die Weiterentwicklung der postkeynesianischen Verteilungstheorie* (Europäische Hochschulschriften) (Peter Lang, Berne).

DOUGHERTY, C. R. S. (1972) 'On the Rate of Return and the Rate of Profit', *Economic Journal*, pp. 1324–50.

—— (1980) *Interest and Profit* (Methuen, London).

DOW, S. C. (1985) *Macro-Economic Thought. A Methodological Approach* (Cambridge University Press, Cambridge).

DRANDAKIS, E. M., and PHELPS, E. S. (1966) 'A Model of Induced Invention, Growth and Distribution', *Economic Journal*, pp. 823–39.

DRÈZE, J. H., and MODIGLIANI, F. (1972) 'Consumption Decisions under Uncertainty', *Journal of Economic Theory*, pp. 308–35.

DUESENBERRY, J. (1952) *Income, Savings and the Theory of Consumer Behavior* (Harvard University Press, Cambridge, Mass.).

EDEN, B., and PAKES, A. (1981) 'On Measuring the Variance-Age Profile of Lifetime Earnings', *Review of Economic Studies*, pp. 385–94.

EICHNER, A. S. (1973) 'A Theory of the Determination of the Mark-up under Oligopoly', *Economic Journal*, pp. 1184–1200.

—— (1976) *The Megacorp and Oligopoly: Micro-Foundations of Macro Dynamics* (Cambridge University Press, Cambridge).

—— (ed.) (1979) *A Guide to Post-Keynesian Economics* (Macmillan, London).

—— (1986) *Toward a New Economics: Essays in Post-Keynesian and Institutionalist Theory* (Macmillan, London).

—— and KREGEL, J. A. (1975) 'An Essay on Post-Keynesian Theory: A New

Paradigm in Economics', *Journal of Economic Literature*, pp. 1293–314.

ELTIS, W. A. (1973) *Growth and Distribution* (Macmillan, London).

—— (1984) *The Classical Theory of Economic Growth* (Macmillan, London).

EWIJK, C. VAN (1982) 'Stability in Keynesian and Neoclassical Growth Models: A Comment on Kuipers', *De Economist*, pp. 101–22.

—— (1989) *On the Dynamics of Growth and Debt: A Post-Keynesian Analysis* (Kanters, Alblasserdam, Netherlands).

FAMA, E. F. (1968) 'Multi-Period Consumption Investment Decisions', Report 6830 (Center for Mathematical Studies in Business and Economics, Chicago).

FARRELL, M. J. (1959) 'The New Theories of the Consumption Function', *Economic Journal*, pp. 678–96.

—— (1970) 'The Magnitude of "Rate-of-Growth" Effects on Aggregate Savings', *Economic Journal*, pp. 873–94.

FAZI, E., and SALVADORI, N. (1981) 'The Existence of a Two-Class Economy in the Kaldor Model of Growth and Distribution', *Kyklos*, pp. 582–92.

—— —— (1985) 'The Existence of a Two-Class Economy in a General Cambridge Model of Growth and Distribution', *Cambridge Journal of Economics*, pp. 155–64.

FELDSTEIN, M. S. (1970) 'Corporate Taxation and Dividend Behavior', *Review of Economic Studies*, pp. 57–72.

—— (1973) 'Tax Incentives, Corporate Saving and Capital Accumulation in the United States', *Journal of Public Economics*, pp. 159–71.

—— and PELLECHIO, A. (1979) 'Social Security and Household Wealth Accumulation: New Microeconomic Evidence', *Review of Economics and Statistics*, pp. 361–8.

FERGUSON, C. E. (1969) *The Neoclassical Theory of Production and Distribution* (Cambridge University Press, Cambridge).

—— (1972) 'The Current State of Capital Theory: A Tale of Two Paradigms', *Southern Economic Journal*, pp. 160–76.

FIELD, B. C. (1989) 'The Evolution of Property Rights', *Kyklos*, pp. 319–45.

FINDLAY, R. (1959/60) 'Economic Growth and Distributive Shares', *Review of Economic Studies*, pp. 167–78.

FISHER, I. (1907) *The Rate of Interest* (Macmillan, London).

—— (1930) *The Theory of Interest* (Macmillan, London).

FLECK, F. H., and DOMENGHINO, C.-M. (1987) 'Cambridge (UK) versus Cambridge (Mass.): A Keynesian Solution of "Pasinetti's Paradox"', *Journal of Post-Keynesian Economics*, pp. 22–36.

FLEMMING, J. S. (1969) 'The Utility of Wealth and Utility of Windfalls', *Review of Economic Studies*, pp. 55–66.

—— (1971) 'Portfolio Choice and Taxation in Continuous Time', mimeo (Nuffield College, Oxford).

—— (1974) 'Portfolio Choice and Liquidity Preference; a Continuous-Time Treatment', in H. Johnson and A. Nobay, *Issues in Monetary Economics* (Oxford University Press, Oxford), pp. 137–50.

—— (1979) 'The Effects of Earnings Inequality, Imperfect Capital Markets, and Dynastic Altruism on the Distribution of Wealth in Life Cycle Models', *Economica*, pp. 363–80.

FLEMMING, J. S. and LITTLE, I. M. D. (1974) *Why We Need a Wealth Tax* (Methuen, London).

FOLKERS, C. (1974a) 'Die Wirkungen einer verstärkten Beteiligung der Arbeitnehmer am Vermögenszuwachs auf die Verteilung des Vermögensbestandes', *Finanzarchiv*, NS, pp. 194–217.

—— (1974b) 'Vermögensverteilung und Profitrate im gleichgewichtigen Wirtschaftswachstum', *Zeitschrift für die gesamte Staatswissenschaft*, pp. 373–93.

FRANKE, R. (1984) 'On the Upper- and Lower-Bounds of Workers' Propensity to Save in a Two-Class Pasinetti Model', *Australian Economic Papers*, pp. 271–7.

—— (1987) 'Integrating Financing of Production and a Rate of Interest into Production Price Models', mimeo (University of Bremen).

FREY, B. S. (1970) 'Probleme von Heute und die Theorie des optimalen Wirtschaftswachstums', *Revue Suisse d'Économie Politique et de Statistique*, pp. 149–65.

FRIEDMAN, M. (1957) *A Theory of the Consumption Function* (Princeton University Press, Princeton).

FRIEND, I., and BLUME, M. E. (1975) 'The Demand for Risky Assets', *American Economic Review*, pp. 900–22.

FURONO, Y. (1970) 'Convergence Time in the Samuelson–Modigliani Model', *Review of Economic Studies*, pp. 221–32.

FUSFELD, D. R. (1982) *Economics, Principles of Political Economy* (Scott, Foresman & Co., Glenview).

GAREGNANI, P. (1960) *Il capitale nelle teorie della distribuzione* (Giuffrè, Milan).

—— (1970) 'Heterogeneous Capital, the Production Function and the Theory of Distribution', *Review of Economic Studies*, pp. 407–36.

—— (1984) 'Value and Distribution in the Classical Economists and Marx', *Oxford Economic Papers*, pp. 291–325.

GEORGESCU-ROEGEN, N. (1990) 'Production Process and Dynamic Economics', in Baranzini and Scazzieri (1990a), pp. 198–226.

GOLDBERGER, A. S. (1979) 'Heritability', *Economica*, pp. 327–47.

GOODWIN, R. M. (1967) 'A Growth Cycle', in C. H. Feinstein (ed.) *Socialism, Capitalism and Economic Growth* (Cambridge University Press, Cambridge), repr. in Goodwin (1982).

—— (1982) *Essays in Economic Dynamics* (Macmillan, London).

—— (1983) *Essays in Linear Economic Structures* (Macmillan, London).

—— and PUNZO, L. F. (1987) *The Dynamics of a Capitalist Economy* (Polity Press and Blackwell, Oxford and New York).

GRAM, H., and WALSH, V. (1983) 'Joan Robinson's Economics in Retrospect', *Journal of Economic Literature*, pp. 518–50.

GREEN, G. F. (1979) 'The Relationship between Corporate and Personal Saving: An Empirical Investigation', Kingston Polytechnic Discussion Papers in Political Economy, No. 10.

GREEN, H. A. J. (1971) *Consumer Theory* (Penguin, Harmondsworth).

GUHA, A. (1972) 'The Global Stability of Two-Class Neoclassical Growth', *Quarterly Journal of Economics*, pp. 687–90.

GUNDER, F. A. (1978) *World Accumulation 1492–1789* (Macmillan, London).

GUPTA, K. L. (1976) 'Differentiated Interest Rate and Kaldor–Pasinetti Paradoxes', *Kyklos*, pp. 310–14.

—— (1977) 'On the Existence of a Two-Class Economy in the Kaldor and Pasinetti Models of Growth and Distribution', *Jahrbücher für Nationalökonomie und Statistik*, pp. 68–72.

HAGEMANN, H. (1987) 'A Kaldorian Saving Function in a Two-Sectoral Linear Growth Model', Paper Presented at the Kaldor Conference, New School for Social Research, New York.

—— (1990) 'The Structure Theory of Economic Growth', in Baranzini and Scazzieri (1990*a*), pp. 144–71.

—— and KURZ, H. D. (1976) 'Reswitching of Techniques in Neo-Austrian Models', *Kyklos*, pp. 678–708.

—— —— (eds.) (1984) *Beschäftigung, Verteilung und Konjunktur*, Festschrift für Adolph Lowe (Bremen University Press, Bremen).

HAHN, F. H. (ed.) (1971) *Readings in the Theory of Growth* (Macmillan, London).

—— (1972) *The Share of Wages in the National Income* (Weidenfeld & Nicolson, London).

—— (1982) 'The Neo-Ricardians', *Cambridge Journal of Economics*, pp. 353–74.

—— (1984) *Equilibrium and Macroeconomics* (Blackwell, Oxford).

HALL, R. E. (1978) 'Stochastic Implications of the Life-Cycle Permanent Income Hypothesis: Theory and Evidence', *Journal of Political Economy*, pp. 971–87.

—— (1981) 'Intertemporal Substitution in Consumption' (Working Paper No. 720, National Bureau of Economic Research, Washington, DC).

HAMADA, K. (1967) 'On the Optimal Transfer and Income Distribution in a Growing Economy', *Review of Economic Studies*, pp. 295–9.

HAMBERG, D. (1971) *Models of Economic Growth* (Harper & Row, New York).

HAMERMESH, D. S. (1982) 'Consumption during Retirement: The Missing Link in the Life-Cycle', mimeo (University of Michigan, Ann Arbor).

HAMOUDA, O. F. (1984) 'On the Notion of Short-Run and Long-Run: Marshall, Ricardo and Equilibrium Theories', *British Review of Economic Issues*, pp. 55–82.

—— and HARCOURT, G. C. (1988) 'Post Keynesianism: From Criticism to Coherence?', *Bulletin of Economic Research*, pp. 1–33.

HARBURY, C. D. (1962) 'Inheritance and the Distribution of Personal Wealth in Britain', *Economic Journal*, pp. 845–68.

—— and HITCHENS, D. M. W. M. (1976) 'The Inheritance of Top Wealth Leavers: Some Further Evidence', *Economic Journal*, pp. 321–6.

—— and McMAHON, P. C. (1973) 'Inheritance and the Characteristics of Top Wealth Leavers in Britain', *Economic Journal*, pp. 810–33.

HARCOURT, G. C. (1969) 'Some Cambridge Controversies in the Theory of Capital', *Journal of Economic Literature*, pp. 369–405; repr. in Harcourt (1986), pp. 145–206.

—— (1971) Book review of the *Theory of Economic Growth* by Michio

Morishima, *Journal of Economic Literature*, pp. 91–2.

HARCOURT, G. C. (1972) *Some Cambridge Controversies in the Theory of Capital* (Cambridge University Press, Cambridge).

—— (1973) 'The Rate of Profits in Equilibrium Models: A Review Article', *Journal of Political Economy*, pp. 1261–77.

—— (1976) 'The Cambridge Controversies: Old Ways and New Horizons—or Dead End?', *Oxford Economic Papers*, pp. 25–65.

—— (1977) *The Microeconomic Foundations of Macroeconomics* (Macmillan, London).

—— (1980) 'Appraisal of Post-Keynesian Economics: Discussion', *American Economic Review*, Papers and Proceedings, pp. 27–8.

—— (1982*a*) *The Social Science Imperialists*, ed. Prue Kerr (Routledge & Kegan Paul, London).

—— (1982*b*) 'Post-Keynesianism: Quite Wrong and/or Nothing New?' *Thames Papers in Political Economy*, repr. in Arestis and Skouras (1985), pp. 125–45.

—— (ed.) (1985) *Keynes and his Contemporaries*, Sixth and Centennial Keynes Seminar, University of Kent (Macmillan, London).

—— and KENYON, P. (1976) 'Pricing and Investment Decision', *Kyklos*, pp. 449–77; repr. in Harcourt (1982*a*), pp. 104–26.

—— and LAING, N. F. (eds.) (1971) *Capital and Growth: Selected Readings* (Penguin, Harmondsworth).

—— and O'SHAUGHNESSY, T. J. (1985) 'Keynes's Unemployment Equilibrium: Some Insights from Joan Robinson, Piero Sraffa and Richard Kahn', in Harcourt (1985), pp. 3–41.

HARK, S. (1990) 'Boulding's Theory of Distribution Revisited: Kaldor's Neo-Boulding Theorem', mimeo (University of Aarhus, Denmark).

HARRIS, D. J. (1974) 'The Price Policy of Firms, the Level of Employment and the Distribution of Income in the Short Run', *Australian Economic Papers*, pp. 144–57.

—— (1975) 'The Theory of Economic Growth: A Critique and Reformulation', *American Economic Review*, Papers and Proceedings, pp. 329–37.

—— (1978) *Capital Accumulation and Income Distribution* (Stanford University Press, Stanford; Routledge & Kegan Paul, London).

—— (1982) 'Structural Change and Economic Growth: A Review Article', *Contributions to Political Economy*, pp. 25–46.

HARROD, R. F. (1936) *The Trade Cycle: An Essay* (Clarendon Press, Oxford).

—— (1939) 'An Essay in Dynamic Theory', *Economic Journal*, pp. 14–33.

—— (1948) *Towards a Dynamic Economics* (Macmillan, London).

HATTORI, Y. (1975) 'A Note on Pasinetti's Theorem', *Bulletin of University of Osaka Prefecture*, pp. 13–15.

HAUSMAN, J. A. (1981) 'Exact Consumer's Surplus and Deadweight Loss', *American Economic Review*, pp. 662–76.

HAYASHI, F. (1982) 'The Permanent Income Hypothesis: Estimation and Testing by Instrumental Variables', *Journal of Political Economy*, pp. 895–918.

—— ANDO, A., and FERRIS, R. (1989) 'Life-Cycle and Bequest Savings: A Study of Japanese and U.S. Households based on Data from 1984 NSFIE and the 1983 Survey of Consumer Finances', *Journal of Japanese and International Economies*.

HICKS, J. (1932) *The Theory of Wages* (Macmillan, London).

—— (1965) *Capital and Growth* (Oxford University Press, Oxford).

—— (1970) 'A Neo-Austrian Growth Theory', *Economic Journal*, pp. 257–81.

—— (1974) *Value and Capital: An Inquiry into Some Fundamental Principles of Economic Theory*, 1st edn. 1939 (Clarendon Press, Oxford).

—— (1975) 'The Scope and Status of Welfare Economics', *Oxford Economic Papers*, pp. 307–26.

—— (1976) '"Revolutions" in Economics', in S. J. Latsis (ed.), *Method and Appraisal in Economics* (Cambridge University Press, Cambridge), pp. 207–18.

—— (1977) *Economic Perspectives* (Clarendon Press, Oxford).

—— (1979) *Causality in Economics* (Blackwell, Oxford).

—— (1983) 'A Discipline not a Science', in *Collected Essays on Economic Theory*, iii: *Classics and Moderns* (Blackwell, Oxford), pp. 365–75.

—— (1985) *Methods of Dynamic Economics* (Clarendon Press, Oxford).

—— (1986) 'Is Economics a Science?' in Baranzini and Scazzieri (1986), pp. 91–101.

HOWARD, M. C. (1979) *Modern Theories of Income Distribution* (Macmillan, London).

ISHIKAWA, T. (1980) 'Corporate Savings, Financial Market Equilibrium and Macro Distribution of Income', mimeo (University of Tokyo), pp. 68.

—— (1984*a*) 'The Role of Finance and Wealth Holdings in Cambridge Growth and Distribution Models', mimeo (University of Tokyo).

—— (1984*b*) 'The Pasinetti Theorem Revisited: The Case of Two Financial Assets', mimeo (University of Tokyo).

JARSULIC, M. (1988) *Effective Demand and Income Distribution* (Polity Press, Oxford).

JENKS, C. (1972) *Inequality: A Reassessment of the Effect of Family and Schooling in America* (Basic Books, New York).

JONES, H. G. (1975) *An Introduction to Modern Theories of Economic Growth* (Nelson, London).

KAHN, R. F. (1959) 'Exercises in the Analysis of Growth', *Oxford Economic Papers*, pp. 143–56.

—— (1972) *Selected Essays on Employment and Growth* (Cambridge University Press, Cambridge).

—— (1984) *The Making of Keynes' General Theory* (Cambridge University Press, Cambridge).

KALDOR, N. (1956) 'Alternative Theories of Distribution', *Review of Economic Studies*, pp. 83–100; repr. in Kaldor (1960*a*).

—— (1957) 'A Model of Economic Growth', *Economic Journal*, pp. 591–624.

—— (1960*a*) *Essays on Value and Distribution* (Duckworth, London).

—— (1960*b*) *Essays on Economic Stability and Growth* (Duckworth, London).

—— (1960*c*) 'A Rejoinder of Mr. Atsumi and Professor Tobin', *Review of Economic Studies*, pp. 121–3.

KALDOR, N. (1961) 'Capital Accumulation and Economic Growth', in F. A. Lutz and D. C. Hague (eds.), *The Theory of Capital* (Macmillan, London), pp. 177–222.

—— (1966) 'Marginal Productivity and the Macro-Economic Theories of Distribution', *Review of Economic Studies*, pp. 309–19.

—— (1970) 'Some Fallacies in the Interpretation of Kaldor', *Review of Economic Studies*, pp. 1–7.

—— (1972) 'The Irrelevance of Equilibrium Economics', *Economic Journal*, pp. 1237–55.

—— (1976) 'Inflation and Recession in the World Economy', *Economic Journal*, pp. 703–14.

—— (1985) *Economics Without Equilibrium* (Cardiff University Press, Cardiff; M. E. Sharpe, Armonk, New York).

—— (1986) *Ricordi di un economista*, ed. M. C. Marcuzzo (Garzanti Editore, Turin).

—— and MIRRLEES, J. A. (1962) 'A New Model of Economic Growth', *Review of Economic Studies*, pp. 174–92.

KALECKI, M. (1939) *Essays in the Theory of Economic Fluctuations* (Allen & Unwin, London).

—— (1971a) *Selected Essays on the Dynamics of the Capitalist Economy* (Cambridge University Press, Cambridge).

—— (1971b) 'Class Struggle and the Distribution of National Income', *Kyklos*, pp. 1–9.

KAMIN, L. (1974) *The Science and Politics of I.Q.* (Halstead Press, New York).

KANO, M. (1985) 'Money, Financial Assets and Pasinetti's Theory of Profit', *Economic Studies Quarterly*, pp. 169–77.

KEMP, M. C., and THANH, P. C. (1966) 'On a Class of Growth Models', *Econometrica*, pp. 257–82.

KENNEDY, C. (1964) 'Induced Bias in Innovation and the Theory of Distribution', *Economic Journal*, pp. 541–7.

KESSLER, D., and MASSON, A. (eds.) (1988) *Modelling the Accumulation and Distribution of Wealth* (Oxford University Press, Oxford).

KEYNES, J. M. (1930) *A Treatise on Money*, 2 vols. (Macmillan, London).

—— (1936) *The General Theory of Employment, Interest and Money* (Macmillan, London).

—— (1973–) *The Collected Writings of John Maynard Keynes*, ed. A. Robinson and D. Moggridge (Macmillan, London; Cambridge University Press, Cambridge).

KING, M. A. (1985) 'The Economics of Saving: A Survey of Recent Contributions', in K. J. Arrow and S. Honkapohja (eds.), *Frontiers of Economics* (Blackwell, Oxford and New York), pp. 227–94.

—— and DICKS-MIREAUX, L. D. L. (1982) 'Asset Holdings and the Life-Cycle', *Economic Journal*, pp. 1–21.

KIRMAN, A. (1989) 'The Intrinsic Limits of Modern Economic Theory: The Emperor has no Clothes', *Economic Journal*, pp. 126–39.

KOHLBERG, E. (1976) 'A Model of Economic Growth with Altruism between Generations', *Journal of Economic Theory*, pp. 1–13.

KOOPMANS, T. C. (1967) 'Objectives, Constraints, and Outcomes in Optimal Growth Models', *Econometrica*, pp. 1–15.

KOTLIKOFF, L. J., and SUMMERS, L. H. (1980) 'The Role of Intergenerational Transfers in Aggregate Capital Accumulation' (Working Paper No. 445, National Bureau of Economic Research, Washington, DC).

—— —— (1981) 'The Role of Intergenerational Transfers in Aggregate Capital Accumulation', *Journal of Political Economy*, pp. 706–32.

—— —— (1988) 'The Contribution of Intergenerational Transfers', in Kessler and Masson (1988), pp. 53–67.

KREGEL, J. A. (1971) *Rate of Profit, Distribution and Growth: Two Views* (Macmillan, London).

—— (1972) 'Review of Eltis' *Growth and Distribution*', *Economica*, pp. 345–6.

—— (1973) *The Reconstruction of Political Economy: An Introduction to Post-Keynesian Economics* (Macmillan, London).

—— (1976) 'Economic Methodology in the Face of Uncertainty: The Modelling Methods of Keynes and the Post-Keynesians', *Economic Journal*, pp. 209–25.

—— (1978) 'Post-Keynesian Theory: Income Distribution' *Challenge*, pp. 37–43.

KRELLE, W. (1972) *Wachstumstheorie* (Springer–Verlag, Berlin).

KUBOTA, K. (1968) 'A Re-Examination of the Existence and Stability Propositions in Kaldor's Growth Models', *Review of Economic Studies*, pp. 353–60.

KURZ, M. (1968a) 'Optimal Growth and Wealth Effects', *International Economic Review*, pp. 348–57.

—— (1968b) 'The General Instability of a Class of Competitive Growth Processes', *Review of Economic Studies*, pp. 155–74.

—— (1984) 'Capital Accumulation and the Characteristics of Private Intergenerational Transfer', *Economica*, pp. 1–22.

LAING, N. F. (1969) 'Two Notes on Pasinetti's Theorem', *Economic Record*, pp. 373–85.

LAITNER, J. P. (1979) 'Bequests, Golden-Age Accumulation and Government Debt', *Economica*, pp. 403–14.

LANDESMANN, M. A., and SCAZZIERI, R. (1990) 'Specification of Structure and Economic Dynamics', in Baranzini and Scazzieri (1990a), pp. 95–121.

LEIJONHUFVUD, A. (1968) *On Keynesian Economics and the Economics of Keynes* (Oxford University Press, New York).

LEON, P. (1967) *Structural Change and Growth in Capitalism* (Johns Hopkins University Press, Baltimore).

LEVHARI, D. and MIRMAN, J. (1977) 'Savings and Consumption with an Uncertain Horizon', *Journal of Political Economy*, pp. 265–81.

—— and PATINKIN, D. (1968) 'The Role of Money in a Simple Growth Model', *American Economic Review*, pp. 713–53.

—— and SRINIVASAN, T. N. (1969) 'Optimal Savings under Uncertainty', *Review of Economic Studies*, pp. 153–63.

—— and WEISS, Y. (1974) 'The Effect of Risk on the Investment in Human Capital', *American Economic Review*, pp. 950–63.

LEWELLIN, W. G., LEASE, R. C., and SCHLARBAUM, G. G. (1974) 'Patterns of Investment Strategy and Behaviour among Individual Investors', mimeo (Purdue University, West Lafayette).

LICHTENSTEIN, P. M. (1983) *An Introduction to Post-Keynesian and Marxian Theories of Value and Price* (Macmillan, London).

LOMBARDINI, S. (1953) *Il monopolio nella teoria economica* (Vita e Pensiero, Milan).

LOMBARDINI, S. (1968) 'Competition, Free Entry, and General Equilibrium Models', *Economia Internazionale*, pp. 1–26.

—— (1987) 'Prolegomena to a Theory of Economic Development', *Rivista Internazionale di Scienze Economiche e Commerciali*, 34, pp. 1001–24.

—— and QUADRIO-CURZIO, A. (eds.) (1972) *La distribuzione del reddito nella teoria economica* (Franco Angeli, Milan).

LÖWE, A. (1976) *The Path of Economic Growth* (Cambridge University Press, Cambridge).

LUXEMBURG, R. (1951) *The Accumulation of Capital* (Routledge & Kegan Paul, London). German original published in 1913.

LYDALL, H. (1955) 'The Life Cycle in Income, Saving and Asset Ownership', *Econometrica*, pp. 131–50.

—— (1979) *A Theory of Income Distribution* (Clarendon Press, Oxford).

McCALLUM, B. T. (1969) 'The Instability of Kaldorian Models', *Oxford Economic Papers*, pp. 56–65.

MAINWARING, L. (1980) 'International Investment and the Pasinetti Process', *Oxford Economic Papers*, pp. 99–101.

MANESCHI, A. (1974) 'The Existence of a Two-Class Economy in the Kaldor and Pasinetti Models of Growth and Distribution', *Review of Economic Studies*, pp. 149–50.

MARANGONI, G. D. (1985) *Il modello di produzione di merci a mezzo di merci di Piero Sraffa* (Cedam, Padua).

MARGLIN, S. A. (1984) *Growth, Distribution and Prices* (Harvard University Press, Cambridge, Mass., and London).

MARKOWITZ, H. (1959) *Portfolio Selection: Efficient Diversification of Investments* (Wiley, New York).

MARRELLI, M., and SALVADORI, M. (1979) 'The Rate of Profit in an Expanding Economy: Some Existence, Uniqueness and Stability Conditions', *Australian Economic Papers*, pp. 283–92.

MARRIS, R. L. (1972) 'Why Economics needs a Theory of the Firm', *Economic Journal*, pp. 321–52.

MARX, K. (1983) *Capital: A Critique of Political Economy*, i (Lawrence & Wishart, London). German original published in 1867.

MASAMICHI, K. (1987) 'The Effect of Public Education in Two-Class Models', *Journal of Macroeconomics*.

MASTROMATTEO, G. (1989a) 'Self-financing by Companies and the Outcome of the Pasinetti's Process: A Note', mimeo (Catholic University of Milan).

—— (1989b) 'Government Intervention, Self-Financing by Private Companies and the Pasinetti's Process: A Few Reflections', mimeo (Catholic University of Milan).

MATYAS, A. (1980) *History of Modern Non-Marxian Economics* (Akadémiai Kiadò, Budapest).

MEACCI, F. (1989) 'Irving Fisher and the Classics on the Notion of Capital: Upheaval and Continuity in Economic Thought', *History of Political Economy*, pp. 409–24.

MEADE, J. E. (1963) 'The Rate of Profits in a Growing Economy', *Economic Journal*, pp. 665–74.

—— (1964) *Efficiency, Equality and the Ownership of Property* (Allen & Unwin, London).

—— (1966a) 'The Outcome of the Pasinetti Process: A Note', *Economic Journal*, pp. 161–5.

—— (1966b) 'Life-Cycle Savings, Inheritance and Economic Growth', *Review of Economic Studies*, pp. 61–78.

—— (1968) *The Growing Economy* (Allen & Unwin, London).

—— (1973) *The Inheritance of Inequalities*, Third Keynes Lecture in Economics (Oxford University Press, Oxford).

—— (1976) *The Just Economy* (Allen & Unwin, London).

—— and HAHN, F. H. (1965) 'The Rate of Profit in a Growing Economy', *Economic Journal*, pp. 445–8.

MEHRLING, P. G. (1986) 'A Classical Model of the Class Struggle: A Game-Theoretic Approach', *Journal of Political Economy*, pp. 1280–303.

MENCHIK, P. L. (1979) 'Inter-Generational Transmission of Inequality: An Empirical Study of Wealth Mobility', *Economica*, pp. 349–62.

—— (1988) 'Unequal Estate Division: Is it Altruism, Reverse Bequest, or Simply Noise?' in Kessler and Masson (1988), pp. 105–16.

—— and DAVID, M. (1983) 'Income Distribution, Lifetime Saving and Bequests', *American Economic Review*, pp. 672–90.

MERTON, R. C. (1969) 'Lifetime Portfolio Selection under Uncertainty: The Continuous-Time Model', *Review of Economics and Statistics*, pp. 247–57.

—— (1971) 'Optimum Consumption and Portfolio Rules in a Continuous-Time Model', *Journal of Economic Theory*, pp. 373–413.

MILL, J. S. (1965) *Principles of Political Economy with Some of their Applications to Social Philosophy*, ed. J. M. Robson, with an introduction of R. F. Rae (University of Toronto Press, Toronto; Routledge & Kegan Paul, London). 1st edn. 1848.

MINCER, J. (1958) 'Investment in Human Capital and Personal Income Distribution', *Journal of Political Economy*, pp. 281–302.

MINSKY, H. P. (1975) *John Maynard Keynes* (Columbia University Press, New York).

—— (1982) *Can it Happen Again?* (M. E. Sharpe, Armonk, New York).

MIRER, T. W. (1979) 'The Wealth–Age Relation among the Aged', *American Economic Review*, pp. 435–43.

MIRRLEES, J. A. (1965) 'Optimum Accumulation under Uncertainty', mimeo (Trinity College, Cambridge).

—— (1967) 'Optimum Growth when Technology is Changing', *Review of Economic Studies*, pp. 95–124.

—— and STERN, N. H. (eds.) (1973) *Models of Economic Growth* (Macmillan, London).

MIYAZAKI, K. (1986) 'The Differentiated Rate of Interest and Income Distribution in the Pasinetti Model of Growth and Income Distribution', mimeo (Hosei University, Tokyo).

—— (1987*a*) 'A Note on Income Distribution in the Pasinetti Growth Model', mimeo (Hosei University, Tokyo).

—— (1987*b*) 'Income Distribution in the Pasinetti Growth Model: The Case of Two Types of Workers with Different Propensities to Save', mimeo (Hosei University, Tokyo).

—— (1988) 'The Post-Keynesian View about the Neoclassical Anti-Pasinetti Theory', mimeo (Hosei University, Tokyo); *Oxford Economic Papers*, forthcoming.

MODIGLIANI, F. (1975) 'The Life-Cycle Hypothesis of Saving Twenty Years Later', in M. Parkin (ed.), *Contemporary Issues in Economics* (Manchester University Press, Manchester), pp. 1–36.

—— (1986) 'Life Cycle, Individual Thrift, and the Wealth of Nations', *American Economic Review*, pp. 297–313.

—— (1988) 'Measuring the Contribution of Intergenerational Transfers to Total Wealth: Conceptual Issues and Empirical Findings', in Kessler and Masson (1988), pp. 21–52.

—— and BRUMBERG, R. (1954) 'Utility Analysis and the Consumption Function: An Interpretation of Cross-Section Data', in K. K. Kurihara (ed.), *Post-Keynesian Economics* (Rutgers University Press, New Brunswick).

MOORE, A. M. (1967) 'A Reformulation of the Kaldor Effect', *Economic Journal*, pp. 84–99.

MOORE, B. J. (1974) 'The Pasinetti Paradox Revisited', *Review of Economic Studies*, pp. 297–9.

—— (1975) 'Equities, Capital Gains, and the Role of Finance in Accumulation', *American Economic Review*, pp. 872–86.

—— (1978/9) 'Life-Cycle Saving and Bequest Behavior', *Journal of Post-Keynesian Economics*, pp. 79–99.

—— (1983) 'Unpacking the Post-Keynesian Black Box: Bank Lending and the Money Supply', *Journal of Post Keynesian Economy*, pp. 537–56.

MORISHIMA, M. (1964) *Equilibrium, Stability and Growth* (Clarendon Press, Oxford).

—— (1969) *Theory of Economic Growth* (Clarendon Press, Oxford).

—— (1977) 'Pasinetti's Growth and Income Distribution Revisited', *Journal of Economic Literature*, pp. 56–61.

—— (1989) 'The Economic Theory of Industrial Evolution', in Baranzini and Scazzieri (1990*a*), pp. 175–97.

MOSS, S. J. (1978) 'The Post Keynesian Theory of Income Distribution in the Corporate Economy', *Australian Economic Papers*, pp. 303–22.

MOTT, T. (1985/6) 'Towards a Post-Keynesian Formulation of Liquidity Preference', *Journal of Post-Keynesian Economics*, pp. 222–32.

MÜCKL, W. J. (1972) 'Die Gewinnquote im Pasinetti-Model', *Zeitschrift für die Gesamte Staatswissenschaft*, pp. 525–55.

—— (1975) 'Die Zeitdauer des langfristigen Anpassungsprozessen im

Verteilungsmodell von L. L. Pasinetti', *Zeitschrift für die gesamte Staatswissenschaft*, pp. 134–45.

—— (1978) 'On the Existence of a Two-Class Economy in the Cambridge Models of Growth and Distribution', *Jahrbücher für Nationalökonomie und Statistik*, pp. 508–17.

MURFIN, A. J. (1980) 'Savings Propensities from Wage and Non-Wage Income', *Warwick Economic Research Papers*, No. 174 (Dept. of Economics, University of Warwick, Coventry).

NACHMAN, D. C. (1975) 'Risk Aversion, Impatience, and Optimal Timing Decisions', *Journal of Economic Theory*, pp. 196–246.

NARDOZZI, G. (1985) 'Schumpeter e l'economia monetaria', in C. Filippini and P. Porta (eds.), *Società, Sviluppo, Impresa; Saggi su Schumpeter* (Istituto IPSOA, Milan), pp. 307–14.

NÄSLUNG, B. (1973) 'Labour Power and Income Distribution', *Swedish Journal of Economics*, pp. 128–42.

NELL, E. (1982) 'Growth, Distribution and Inflation', *Journal of Post-Keynesian Economics*, pp. 104–13.

—— (1984) 'Structure and Behavior in Classical and Neo-Classical Theory', *Eastern Economic Journal*, pp. 139–55.

—— (1987) 'Accumulation of Capital', in J. Eatwell, M. Milgate, and P. Newman (eds.), *The New Palgrave Dictionary of Economics*, i. pp. 14–18.

—— (1989) 'On Long-Run Equilibrium in Class Society', in G. R. Feiwel (ed.), *Joan Robinson and Modern Economic Theory* (Macmillan, London), pp. 323–43.

NG, Y. K. (1974) 'The Neoclassical and Neomarxist Keynesian Theories of Income Distribution: A Non-Cambridge Contribution to the Cambridge Controversy in Capital Theory', *Australian Economic Papers*, pp. 124–32.

NODA, T. (1987) 'The Pasinetti Theorem in a Mixed Economy', mimeo (University of Tokyo).

NUTI, D. M. (1974) 'On the Rates of Return on Investment', *Kyklos*, pp. 345–66.

O'CONNELL, J. (1985) 'Undistributed Profits and the Pasinetti and Dual Theorems', *Journal of Macroeconomics*, pp. 115–19.

—— (1987) 'Kaldor's Distribution Theory', *Journal of Post-Keynesian Economics*, pp. 572–5.

ODA, S. H. (1986) 'Income Distribution in Growing Economies with Firms and Households: An Analysis of the Stability of the Valuation Ratio', mimeo (University of Tokyo and Catholic University of Milan).

—— (1990) 'A Theoretical Study of Non-Proportionally Growing Economies with Technical Progress', unpublished Ph.D. thesis, Science Policy Research Unit, University of Sussex.

OLSON, M. and BAILEY, N. J. (1981) 'Positive Time Preference', *Journal of Political Economy*, pp. 1–37.

OULTON, N. (1976) 'Inheritance and the Distribution of Wealth', *Oxford Economic Papers*, pp. 86–101.

PANICO, C. (1980) 'Marx's Analysis of the Relationship between the Rate of

Interest and the Rate of Profits', *Cambridge Journal of Economics*, pp. 363–78.

PANICO, C. (1984) 'Interest and Profit in the Theories of Value and Distribution', Ph.D. dissertation, University of Cambridge.

—— (1985) 'Market Forces and the Relation between the Rates of Interest and Profits', *Contributions to Political Economy*, pp. 37–60.

PARKIN, F. (1985) *Class Inequality and Political Order* (Paladin Books, London).

PASINETTI, L. L. (1960) 'A Mathematical Formulation of the Ricardian System', *Review of Economic Studies*, pp. 78–98.

—— (1962) 'The Rate of Profit and Income Distribution in Relation to the Rate of Economic Growth', *Review of Economic Studies*, pp. 267–79.

—— (1964*a*) 'A Reply to Professor Chang', *Review of Economic Studies*, p. 106.

—— (1964*b*) 'A Comment on Professor Meade's "Rate of Profit in a Growing Economy"', *Economic Journal*, pp. 488–9.

—— (1964/5) 'Causalità e interdipendenza nell'analisi economica', *Annuario dell'Università Cattolica de S. Cuore* (Milan), pp. 233–50.

—— (1965) 'A New Theoretical Approach to the Problems of Economic Growth', in *Econometric Approach to Development Planning* (North Holland, Amsterdam), pp. 571–696.

—— (1966*a*) 'New Results in an Old Framework: Comment on Samuelson and Modigliani', *Review of Economic Studies*, pp. 303–6.

—— (1966*b*) 'The Rate of Profit in a Growing Economy: A Reply', *Economic Journal*, pp. 158–60.

—— (1966*c*) 'Changes in the Rate of Profit and Switches of Techniques', *Quarterly Journal of Economics*, pp. 503–17.

—— (1969) 'Switches of Techniques and the "Rate of Return" in Capital Theory', *Economic Journal*, pp. 508–31.

—— (1970) 'Again on Capital Theory and Solow's "Rate of Return"', *Economic Journal*, pp. 428–31.

—— (1972) 'Reply to Mr Dougherty', *Economic Journal*, pp. 1351–2.

—— (1974*a*) *Growth and Income Distribution. Essays in Economic Theory* (Cambridge University Press, Cambridge).

—— (1974*b*) 'A Reply to Dr Nuti on the Rate of Return', *Kyklos*, pp. 370–3.

—— (1975) 'Determinatezza del saggio di profitto nella teoria post-Keynesiana: risposta al Prof. Campa', *Giornale degli economisti e annali di economia*, pp. 639–47.

—— (1977*a*) *Essays on the Theory of Joint Production* (Macmillan, London; Columbia University Press, New York).

—— (1977*b*) 'Reply to Professor Stiglitz', in M. Morishima, 'Pasinetti's *Growth and Distribution* Revisited', *Journal of Economic Literature*, pp. 57–8.

—— (1980*a*) 'The Rate of Interest and Distribution of Income in a Pure Labour Economy', *Journal of Post-Keynesian Economics*, pp. 170–82.

—— (1981) *Structural Change and Economic Growth: A Theoretical Essay on the Dynamics of the Wealth of Nations* (Cambridge University Press, Cambridge).

—— (1982) 'A Comment on the "New View" of the Ricardian Theory', in Baranzini (1982*b*), pp. 240–2.

—— (1983*a*) 'Conditions of Existence of a Two Class Economy in the Kaldor and More General Models of Growth and Income Distribution', *Kyklos*, pp. 91–102.

—— (1983*b*) 'The Accumulation of Capital', *Cambridge Journal of Economics*, pp. 405–11.

—— (1984/5) 'The Difficulty, and yet the Necessity, of Aiming at Full Employment: A Comment on Nina Shapiro's Note', *Journal of Post-Keynesian Economics*, pp. 246–8.

—— (1985) 'Technical Progress and the Wealth of Nations', in H. Bortis and L. Bosshart (eds.), *Technological Change in Economics and Society* (Presses Universitaires, Fribourg), pp. 47–66.

—— (1986*a*) 'Theory of Value: A Source of Alternative Paradigms in Economic Analysis', in Baranzini and Scazzieri (1986), pp. 409–31.

—— (1986*b*) 'Sraffa's Circular Process and the Concept of Vertical Integration', *Political Economy (Studies in the Surplus Approach)*, pp. 3–16.

—— (1987) '"Satisfactory" versus "Optimal" Economic Growth', *Rivista Internazionale di Scienze Economiche e Commerciali*, 34, pp. 989–99.

—— (1988*a*) 'Sraffa on Income Distribution', *Cambridge Journal of Economics*, pp. 135–8.

—— (1988*b*) 'Growing Sub-Systems, Vertically Hyper-Integrated Sectors and the Labour Theory of Value', *Cambridge Journal of Economics*, pp. 125–34.

—— (1989*a*) 'Ricardian Debt/Taxation Equivalence in the Kaldor Theory of Profits and Income Distribution', *Cambridge Journal of Economics*, pp. 25–36.

—— (1989*b*) 'Government Deficit Spending is not Incompatible with the Cambridge Theory of the Rate of Profit: A Reply to Fleck and Domenghino', *Journal of Post-Keynesian Economics*, pp. 641–7.

—— (1990) 'At the Roots of Post-Keynesian Thought: Keynes' Break with Tradition', 10th Annual Conference of the Association of Post-Keynesian Studies, mimeo (Catholic University of Milan).

—— and LLOYD, P. (eds.) (1987) *Structural Change, Economic Interdependence and World Development* (Macmillan, London).

—— and SCAZZIERI, R. (1984) 'Dinamica Economica Strutturale', *Scienze e Tecnica. Annuario della Est* (Mondadori, Milan), pp. 357–60.

—— —— (1987*a*) 'Capital Theory: Paradoxes', *The New Palgrave, A Dictionary of Economics*, Macmillan, Basingstoke, i. 363–8.

—— —— (1987*b*) 'Structural Economic Dynamics', *The New Palgrave, A Dictionary of Economics*, Macmillan, Basingstoke, iv. 525–8.

PETTENATI, P. (1967) 'Il teorema di Pasinetti in un diverso quadro di riferimento', *Studi Economici*, pp. 581–8.

PHELPS, E. S. (1965) 'Second Essay on the Golden Rule of Accumulation', *American Economic Review*, pp. 793–814.

—— (1966) *Golden Rules of Economic Growth* (W. W. Norton, New York).

PHELPS BROWN, H. (1988) *Egalitarianism and the Generation of Inequality* (Clarendon Press, Oxford).

PRATT, J. W. (1964) 'Risk Aversion in the Small and Large', *Econometrica*, pp. 122–36.

QUADRIO-CURZIO, A. (1967) *Rendita e distribuzione in un modello economico plurisettoriale* (Giuffrè, Milan).

QUADRIO-CURZIO, A. (1980) 'Rent, Income Distribution, Orders of Efficiency and. Rentability', in L. L. Pasinetti (ed.), *Essays on the Theory of Joint Production* (Macmillan, London), pp. 218–40.

—— (1986) 'Technological Scarcity: An Essay on Production and Structural Change', in Baranzini and Scazzieri (1986), pp. 311–38.

—— and SCAZZIERI, R. (eds.) (1977–82) *Protagonisti del pensiero economico*, vols. i–iv (Il Mulino, Bologna).

RAMANATHAN, R. (1976) 'The Pasinetti Paradox in a Two-Class Monetary Growth Model', *Journal of Monetary Economics*, pp. 389–97.

RAMSER, H. J. (1969) 'Zur verteilungstheoretischen Relevanz der Kaldor-Formel', *Kyklos*, pp. 585–8.

—— (1979) 'Keynessche Inflations- und Kaldorsche Verteilungstheorie', *Kyklos*, pp. 205–18.

RAMSEY, F. P. (1928) 'A Mathematical Theory of Savings', *Economic Journal*, pp. 543–59.

RAU, N. (1972) 'Two-Class Neoclassical Growth: A Conjecture Proved', *Quarterly Journal of Economics*, pp. 344–5.

RIESE, H. (1981) 'Theorie der Produktion und Einkommensverteilung', *Kyklos*, pp. 540–62.

RIMMER, R. J. (1987) 'Boulding's Theory of Distribution in a Neo-Pasinetti Framework', mimeo (Footscray Institute of Technology, Australia).

ROBINSON, J. (1956) *The Accumulation of Capital* (Macmillan, London).

—— (1962) *Essays in the Theory of Economic Growth* (Macmillan, London).

—— (1966) 'Comment on Samuelson and Modigliani', *Review of Economic Studies*, pp. 307–8.

ROSS, S. A. (1975) 'Uncertainty and the Heterogeneous Capital Goods Model', *Review of Economic Studies*, pp. 133–46.

RUSSELL, R. R. (1988) 'Comments on Chapter 10', in Kessler and Masson (1988), pp. 281–5.

SALVADORI, N. (1985) 'The Existence of a Two-Class Economy in a General Cambridge Model of Growth and Distribution: Further Generalizations', mimeo (University of Catania).

SAMUELSON, P. A. (1966) 'A Summing Up', *Quarterly Journal of Economics*, pp. 568–83.

—— (1967) 'Indeterminacy of Development in a Heterogeneous-Capital Model with Constant Savings Propensity', in K. Shell (ed.), *Essays on the Theory of Optimal Economic Growth* (MIT Press, Cambridge, Mass.).

—— (1969) 'Lifetime Portfolio Selection by Dynamics Stochastic Programming', *Review of Economics and Statistics*, pp. 239–46.

—— (1990) 'Extirpating Error Contamination concerning the Post-Keynesian Anti-Pasinetti Equilibrium', *Oxford Economic Papers*, forthcoming.

—— and MODIGLIANI, F. (1966a) 'The Pasinetti Paradox in Neo-Classical and More General Models', *Review of Economic Studies*, pp. 269–301.

—— —— (1966b) 'Reply to Pasinetti and Robinson', *Review of Economic Studies*, pp. 321–30.

SANDMO, A. (1969) 'Capital Risk, Consumption and Portfolio Choice', *Econometrica*, pp. 586–99.

—— (1970) 'The Effects of Uncertainty on Saving Decisions', *Review of Economic Studies*, pp. 353–60.

—— (1971) 'On the Theory of the Competitive Firm Under Price Uncertainty', *American Economic Review*, pp. 65–73.

SATO, K. (1966) 'The Neoclassical Theorem and Distribution of Income and Wealth', *Review of Economic Studies*, pp. 331–5.

SCAZZIERI, R. (1983) 'Economic Dynamics and Structural Change: A Comment on Pasinetti', *Rivista Internazionale di Scienze Economiche e Commerciali*, pp. 73–90.

—— (1987*a*) 'Reswitching of Technique', *The New Palgrave, A Dictionary of Economics*, iv. 162–4.

—— (1987*b*) 'Reverse Capital Deepening', *The New Palgrave, A Dictionary of Economics*, iv. 172–3.

—— (1990) 'Vertical Integration in Economic Theory', *Journal of Post-Keynesian Economics*, pp. 1–15.

SCHEFOLD, B. (1976) 'Nachworte', in P. Sraffa, *Warenproduktion mittels Waren* (Suhrkamp 780, Frankfurt), pp. 129–226.

—— (1981) 'Die Relevanz der Cambridge-Theorie für die ordnungs-politische Diskussion', *Schriften für Sozialpolitik*, NS, pp. 689–715.

SCHIANCHI, A. (1978) 'Crescita e distribuzione in un modello a tre classi: una nota', *Ricerche Economiche*, pp. 103–6.

SCHLICHT, E. (1975) 'A Neoclassical Theory of Wealth Distribution', *Jahrbücher für Nationalökonomie*, pp. 78–96.

SCHMITT, B. (1984) *Inflation, Chômage et Malformation du Capital* (Economica, Paris).

SCHULTZ, TH. W. (1971) *Investment in Human Capital* (Free Press, New York).

SCOTT, M. F. (1989) *A New View of Economic Growth* (Oxford University Press, Oxford).

SEN, A. K. (1963) 'Neo-Classical and Neo-Keynesian Theories of Distribution', *Economic Record*, pp. 53–64.

—— (ed.) (1970) *Growth Economics: Selected Readings* (Penguin, London).

SHASTRI, R. A., and NAGARY, A. (1984) 'The Pasinetti Paradox', mimeo (National Academy of Development, Hyderabad, India).

SHEA, K.-L. (1981) 'An Alternative Theory of Inflation', *Kyklos*, pp. 611–28.

SHENG CHENG HU (1973) 'On Optimal Capital Accumulation in a Two Class Model of Economic Growth', *Metroeconomica*, pp. 229–49.

SHORROCKS, A. F. (1975) 'The Age–Wealth Relationship: A Cross-Section and Cohort Analysis', *Review of Economics and Statistics*, pp. 155–63.

—— (1979) 'On the Structure of Inter-Generational Transfers between Families', *Economica*, pp. 415–25.

SIDRAUSKI, M. (1967) 'Inflation and Economic Growth', *Journal of Political Economy*, pp. 796–810.

—— (1967) 'Rational Choice and Patterns of Growth in a Monetary Economy', *American Economic Review*, pp. 534–44.

SIEGEL, F. W., and HOBAN, J. P. (1982) 'Relative Risk Aversion Revisited', *Review of Economics and Statistics*, pp. 481–7.

SKOTT, P. (1981) 'An Examination of Kaldor's Growth and Distribution Models 1956–1966', unpublished thesis, University of Aarhus.

SOLDATOS, G. T. (1988) 'Income Inequality and Public Debt Neutrality', mimeo (University of Athens).

SOLOW, R. M. (1956) 'A Contribution to the Theory of Economic Growth', *Quarterly Journal of Economics*, pp. 65–94.

—— (1970) *Growth Theory: An Exposition* (Oxford University Press, Oxford and New York).

SPAVENTA, L. (1962) 'Effetti di variazioni strutturali nella composizione della domanda sulla produttività del lavoro e sulla occupazione', in L. Spaventa (ed.) *Nuovi problemi di sviluppo economico* (Boringhieri, Turin), pp. 229–49.

STAMP, J. (1926) 'Inheritance as an Economic Factor', *Economic Journal*, pp. 339–74.

STEEDMAN, I. (1972) 'The State and the Outcome of the Pasinetti Process', *Economic Journal*, pp. 1387–95.

—— (1975) 'Positive Profits with Negative Surplus Value', *Economic Journal*, pp. 114–23.

STIGLITZ, J. E. (1967) 'A Two Sector Two Class Model of Economic Growth', *Review of Economic Studies*, pp. 227–38.

—— (1968) Review of K. J. Arrow's *Aspects of the Theory of Risk Bearing*, *Econometrica*, pp. 742–3.

—— (1969a) 'Distribution of Income and Wealth Among Individuals', *Econometrica*, pp. 382–97.

—— (1969b) 'Behaviour Towards Risk with Many Commodities', *Econometrica*, pp. 660–7.

—— (1969c) 'The Effects of Income, Wealth and Capital Gains Taxation on Risk-Taking', *Quarterly Journal of Economics*, pp. 263–83.

—— and UZAWA, H. (eds.) (1969) *Readings in the Modern Theory of Economic Growth* (MIT Press, Cambridge, Mass.).

STOKER, T. M. (1984) 'Completeness, Distribution Restrictions and the Form of Aggregate Functions', *Econometrica*, pp. 887–907.

SWAN, T. W. (1956) 'Economic Growth and Capital Accumulation', *Economic Record*, pp. 343–61.

SYLOS-LABINI, P. (1962) *Oligopoly and Technical Progress* (Harvard University Press, Cambridge, Mass.).

—— (ed.) (1973) *Prezzi relativi e distribuzione del reddito* (Boringhieri, Turin).

—— (1974) *Trade Unions, Inflation and Productivity* (Lexington Books, Lexington).

—— (1979) 'Prices and Income Distribution in Manufacturing Industry', *Journal of Post-Keynesian Economics*, pp. 3–25.

—— (1984) *The Forces of Economic Growth and Decline* (MIT Press, Cambridge, Mass. and London).

TANIGUCHI, K. (1987) 'The Existence of Traverse in Pasinetti's Model of Growth and Distribution', mimeo (Discussion Paper No. 11, University of Osaka Prefecture).

TARGETTI, F. (1988) *Nicholas Kaldor: Teoria e politica economica di un capitalismo in mutamento* (Il Mulino, Bologna). Oxford University Press, forthcoming.

TOBIN, J. (1958) 'Liquidity Preference as Behavior Towards Risk', *Review of Economic Studies*, pp. 65–86.

—— (1960) 'Towards a General Kaldorian Theory of Distribution', *Review of Economic Studies*, pp. 11–20.

—— (1965) 'Money and Economic Growth', *Econometrica*, pp. 671–84.

—— (1967a) 'Life Cycle Saving and Balanced Growth', in W. Fellner *et al.*, *Ten Economic Studies in the Tradition of Irving Fisher* (Wiley, London and New York), pp. 231–56.

—— (1967b) 'The Neutrality of Money in Growth Models: A Comment', *Economica*, pp. 69–72.

—— (1984) *Asset Accumulation and Economic Activity* (Blackwell, Oxford and New York).

TOMES, N. (1981) 'The Family, Inheritance and the Intergenerational Transmission of Inequality', *Journal of Political Economy*, pp. 928–50.

—— (1982) 'On the Intergenerational Savings Function', *Oxford Economic Papers*, pp. 108–34.

—— (1988) 'Inheritance and Inequality within the Family: Equal Division among Unequals, or do the Poor get More?' and 'The Intergenerational Transmission of Wealth and the Rise and Fall of Families', in Kessler and Masson (1988), pp. 79–104 and 147–165.

UPADHYAY, V. (1978) 'Tobin on Kaldor: A Comment', McMaster Working Paper, No. 78-32.

UZAWA, B. (1969) 'Time Preference and the Penrose Effect in a Two-Class Model of Economic Growth', *Journal of Political Economy*, pp. 628–52.

VAN HORNE, J. C. (1975) 'The Asset Structure of Individual Portfolios and Some Implications for Utility Functions', *Journal of Finance*, pp. 585–603.

VAUGHAN, R. N. (1971) 'The Pasinetti Paradox in Neoclassical and More General Models: A Correction', *Review of Economic Studies*, p. 271.

—— (1979) 'Class Behavior and the Distribution of Wealth', *Review of Economic Studies*, pp. 447–65.

—— (1988) 'Distributional Aspects of the Life Cycle Theory of Saving', in Kessler and Masson (1988), pp. 193–235.

VICKERS, D. (1968) *The Theory of the Firm, Production, Capital and Finance* (McGraw-Hill, New York).

WALSH, V., and GRAM, H. (1980) *Classical and Neoclassical Theories of General Equilibrium* (Oxford University Press, Oxford).

WAN, H. Y. (1971) *Economic Growth* (Harcourt Brace Jovanovich, New York).

WEDGWOOD, J. (1928) 'The Influence of Inheritance on the Distribution of Wealth', *Economic Journal*, pp. 38–55.

—— (1929) *The Economics of Inheritance* (Routledge & Kegan Paul, London).

WEINTRAUB, S. (1966) *A Keynesian Theory of Employment, Growth and Income Distribution* (Chilton, Philadelphia).

—— (1979) 'The Naked and the Nude: Professor Brems on Post-Keynesian', *Journal of Post-Keynesian Economics*, pp. 138–9.

WEIZSÄCKER, C. C. VON (1966) 'Tentative Notes on a Two-Sector Model with Induced Technical Progress', *Review of Economic Studies*, pp. 245–51.

WOLFF, E. N. (1988) 'Life-Cycle Savings and the Individual Distribution of Wealth by Class', in Kessler and Masson (1988), pp. 261–80.

WOOD, A. J. B. (1972) 'An Analysis of Income Distribution', Ph.D. thesis, University of Cambridge.

—— (1975) *A Theory of Profits* (Cambridge University Press, Cambridge).

—— (1978) *A Theory of Pay* (Cambridge University Press, Cambridge).

WOODFIELD, A., and McDONALD, J. (1979) 'On Relative Income Shares in the Pasinetti and Samuelson–Modigliani Systems', *Economic Journal*, pp. 329–35.

———— (1981) 'Income Distribution in the Pasinetti Model: An Extension', *Australian Economic Papers*, pp. 104–14.

———— (1982) 'Income Distribution in the Pasinetti Model: Reply to Baranzini', *Australian Economic Papers*, pp. 207–13.

WORSWICK, D., and TREVITHICK, J. (eds.) (1983) *Keynes and the Modern World* (Cambridge University Press, Cambridge).

YAARI, M. E. (1965) 'Uncertain Lifetime, Life Insurance and the Theory of the Consumer', *Review of Economic Studies*, pp. 137–50.

YELLEN, J. L. (1980) 'On Keynesian Economics and the Economics of Post-Keynesians', *American Economic Review*, Papers and Proceedings, pp. 15–19.

NAME INDEX

SUBJECT INDEX